Robert E Sullivan

DEFENCE OF THE WEST

OTHER BOOKS BY CAPTAIN LIDDELL HART

B. H. LIDDELL HART

DEFENCE OF THE WEST

 WILLIAM MORROW & CO., 1950
NEW YORK

To GEORGE LINDSAY
and CHARLES BROAD
two soldiers of vision and
comrades in the struggle
for military progress

CONTENTS

PART FOUR: THE TIME FACTOR
SOME CURRENT MILITARY PROBLEMS

PART FIVE: TIMELESS
SOME BASIC PROBLEMS OF YESTERDAY AND TOMORROW

THIS book deals with the immediate problems of an effective "Defence of the West" and some basic problems of the human search for security against aggression. It may thus be worth while to explain why the book begins by dealing with the immediate past—with some of the principal puzzles of World War II. My original intention was to summarize the investigation of these questions in a separate small book. But my publishers expressed a strong preference for incorporating it as Part One of this book, and of other friends whom I consulted the majority agreed with the publishers' view. I hope that they may be right in their judgment of readers' taste—for while I cannot presume to gauge other people's taste, I have become convinced in my own experience of the value of the historical approach to current problems. In trying to solve such problems, or make forecasts, it has repeatedly proved helpful to get a projection from the past through the present into the future.

However, if any reader does not care for this approach, the remedy is simple—he can skip Part One and start at Part Two.

This book was completed before the outbreak of war in Korea. That event has dispelled illusions which were widely prevalent, and shattered hopes built on the effect of much-publicized new weapons not yet in production. What has happened in Korea, however, does not call for any amendment of this book. Indeed, experience there has confirmed what I have written about a number of important factors—for instance, about the continued value of tanks; about the limitations of an air force in checking land invasion, particularly by troops of Soviet type; about the crucial importance of superior training; about the formidable quality of Soviet-trained troops, which Western military authorities were too inclined to disparage; and about the handicap which Western armies impose on themselves by their excessive scale of road-bound vehicles and over-elaborate supply organization.

Recent admissions by leading statesmen have also confirmed my indictment of the utter inadequacy of the existing defence of the West—the "paper screen" that faces the Iron Curtain.

In conclusion, I would express grateful appreciation to my friends John Brophy, Sir Frederick Pile and Lieut.-General Sir Francis Tuker, as well as to my wife, for their valuable help in reading and checking the book in proof stage.

B. H. Liddell Hart.

Wolverton Park,
Buckinghamshire,
England.

PART ONE

YESTERDAY

Riddles of the Immediate Past

CHAPTER I

WAS THE 1940 COLLAPSE AVOIDABLE?

How different the state of the world would be if the Western Front had not collapsed in May, 1940. The collapse occurred in six days, but resulted in the war lasting six years, and spreading over the world—with consequences that were terrible for many millions of people, and most of all for those who were the momentary victors. Yet Hitler's victory was by no means inevitable, though it looked so after the event. The 1940 collapse in the West gave rise to the wildest notions and explanations. More nonsense has been written about it than about any other event of the war. That is not surprising, because it was the greatest of all shocks.

Throughout the first winter of the war the public had been lulled and gulled by an unceasing flow of "hot air" —in Government circles, in the press, and on the radio— about the strength of France and Britain. There was far more talk and thought of what they were going to do to Germany than of what she might do. Acutely conscious how unjustified such talk was, I kept a day to day record of what the leaders of the nations and of national opinion

3

were saying. The record looks almost unbelievably absurd now. Never did so many boast so much about so little.

When the shock of disillusionment came, opinion swung to the other extreme. The collapse came to be regarded as having been certain from the start, and the inevitable result of factors that were magnified out of all proportion to the facts. For in such a climate, legends quickly grow. Truth is slow to catch up with legend, and has not done so yet.

The first legend sprouted in the very first days of the invasion. Hosts of parachutists were said to be dropping in all the invaded countries, often disguised as priests or nuns—a religious vocation became a dangerous profession in those feverish days. Such stories are widely believed even today. In reality there were only some 4,500 German parachutists altogether, of whom 4,000 were used in the corner of Holland between Rotterdam and the Hague. The remaining 500 were employed on one short stretch of the Belgium frontier—to capture the crossings of the Albert canal. None were used in France. To supplement the shortage of real parachutists, dummies were dropped at a variety of points. They not only caused a scare for the moment, but fostered a long-lived legend.

A second piece of fanciful history is that the success of the German invasion was due to widespread treachery, and the help received from a vast Fifth Column. While there was reason for the suspicion that Nazi agents and sympathizers hindered the defence at some points, it is clear now that the importance of this factor and the dimensions of the Fifth Column were immensely exaggerated. The defence suffered much more from muddle-headedness and panic than from treachery.

Another myth that became current after the event was that the defeat was due to the Allies, and particularly the French, being too defensive-minded. "Maginot-minded" was the popular term of scorn in subsequent argument. That notion was not easy to reconcile with the fact that the much-discussed Maginot Line covered only the easterly half of the French frontier, and had not been extended westward. It was refuted by the fact that no serious attempt had been made to fortify the sector along the Meuse where the Germans actually broke into France. But those who cherish myths are not concerned with facts and reasonable deductions. In reality, the captured files of the French High Command show that during the first nine months of the war it was occupied in planning offensive moves to outflank Germany, though it lacked the strength needed to give these dreams any chance of success. Moreover, the pattern of the ill-fated Plan D, which the French Command tried to carry out as soon as the Germans moved, clearly bears the mark of being designed by offensive-minded soldiers who are unwillingly reduced to practising defence. That bad compromise was its basic fault.

It is not correct that Hitler's victory was assured by an overwhelming superiority of force. Germany did not mobilize as many men as her opponents did—at the expense of their arms production. The Germans managed to form and equip more divisions than the French did, but had no advantage in numbers over the total array of opposing divisions in the West. That did not matter. For the issue was really decided by the deep-driven thrusts of a picked 8 per cent of their army—their ten armoured divisions—before the bulk had come into action.

That was not due to the German Army having a much greater number of tanks, as was naturally imagined at the time. Whereas the French estimated that it had 7,000-8,000 tanks, we now know that it had less than half this number—and only 2,800 were used in the first, and decisive, phase of the invasion. But they were used to the utmost advantage. The French had almost as many tanks, but they were not so mobile and the greater part of them were scattered as small packets, instead of being concentrated for a powerful punch. The French generals still clung to the 1918 idea that tanks were the servants of the infantry, while Hitler had listened to Guderian, the leader of the new school, who argued that armoured divisions should be the spearhead of the army—Hitler's backing made the older generals more inclined to swallow their doubts and accept the newer idea.

Similarly, Hitler had gone all out for air power. Here he did have a big superiority in numbers, approaching 3 to 1, and he scored most heavily through having developed a mass of dive-bombers to combine with his tanks. The French military chiefs had tended to underrate the value of airpower until it was too late to remedy their prolonged neglect of the air arm.

Even so, much more than this was required to produce such a victory as Hitler gained. Neither his advantage as the aggressor, nor his advantage in forces, counted for as much as certain extraordinary blunders on the other side—blunders of a kind that no planner of aggression could bank on. But even these would not have been decisive save for a string of lucky turns that were quite incalculable.

The invasion of Holland is the first illustration of this fateful combination. It was a subsidiary part of Hitler's plan, and the forces he could spare for it were much smaller than those the Dutch had mobilized. But the Dutch Command reshuffled the disposition of its forces on the very night that the Germans were moving up to attack, and this side-step left a weak spot just where the German Command had placed the solitary armoured division it could spare for the invasion of Holland. As a result, this division was able to push through and race for ninety miles along an almost clear path, to reinforce the parachute troops who had dropped around Rotterdam. Even then, the German forces at this far-advanced point were still greatly outnumbered, but the daring stab at the heart of Holland cloaked the weakness of the invaders and created a paralyzing confusion. Coupled with the threat of air attack on Holland's crowded cities, it led to the Dutch surrendering two days later, although their main front was still unbroken.

The keys of the Maastricht gateway into Belgium were secured by a few hundred airborne troops, silently descending in gliders out of the dark. The two essential bridges over the Albert Canal were captured intact, before they could be blown up. The covering fort of Eben Emael, dominating the canal, was paralyzed by a mere eighty paratroops who "squatted" on top of it and dropped explosives into the gun-muzzles and casemates. This triple coup had been Hitler's own idea, and its possibility had been doubted by most of his generals.

Studying the operation step by step on the ground, after the war, I saw how decisive had been the effect of one big oversight and several chance factors. The bridge-defences and the fort were well prepared to meet anything except the possibility of troops arriving immediately overhead. Thus they could not bring fire to bear on the assailants at the crucial moment. Nevertheless, at the main bridge the fuse was actually lit—but the crew of one glider got into the blockhouse, on the heels of the sentries, just in time to extinguish it. At Eben Emael a

counter-attack that might have cleared the paratroops off
the top of the fort was cancelled through a misunderstood message.

By next morning sufficient Germans had accumulated
beyond the canal to burst through the shallow line of defences behind, while two armoured divisions poured over
the unblown bridges and drove into the plains beyond.
The menace led the Belgian forces to start a general retreat—just as the French and British forces were arriving
on the Dyle to their support.

This break-through near Maastricht was not the decisive stroke of the campaign, but it had an important
bearing on the outcome. It created a whirlpool which
sucked in the French mechanized divisions, so that these
could not be drawn out and switched to check the dead-
lier menace that arose further south. For the bulk of
the German armoured and motorized divisions was
sweeping towards the French frontier, through the
wooded hills of the Ardennes.

It was a daring venture to thrust a mass of tanks
through such difficult country, but the gamble came off—
and caused the downfall of France. We know now that
it was due to a late change in the German plan, suggested
by a staff officer of imagination, General von Manstein,
after he had consulted Guderian and been assured
that a tank drive through the Ardennes was a practicable
operation.

The original plan had been to make the main push in
the north, with the right wing as in 1914. If that plan had
been carried out, it would have run head-on into the best
part of the Anglo-French forces. It might have pushed
them back, but it would hardly have succeeded in cutting them off, as the new plan did.

Manstein felt that the original plan lacked the essential

element of surprise—especially as it repeated the general line of the 1914 plan—and had no promise of proving decisive. The boldness of the new conception appealed to Hitler. But the definite decision to change the original plan was produced by an extraordinary accident when, on January 10, a staff officer who was carrying papers about the plan lost his way in a snowstorm when flying from Münster to Bonn, and landed by mistake in Belgian territory. The German High Command naturally feared that he might have been unable to destroy the papers (and, in fact, his attempt to burn them was a partial failure). Even then the Commander-in-Chief and the Chief of the General Staff hesitated to turn the plan round so completely as Manstein had proposed. Their resistance was only overcome after Manstein, going behind the backs of his superiors, had seen Hitler personally and gained his decisive support for the unconventional project.

Hitler had originally wished to launch his offensive in November, 1939, but successive postponements were caused by the weather, thus providing time for Manstein to pursue his arguments, as well as for the mishap in the snowstorm. In this double way, bad weather contributed much to the eventual success of Hitler's offensive!

During the interval, false alarms had led the Allies to show their hand, and their intention of advancing in force deep into Belgium. That disclosure, too, strengthened the case for changing the German plan in the way Manstein advocated.

Strangely, it did not lead the Allies to vary their plan—which was a further piece of luck for Hitler. But the supreme blunder of the Allies, when rushing forward into Belgium, was to leave the hinge of their advance, facing

the Ardennes, to be guarded by only a few inferior-grade
French divisions. Thereby the plan framed by Gamelin
and Georges fitted perfectly into the new German plan.
That crowned Hitler's run of luck. It was also the clearest
proof of how foolishly offensive-minded the French generals were.

Another example was their attitude to a proposal that
the forest roads leading across the French frontier should
be blocked by the simple and effective expedient of felling thousands of trees. This proposal was turned down,
on the ground that the roads must be kept clear for the
advance of the French cavalry!

Even then, the chance of checking the Germans was
better than it looked subsequently. Only Manstein and
Guderian, besides Hitler, seemed to have been really
confident of success. Most of the generals have frankly
admitted that they were full of doubts beforehand, and
were astonished to find such weak opposition along their
difficult line of advance. They knew the Ardennes contained many awkward bottlenecks and feared they would
find these strongly held.

One of their biggest worries was that air photographs showed a large fortified bridgehead on the Meuse
covering Sedan. But just before the start an Austrian expert re-examined the photographs and detected that the
fortifications were in an unfinished state. This was a great
relief to Kleist, who was in command of the whole mobile
striking force of Rundstedt's Army Group. With such reassurance, Kleist felt that he could race on ahead of the
infantry. That gain of time forestalled the belated movement of the French reserves.

On the way through the Ardennes the German tanks
met only some old-fashioned cavalry, who were easily
swept away. Guderian's panzer corps, which was lead-

ing, reached the river on the 13th, and there found merely a thin chain of pillboxes. Moreover, the defenders, being low-category troops, had been allotted few anti-tank guns.

Despite that luck, the crossings succeeded at only one point out of the three tried that day. The foothold was soon extended, and thus sufficed, as Guderian lost no time in exploiting the opportunity. But the local checks had shown what a general check could have been imposed by any adequate defence.

Another panzer corps got across at Monthermé, a day later. That place lies in a deep gorge where one resolute and well-equipped battalion should have been able to hold up an army corps. But the French division on this sector, besides being composed of old reservists, had not a single anti-tank gun!

Once across the Meuse, the tanks bowled along the roads that led west, meeting scarcely any opposition. In a week they reached the Channel coast, 160 miles distant—and cut off the Allied armies in Belgium. "Dunkirk" and the fall of France were the sequels. It was the easiest-won victory in history.

Why was nothing effective done to stop the invaders during that week? For there were several stop-lines that could have been used by any defence expert who understood tanks.

One reason was that the pace of panzer warfare paralyzed the French Staff, whose minds were still moving at 1918 tempo. The orders they issued might have been effective but for being, repeatedly, twenty-four hours late for the situation they were intended to meet.

Another reason was that the French Staff were always trying to mount massive counter-attacks, instead of hurrying to man the stop-lines. Time after time the Ger-

mans drove over these lines, while the French reserves
were gradually assembling on the flank. The French
Staff were too content to follow an old offensive theory
regardless of what was happening in practice. In that obsession they threw away chance after chance of baulking
Hitler's gamble.

The irony was that the German Staff had not reckoned
on any such complete success as they obtained. Even
Hitler had originally aimed at no more than to give the
French a knock that would incline them to make peace,
and to occupy part of the Channel coast so as to put the
same peace-seeking pressure on England. The aim of
conquering England was not in his mind.

But he became the victim of his own victory. Although
succeeding beyond expectation in his invasion of the
West, he was baffled by the stubbornness of the British.
It is remarkable to find how far he was prepared to go in
conciliating them, at the moment when he was in the
flush of his triumph and they had been almost unarmed.
Unable to understand why they spurned his offers of
peace, he drifted along with the current of the war he
had unloosed, and eventually came to grief.

If Hitler had been checked at the outset, it would not
have saved him, but the world would have been saved
much.

We know now that even his own generals were waiting
for such a check to loosen the trust of his propaganda-fed
people, and give them the chance to overthrow him.

Hitler's fatal success owed much to an extraordinary
run of luck, but it owed even more, at every stage, to the
short-sightedness of his opponents. The statesmen of
France and Britain had smoothed his path by failing to
see where their policy was leading. The soldiers were
equally short-sighted in their sphere. The breakdown of

1940 was basically due to the way that military orthodoxy prevailed over modern ideas, not only at that moment, but for twenty years before. The French and British—except for the small band of modern thinkers who preached the idea of mobile-mechanized warfare—had been preponderantly conservative ever since their victory in 1918, whereas the Germans had been spurred by their defeat in 1918 to become relatively progressive. There is the key to what happened on the battlefields of 1940.

Hitler would have "got nowhere" without the tank forces that Guderian had created and trained. The decisive success of Guderian's break-through at Sedan and swift drive to the Channel coast changed the course of history, and has had far-reaching effects on the future of Europe. Yet it could almost certainly have been checked if the directing minds on the other side had understood the new style of warfare, and thus known how to counter it.

CHAPTER II

COULD AFRICA HAVE BEEN CLEARED IN 1941?

IT was not until late in January, 1943, that the British Eighth Army entered Tripoli, the capital of Italian North Africa. The enemy then retreated into French Tunisia, and a further three months passed before he was finally overcome. The news of Montgomery's capture of Tripoli brought a great surge of joy, and relief —for a few months earlier the enemy had been battering at the inner gateway to Egypt.

That surge of joy drowned a lot of awkward questions. It made people forget the miscarriages and mistakes that preceded the triumph during two years of ebb-and-flow fighting, as well as the heavy cost of the prolonged struggle and the strain it had imposed on Britain's whole situation. In the thrill of the moment, hardly anyone thought to ask how much might have been saved if the clearance of Africa had come two years earlier—as had looked likely.

For in February, 1941, the British forces had an almost open path to Tripoli, after wiping out the last portion of Marshal Graziani's army—in the first week of that month.

14

Only a few Italian oddments survived in North Africa to defend Tripoli. No German troops had yet landed.

But at that moment of opportunity, the British forces were stopped on orders from their Government at home. Why? Because the Prime Minister and the Foreign Minister, Mr. Churchill and Mr. Eden, wanted to send an army to Greece and forestall any German move there, even though it meant halting the advance on Tripoli. That army was quickly thrown out of Greece, but by then the opportunity in Africa had passed.

This is one of the most tangled stories of the war, besides being wrapped up in secrecy and covered by myths. It is time to dispel the myths, remove the wrappings, and unravel the thread.

The first myth was created over the source of the forces that turned the tables on the Italians when they invaded Egypt in the autumn of 1940. It was often said later, notably in speeches by Lord Halifax and Mr. Attlee, that the defeat of the Italians was due to Mr. Churchill's bold action, when England itself was threatened by invasion, in sending to Egypt the only armoured division Britain had at home. Actually, this division did not arrive on the scene until after the campaign was over. It was then split up between Greece and Cyrenaica, and overtaken by defeat in both places, losing all its tanks. The decisive role in the victory over Graziani had been played by the famous 7th Armoured Division which had been formed in Egypt before the war, on Mr. Hore-Belisha's insistence.

These facts must be stated for the sake of true history. They do not bring into question the boldness or wisdom of Mr. Churchill's step in reinforcing Egypt even at the risk of England. The plunge into Greece is a different matter.

A second myth arose over the executive credit for the defeat of Graziani. The press concentrated its spotlight on General Wavell, the Commander-in-Chief in the Middle East as a whole. Mr. Churchill, in speeches, emphasized the part of General Wilson, the Commander in Egypt. But the actual forces at the front were led by General O'Connor, and it was to his brilliant tactics that the troops themselves ascribed the victory, apart from the broad direction given by Wavell. In fast-moving desert battles the man who handled them on the spot naturally counted for more than a remote higher commander who was 300 miles back, in Cairo.

That remoteness had an adverse influence on the sequel. Here we come to one of the strangest revelations of the war. Graziani's army was caught off its balance and overthrown by the surprise shock of a mere couple of divisions—the 7th Armoured and the 4th Indian—which was all that O'Connor had. When the battle was won, the 7th Armoured took up the pursuit of the beaten foe, and the 4th Indian should have backed it up. But at the moment of victory and opportunity, O'Connor received the staggering word from Cairo that the 4th Indian Division must be withdrawn, and go to the Sudan. The extraordinary situation thus followed that as the Italians were fleeing westward, half the victor's force was withdrawing eastward—marching back to back!

As a result, the 7th Armoured Division was held up outside the fortified camp of Bardia, where the Italians had taken refuge after recrossing their own frontier. Nearly a month passed before the arrival of the 6th Australian Division made possible the capture of Bardia, and the continuance of the British advance. That was an unfortunate delay.

Worse still, a fresh drain now developed. Reinforcements and transport that could have been sent to help O'Connor in completing the conquest of North Africa were withheld because they were earmarked for Greece. At the same time a succession of units was even taken away from him while he was driving forward through Cyrenaica.

The Balkan theatre had long fascinated Mr. Churchill, since his boldly conceived but ill-fated Dardanelles venture in World War I. Now, his imagination was fired by the way that the Greeks had withstood Mussolini, and he became filled with the idea of giving Hitler a slap in the face if he pushed his nose into Greece. Mr. Churchill's eagerness outran the practical possibilities, however, and showed little regard to the limited extent of his resources compared with Hitler's.

The account presented to the public after the failure was that the British Government had embarked on the venture at the pressing appeal of the Greeks, and that Britain could not in loyalty abstain, whatever the cost to herself. This was a long way wide of the truth. In reality, the British Cabinet had pressed the Greeks to accept support about which they were very dubious.

When Mr. Churchill pressed his aid on them in mid-January he received a cold douche. General Metaxas, the Greek Prime Minister, rejected the proposal, saying that the forces offered would be likely to provoke German aggression without being anything like strong enough to check it. The Greek Commander-in-Chief, General Papagos, argued that nine divisions were needed, whereas the British Government offered an immediate deposit of two regiments, to be followed by two or three divisions. He thought that the British would be wiser to complete their victory in Africa before attempting anything fresh. To split their effort would be bad strategy.

The British Government still tried to insist on the Greeks accepting the immediate deposit, but Metaxas maintained his refusal. Mr. Churchill then addressed an offer to Turkey, only to meet with another refusal, on similar grounds. Despite these rebuffs, he continued to cherish the schemes.

Meanwhile, permission was given to continue the advance in North Africa and capture Benghazi, if it could be done on the cheap, without additional troops. Despite this handicap, O'Connor pulled off a more striking success than was expected. Sending the 7th Armoured Division on a 150-mile dash through the desert interior to Beda Fomm, beyond Benghazi, he blocked the road to Tripoli and cut off the whole remainder of Graziani's army. After trying in vain to break through this block, the Italians surrendered on February 7.

The victors were burning to drive on towards Tripoli. The few Italian troops who had been left there were panic-stricken by the fate of the main army, and were expecting the British tanks to appear any time. Hitler was tardily sending a light armoured division under Rommel to their rescue, but the first elements of this did not begin to land until a week later. Giving me the view of the German Supreme Command, General Warlimont said: "We could not understand at the time why the British did not exploit the difficulties of the Italians in Cyrenaica by pushing on to Tripoli. There was nothing to check them."

The appeal for permission to push on fell on deaf ears. On the morrow of the victory, the Cabinet sent Wavell a telegram directing him to halt the advance, leave only a minimum force to hold the conquered territory, and prepare to send the largest possible force to Greece. Almost the whole of O'Connor's air force was taken away at once, and only one squadron of fighters left.

What had happened? Metaxas had died suddenly on January 29, and Mr. Churchill was quick to revive his cherished project. The new Greek Prime Minister had sent the British Government a note reaffirming his predecessor's principle of resisting the Germans if they attacked, while reiterating that the dispatch of British troops should not take place unless a German invasion threatened—through the Germans' moving into Bulgaria's intervening territory. That slight sign from the Greek Government was enough for Mr. Churchill—enough to make him abandon the advance on Tripoli in favour of a venture in Greece. The forces in Cyrenaica were already in process of being pulled back when, on February 22, Mr. Eden arrived in Athens accompanied by an imposing military staff, and pressed the new Greek Prime Minister to accept the British offer.

General de Guingand, who was then on the Joint Planning staff in Cairo, and later Montgomery's Chief of Staff, has given an account in his memoirs of what took place:

"I think it was Eden who stressed and enumerated the 'formidable' resources which we were prepared to send over. It sounded pretty good, but if a real expert had carried out a more detailed investigation, I doubt whether those present would have been so satisfied."

General de Guingand says that the figures he had compiled did not appear good enough to one of Mr. Eden's party who was preparing the brief. "He asked that the figures should be swelled into what to my mind were doubtful values. I felt that this was hardly a fair do, and bordering upon dishonesty." He relates that after the conference: "Eden came in looking buoyant. He strode over to the fire and warmed his hands, and then stood with his back to it dictating signals to his staff. They in turn looked nearly as triumphant as he did, and were positively oozing congratulations. Presumably he had done his job, and accomplished what he had set out to achieve. . . . But whether it was a job worth doing and in our best interests seemed to me very doubtful."

The Germans were well informed of Eden's activities, and his visit was made with a provocative flourish that was like "cocking a snook" at Hitler.

On March 1 the Germans moved into Bulgaria. On March 7 the leading contingent of the British expeditionary force, under General Wilson, landed in Greece. On April 6 the Germans invaded Greece, and also Yugoslavia—where General Simovich had been encouraged by British agents to overturn the Government, repudiate the recent pact with Germany, and make a gesture of defiance.

The sequel was that within three weeks Greece and Yugoslavia were overrun, and the British forces driven to a second Dunkirk, leaving all their tanks and most of their equipment behind them. The loss of Crete followed. Meanwhile the diminished British force in Cyrenaica had been taken by surprise and driven out by Rommel, who had been able to land in Tripoli undisturbed. This series of invited disasters spelt a damaging loss of prestige and prospect for Britain. It brought appalling misery on the people of Greece and Yugoslavia—and the bitter fruits are still being harvested in the troubles that have followed the war.

In later years, those who were responsible for the Greek gamble have sought to justify it on the ground that it saved Russia. They argue that the German invasion of Greece caused delay in the invasion of Russia, and thus shortened the period in which Hitler could

achieve his aim there before winter came. This conten-
tion is dubious. The provisional date for the offensive
against Russia was postponed from May to June, but
General Halder, then Chief of the German General Staff,
has said that the weather did not allow an earlier start.
I have discussed the question with several of the commanders on the main front of attack, and they all confirmed the fact that the ground was not dry enough to
begin an offensive until the middle of June.

In any case the apologetic argument is irrelevant, because the British forces were sent to Greece with the
idea of establishing a British lodgment in the Balkans,
not to affect a contingency that had not yet arisen. General de Guingand's comment on the post-dated argument
for the Greek gamble is much to the point—"Such a
method of justification is similar to a punter who, having bought by mistake the wrong ticket at the tote, finds
that horse wins, and then goes about saying, 'What a
clever boy am I'!"

The prime effect of the gamble was the heavy forfeit
in North Africa. General de Guingand states that the
Joint Planning Staff of the Middle East was convinced
that Tripoli could have been reached, and the enemy
cleared out of Africa, before the spring of 1941. General
O'Connor and his staff were equally confident. The possibility depended on using Benghazi as an advanced base
port, and on making available the transport that was
being reserved for the gamble in Greece. But all this had
been worked out.

It may be argued that if the British had captured
Tripoli then, the Germans would have landed in Tunisia,
and from there have advanced eastward to turn them out
of Tripoli. That was an obvious risk, and at that time the
British lacked the resources to maintain their forces so far

forward against a heavy assault. But there is reason to question whether it was a serious risk. For Hitler was not really interested in Africa, nor inclined to send strong forces there. His mind was focused on Russia.

Although his naval chiefs repeatedly urged the importance of the Mediterranean, and the aim of capturing the Suez Canal, Hitler showed little response to their arguments. Besides his obsession with Russia, another influence on his mind was his underlying reluctance to undermine the British Empire, which he regarded as a factor of stability in the world. Strange as it may seem, that reluctance has become clear in evidence that has now come out. Even at the moment of England's greatest weakness, after the fall of France, he talked in private to his generals of the need to maintain the British Empire.

Hitler's military chiefs were equally averse, on military grounds, to the diversion of forces to Africa and disliked the idea of committing troops across the sea—for they had a deep-seated fear of the British navy, and no trust in the Italians. He and they begrudged even the slender detachment that was belatedly sent to Africa, under Rommel, after Graziani's collapse.

So if the British had gone to Tripoli when the opportunity was open, and thus occupied all the ports on that coast, it is unlikely that the Germans would have attempted the much bigger overseas effort required to evict them. If they had, the British Navy and Air Force would have been better placed to interfere, from more advanced bases.

The clearance of Italian North Africa in 1941 would have carried a prospect of great advantages. It would have brought the British into contact with French North Africa, and might have encouraged the French military leaders to make common cause with Britain much earlier than they did. It would have enabled her to use the Mediterranean shipping route, and eased the immense burden of sending her troops and supplies round by the Cape—a long detour which swallowed up so much of Britain's resources. And, once America was brought into the war, the build-up for the Allied invasion of Europe could have been hastened.

CHAPTER III

WAS RUSSIA CLOSE TO DEFEAT?

Since Hitler died in the ruins of Berlin, and Stalin has been the dominant figure in Europe, there has been a general tendency to assume that Hitler's invasion of Russia was foredoomed from the outset. His attempted conquest of Russia has been placed in a historical niche alongside Napoleon's, and regarded as yet another proverbial example of the folly of "trying to bite off more than one can chew."

No such conclusion, however, emerges from examination of the campaign. The failure of Hitler's gamble was not as certain as it looks now. If it had been better prepared, with mechanized resources superior to those he had available, it might have come off. Even as things were, it was not far from success at the first attempt, and perhaps even at the second.

The truth about the campaign is not easy to reach. The Russians, besides being habitually secretive, are not disposed to shed light on weaknesses that developed. But much about the campaign has been revealed in the evidence of the German generals—even more in their admis-

24

sions than in their assertions. Moreover, significant points often emerge indirectly from the accounts published on the Russian side.

The first striking point about the 1941 invasion is the relative slenderness of Hitler's forces. Not only was space against him, but numbers—even at the start. He plunged into the immense depths of Russia, on June 22, in face of the knowledge that his forces were fewer than those opposing him, while they were bound to be increasingly outnumbered if the campaign were prolonged. That is an astonishing fact. In terms of numbers and space, his was a gamble against greater odds than any aggressor in modern history has dared.

When Hitler's plan was unfolded to his generals in February, 1941, they were disturbed to hear that the Red Army had 155 divisions available in Western Russia, whereas the invading forces could muster only 121. Actually, the German intelligence estimate was a little under the mark.

The Germans had not even equality, let alone superiority, in the number of tanks—although Hitler was counting mainly on these for his chance of victory. General von Thoma, then head of the tank side of the General Staff, told me that the invasion was launched with only 2,434 tanks—excluding the very light ones, which he called "sardine-tins"—whereas Russian reports credited the Germans with 12,000.

The Germans concentrated the bulk of their strength on the sector north of the Pripet Marshes, where the highway to Moscow ran. By that concentration, Field-Marshal von Bock's Army Group there had a slight advantage of numbers. But on the southern front, where Field-Marshal von Rundstedt attacked, it was very much otherwise. Field-Marshal von Kleist, who led Rundstedt's panzer drive here, told me that he had only 600 tanks. In Marshal Budenny's opposing Army Group there were 2,400.

What then was Hitler banking on, since he knew that he faced such adverse odds? First, on a superiority of quality—he reckoned that his generals and troops would enjoy a decisive advantage in skill and organization, benefiting from the experience they had gained in practising the new *blitzkrieg* tactics against Poland and France. Second, on his belief that a quick defeat of the opposing armies would produce a political upheaval in Russia and the collapse of Stalin's regime.

He pinned his hopes to a quick success, for he shared his generals' anxiety about the vast space of Russia, and was fearful of getting too deep into it before he had wiped out her armies. So he planned to encircle and destroy them as near the frontier as possible. That aim agreed with the view of his senior generals, though Guderian—who was now commanding a panzer army in Bock's Army Group—would have preferred to drive through to Moscow as quickly as possible.

Hitler refused to think of what might happen if his plan did not succeed and any large part of the opposing armies should retreat deep into Russia. Accordingly, he made no preparations for a prolonged struggle, but gambled on gaining complete victory before the autumn. His generals did not feel happy about this short view.

It has to be recognized that his first calculation was correct—and that it brought his goal in sight. The technical superiority of the German forces was amply demonstrated by the result of the earlier battles.

In just over a week, the panzer forces had penetrated to Minsk, 200 miles on the road to Moscow, and masses of Russians had been trapped between the pincers. Although large numbers managed to wriggle out, over a quarter of a million were put in the bag. Before the end of July the drive had reached Smolensk, only 200 miles from Moscow, and another pincer-manœuvre had been achieved. Half a million were encircled, though once more a large part eventually escaped. Hitler now decided to try a pincer-manœuvre further south, around Kiev. This time the trap was completely closed, and over 600,-000 prisoners were taken. Hitler then switched his efforts northward again, brought off a great encirclement around Vyasma, and made as huge a bag as at Kiev.

Only lack of tactical skill or lack of fighting spirit could account for such colossal defeats. But the German generals themselves admit that the Russians fought hard from the outset—and recall, with a shudder, how tough they proved. So the cause must have been lack of skill.

Yet the startling results which the Germans secured by superior skill were not good enough to attain Hitler's goal. Each of his victories, great as they seemed, was too little or too late for his purpose. That was due partly to factors for which he was inadequately prepared, and partly to his own fumbling—more than the toughness of the Russians. For the stubbornness which made the Russians so hard to overcome, made them easy to encircle.

The first attempted encirclement, near Minsk, was not a complete success as the German pincers did not close in time. The German Intelligence had failed to realize how poor the Russian roads were, and the German transport was not designed to cope with such deep mud as they developed when it rained. The second encirclement, near Smolensk, fell short of full success from similar causes.

By that time Hitler had become anxious about pushing further while a large part of the Red Army was still unbeaten. He wavered in doubt for several weeks, and then decided to swing his weight southward and trap the Russian forces on Rundstedt's front. As already re-marked, that encirclement succeeded perfectly—but it was late in September before the victory here was complete.

Elated by that sweeping victory, he decided to make another bid on the Moscow line, though his generals' doubts were growing. Again the pincer-manœuvre ended in a triumphant success, but the end of October had arrived before the Russian masses round Vyasma were put in the bag. Hitler had lost too much time—two months—through his own hesitation and his Kiev diversion. The autumn rains were already turning the ground into a bog.

The path to Moscow was swept almost clear of defenders, but Russian mud came to Russia's rescue at this critical moment. The victors at Vyasma were tired, and their wheeled transport floundered in the mud. This slowed down the advance during the crucial days. By the time the Germans reached the Nara river, fresh Russian forces had arrived to hold this defence-line, and the Germans were held up.

The German generals wanted to break off the offensive and pull back to a good line where their troops could rest comfortably during the winter. Rundstedt went further, and argued that the wise course was to withdraw to Poland, and give up the idea of conquering Russia. But Hitler, like most gamblers, could not resist the temptation to have another try.

So the push was continued, under increasing difficulties and in face of growing opposition. On December 2 the final effort was made. Some of the attackers actually penetrated into the suburbs of Moscow, but they had shot their bolt and were paralyzed by the icy cold. Hitler's forces were thrown back by the Russian counter-offensive that was now delivered with reserves newly gathered from the interior.

A similar fate befell the German advance in the south. After the triumph at Kiev, Hitler could not resist the temptation to push on there, as well as on the Moscow front, though it meant splitting his effort. The path was swept so clean that before the end of November Kleist's panzer forces had driven 400 miles further to Rostov-on-Don, the gateway to the Caucasus oilfields. But they became stranded in the mud, petrol supplies could not reach them, and the Russians had time to bring up fresh reserves to stop them.

Looking back, these results are apt to look inevitable. But, looking deeper, it can be seen that the margin by which Russian resistance survived was desperately narrow. The bulk of Russia's original armies were wiped out —the most colossal round-up in the history of war. It was touch-and-go whether Stalin could scrape together fresh armies from Russia's immense reservoir of man-power to halt Hitler before the keys of Russia were captured. Time was gained, and barely gained, only through the saving combination of the weather, German weakness, and Hitler's erraticness, with Russian toughness *and* Russian backwardness. The last was perhaps the most decisive factor of all—as will be explained later.

The Germans had to pay an exorbitant price for Hitler's final gamble of 1941. Compelled to stay in exposed positions throughout a terrible winter, for which they were quite unprepared, their sufferings and their wastage were appalling. Neither the Army nor the Air Force ever fully recovered from the strain.

Nevertheless, even with depleted forces, Hitler came dangerously near achieving in 1942 a goal he had missed in 1941. No longer having sufficient strength to attack along the whole front, he concentrated on the southern part, with the aim of capturing the Caucasus oil—which each side needed if it was to maintain its full mobility. If he could gain it, he might subsequently turn north on to the rear of the immobilized Russian armies that were covering Moscow, or even strike at Russia's new war-industrial base in the Urals. But it was a bigger gamble, because if he became stuck, the flank of this southern drive would be exposed to a counterstroke anywhere along its almost thousand-mile stretch.

At the outset the *blitzkrieg* tactics scored once again—but for the last time. A quick break-through was achieved in the Kursk-Kharkov sector, and then Kleist's panzer army poured like a torrent down the corridor between the Don and Donetz rivers. Surging through the gateway to the Caucasus, it reached the more westerly oilfields round Maikop in six weeks. Russian resistance had crumbled badly, and Kleist met hardly any opposition during the later stage.

This was Russia's weakest hour. Only an instalment of her newly raised armies was yet ready for action, and even that was seriously short of equipment. The lack of artillery was such that mortars, brought up on lorries, had largely to serve as a substitute. The tremendous losses of 1941 could not be quickly replaced, hard though the new factories were working. Many of the troops, too, showed a lack of "guts" compared with the year before. Once they were by-passed, they drifted back as homeward-bound fugitives, instead of fighting on stubbornly at the road centres to obstruct the enemy's communications.

Fortunately for Russia, the attackers were also much weaker than in 1941. Hitler tried to fill the gaps with Rumanian, Italian and Hungarian troops, using them to cover his long flank—and that substitution turned into a fatal liability at the end of the year. It was fortunate for Russia, too, that Hitler split his effort between the Caucasus and Stalingrad.

When Kleist drove on from Maikop towards the main oilfields of the Caucasus he was first halted by running short of petrol, and then hung up in the mountains, where he met stiffer resistance as well as a stiffer obstacle. In giving me his account, he said: "The forces we met there were local troops, who fought more stubbornly because they were fighting to defend their homes." At the same time his own forces were progressively drained in order that Hitler might reinforce the divergent attack on Stalingrad.

Here, the first onset was barely checked, but the resistance hardened with repeated hammering, while the obviousness and directness of the German strokes simplified the Russians' problem in meeting the threat. Hitler could not bear to be defied by the "city of Stalin," and wore down his forces in the prolonged effort to storm it. Meanwhile the new Russian armies were gathering on the flanks.

When winter came, Stalin gave the signal for a counter-offensive, which was shrewdly directed against the troops of Germany's inferior allies. Their collapse and Hitler's obstinacy sealed the fate of the isolated German army at Stalingrad. Following this disaster, the scales of the war turned against Hitler.

Yet it had been touch-and-go in the summer. A little greater impetus might have spread the many local collapses of Russian resistance into a general collapse. Civil as well as military morale was low, especially in Southern Russia, before the inspiring example of the defenders of Stalingrad and the Caucasus, and the diminished momentum of the invaders, helped to revive it.

It is difficult to tell whether there was ground for Hitler's belief in the possibility of a political upheaval in Russia, for signs of anything like that do not emerge in a totalitarian state unless and until the iron surface cracks. It is evident that Hitler overestimated the prospects. But it would also seem that there was often less inclination to resist the invaders than Stalin desired. The stern admonitions that were addressed, and the subsequent punishment administered, to a number of areas told their own tale. They tend to bear out the evidence of the German generals as to the lack of trouble they had when and where they were allowed to practise a policy of conciliation.

Hitler might have had more success if he had been as ready to try on the velvet glove—as he was in the West. His instinctive tendency to "treat the Russians rough" played into Stalin's hand at a critical period.

Weighing up the military factors, one is led to a startling conclusion. Russia owed her survival more to her continued primitiveness than to all the technical development achieved since the Soviet revolution. That reflection applies not only to the toughness of her people and soldiers—their capacity to endure hardships and carry on under shortages that would have been paralyzing to Western peoples and Western armies. A greater asset still was the primitiveness of the Russian roads. Most of them were no better than sandy tracks. The way that they dissolved into bottomless mud, when it rained, did more to check the German invasion than all the Red Army's heroic sacrifices.

Yet the final reflection remains that Hitler might have won in spite of this heavy handicap, if he had been better prepared. He lost chance after chance because the mobility of the German Army was based on wheels instead of on tracks. Its wheeled transport was repeatedly bogged when the tanks could move on.

Tank forces that had tracked transport could have overrun Russia's vital centres long before the autumn. World War I had shown this need to anyone who used his eyes and his imagination. Britain was the birthplace of the tank, and the leaders of the new school of military thought there who preached the idea of mobile mechanized warfare after 1914-1918 urged that the new model forces should have tracked vehicles throughout. The German Army went further than the British Army, or any other, in adopting the idea of fast and deep armoured thrusts. It fell short in the vital respect, however, of neglecting to develop such cross-country transport. In brief, the German Army was more modern than any other in 1940-41, but missed its goal because it had not yet caught up with ideas that were twenty years old.

Even as things were, Hitler might have got to Moscow in the first summer if he had given the tank forces free rein to drive ahead as Guderian urged. But the senior generals considered this a dangerously unorthodox plan, and Hitler here came down on the side of orthodoxy—thus forfeiting his best chance.

CHAPTER IV

COULD HITLER HAVE AVOIDED DEFEAT
AFTER STALINGRAD?

I**T IS** clear that the tide of the war turned
against Germany after her frustration at Stalingrad in the
autumn of 1942. From that time onward her strength
was ebbing, her front receding, her armies retreating—
except for intermittent pauses and a few flash-in-the-pan
retorts. It has thus come to be assumed that she was
henceforth doomed to defeat, and that Stalingrad sealed
her doom. But deeper examination of events suggests that
her fate was not so inevitable as it appears.

In the first place, the failure of Hitler's 1942 offensive
in Russia—his second gamble on victory—did not itself
produce the disaster which followed in the winter. The
fatal step was Hitler's obstinate refusal when winter came
to let Field-Marshal Paulus's army withdraw from its far
advanced position on the edge of the Volga at Stalingrad.
His generals begged him to permit its withdrawal, declaring that it was impossible to maintain that army so
far forward during the winter, with its communications
exposed for several hundred miles back. But their master

could not bear the thought of "losing face" by drawing back after he had come so close to capturing the city. Its very name acted on him like a cocksnook of defiance, and became a deadly temptation.

In September the Chief of the General Staff, Franz Halder, had been sacked because he fretted Hitler by his persistent protests against continuing the offensive with winter approaching. Hitler filled Halder's place by selecting a much younger man, Kurt Zeitzler, feeling that he would be so dazzled by the jump in promotion that he would do what he was bidden without argument. But by December Zeitzler was in disfavour because he dared to urge that Paulus's army should be withdrawn.

Even when the Russians launched their winter counter-offensive and encircled that army, Hitler angrily refused to allow it to abandon its ground and fight its way out westward before the ring was cemented. As a result, it was forced to surrender. This was a crippling loss and left a gap that was hard to fill.

How the Stalingrad army could have saved itself was shown by the way that the Caucasus army did save itself, under worse conditions—for it had pushed much deeper. The Russians surged down the valley of the Don from Stalingrad towards the Black Sea, after Paulus had been cut off, and came within barely 40 miles of the Rostov bottleneck when Kleist's army in the Caucasus was 400 miles *east* of Rostov. Hitler had just previously insisted that it must hang on where it was, but now, at this desperate moment, was induced to permit a withdrawal. Although constantly menaced in flank and rear, Kleist's army got back to safety through the bottleneck, while the Russians were held at bay. That long retreat in the depths of winter was one of the most remarkable feats of extrication from a trap in all history. At the end of it

Kleist was able to mount a counterstroke which temporarily turned back the Russian tide of advance.

This was proof of the *defensive* capacity which the Germans still possessed. But it had a too exhilarating effect on Hitler. He would not listen to his generals' arguments for changing over to a defensive strategy. In the summer he determined to try the offensive again, though his own strength was much depleted and the Russians' was increasing all the time.

Before this last offensive in the East was launched, however, there was a diplomatic move that would have startled the world if it had become known at the time. It was a move to negotiate a privy peace or truce between Germany and Russia. I had an account of it from an officer who was one of the technical advisers on Ribbentrop's staff. The proposal of a concealed truce had behind it the ultra-ingenious idea that it would enable Russia to go on drawing American and British supplies, and pass part of them on to Germany to help the latter in checking the American and British forces! But the Nazi leaders were not prepared to make any large concessions to Russia on their own part, or even to hand back all their ill-gotten gains. They still contemplated a frontier that should extend as far east as the Dnieper.

It is hard to understand how they could have imagined such proposals would be acceptable to Stalin. The story of this backstairs move is still fragmentary, but we know that it was abortive, and no other result could reasonably have been expected.

Close on its heels the final German offensive was delivered in July, 1943. The plan was to pinch off the Kursk salient and thus create a yawning hole in the Russian front. A few weeks earlier it might have had a somewhat better chance, but in the interval the Russians had

covered the threatened sector with a deep layer of minefields, and withdrawn their main forces behind it. When
the Germans had become deeply entangled, and exhausted, the Russians launched their own offensive—as a
counterstroke. They now had ample reserves to maintain
the momentum, whereas Hitler had thrown almost all his
remaining reserves, especially of tanks, into this further
gamble, and thus squandered the strength that might
have still enabled him to check the Russian advance. This
rolled on westward during the autumn and winter with
only short pauses, and by the beginning of 1944 the invaders had been driven out of most of Southern Russia.

How, instead, a stalemate might have been produced
but for that suicidal German offensive at Kursk, was
shown by the dramatic contrast of the results on the
northern part of the Russian front. Here the Germans
had stayed on the defensive, and the Russian attacks
broke down time after time. It was the more notable because these checks to the Russians followed a lengthy
step-back by the Germans. After evacuating Smolensk
the latter fell back, not to a long-prepared position, but
to a hastily improvised one consisting at first of only a
single trench-line. That sufficed, however. The German
step-back took the sting out of the Russian offensive, and
gained time for the Germans to improve their defences
before the next attack came.

I had a striking account of this period from General
Heinrici, who then commanded the German 4th Army,
astride the great highway from Moscow to Minsk and
Warsaw. "In the autumn of 1943 we had to meet a series
of strong Russian offensives, beginning in October and
continuing until December. There were five successive
offensives. I had only 10 divisions to hold a sector that
was over a hundred miles wide, and was without any

reserves. In the first offensive the Russians employed
20-22 divisions; in the second 30 divisions; and in the
next three about 36 divisions apiece. Part of them were
the original ones, but most of them were fresh.

"To meet this assault I used 3½ divisions to hold the
twelve miles frontage where the attack came, leaving 6½
to hold the remainder of my very wide front. Every attack was checked. These five successive battles each
lasted five or six days, but the crisis usually came about
the third or fourth day—after which the attack began to
peter out.

"I reckoned that there were three main factors that
contributed to the success of the defence. First, I formed
narrow divisional sectors, with a high ratio of force to
space, on the actual frontage of the Russian assault. Secondly, I managed to form a very powerful artillery
grouping, of 380 guns, to cover the threatened sector.
This was controlled by a single commander, at Army
Headquarters, and was able to concentrate its fire on any
required point of that 12-mile frontage. The Russian offensives were supported by up to a thousand guns, but
their fire was not so concentrated. Thirdly, the losses of
the German divisions engaged—which had to be reckoned as the equivalent of about one battalion per division in each day of battle—were compensated by a system of drawing battalions from the divisions on other
parts of the Army front. I always tried to have three fresh
battalions—one for each of the divisions holding the
battle front—ready behind this before the attack started."

In March, 1945, Heinrici was given command of the
Army Group that faced the Russians' final push for Berlin. With this he fought the battle of the Oder and the
battle of Berlin.

In this later stage, he said, he had further developed

the defensive methods. "When the Russians were found to be concentrating for an attack, I withdrew my troops from the first line under cover of night, to the second line—usually about two miles behind. The result was that the Russian blow hit the air, and its further attack did not have the same impetus. This system worked very well in the battle of the Oder—the only drawback was our scanty strength, after so much had been wasted needlessly by the rigid defence of positions impossible to hold.

"The German defeat in the East was, in my opinion, due to one main reason—that our troops were compelled to cover immense spaces without the flexibility, in the command, that would have enabled them to concentrate on holding decisive points.

"My first experience after taking over command of the 4th Army in 1942, opened my eyes. I withdrew a small detachment from an awkward position it was holding—whereupon I received a warning that if I did anything of the sort again the least that would happen to me would be a court martial.

"Hitler always tried to make us fight for every yard, threatening to court-martial anyone who didn't. No withdrawal was officially permitted without his approval—even a small scale withdrawal. This principle was so hammered into the Army that it was a common saying that battalion commanders were afraid 'to move a sentry from the window to the door.' These rigid methods cramped us at every turn. Time after time, forces stayed in impossible positions until they were surrounded and captured. But some of us ventured to evade his orders as far as we could."

Such evasion was only possible in a local and limited way. Tippelskirch, who succeeded Heinrici in command of the 4th Army, bore witness to the value of elastic defence, but also to the disastrous consequences of being unable to practice it to an adequate extent. "At Mogilev in March, 1944, I was commanding the 12th Corps—which consisted of three divisions. In the offensive the Russians then launched, they used ten divisions in the assault on the first day, and by the sixth day had used twenty divisions. Yet they only captured the first line, and were brought to a halt before the second. In the lull that followed I prepared a counter-stroke, delivered it by moonlight, and recovered all the ground that had been lost—with comparatively few casualties."

Tippelskirch then went on to relate what happened in the Russians' summer offensive in 1944. He took over command of the 4th Army three weeks before it opened. The army commanders on that front begged for permission to withdraw to the line of the Beresina—a long step-back that would have taken the sting out of the Russian blow. But their proposals were rejected. Tippelskirch nevertheless made a short step-back that sufficed to keep his front intact. But the fronts of both the armies on his right and left were ruptured, and a general collapse followed. The retreat did not stop until the Vistula had been reached, near Warsaw.

"It would have been much wiser strategy to withdraw the whole front in time. The Russians always needed a long pause for preparation after any German withdrawal, and they always lost disproportionately when attacking. A series of withdrawals by adequately large steps would have worn down the Russian strength, besides creating opportunities for counter-strokes at a time when the German forces were still strong enough to make them effective.

"The root cause of Germany's defeat was the way that her forces were wasted in fruitless efforts, and above all

in fruitless resistance at the wrong time and place. That
was due to Hitler."

The German collapse in North Africa was precipitated
in the same way. When Rommel's invasion of Egypt became stuck at El Alamein, the gateway to the Nile, the
British reinforcements rapidly grew while the Germans'
strength and supplies dwindled—owing to their far-
stretched communications and the sinking of their supply
ships and tankers in running the gauntlet of the Mediterranean crossing. The wise course would have been to
withdraw before Montgomery struck, and leave him to
"hit the air," but Hitler vetoed any such timely step-back.
When the German front began to crack under the strain
of Montgomery's offensive, Rommel decided to fall back
to a line fifty miles to the west. The stealthy withdrawal
had already begun, by night, when a wireless order came
from Hitler insisting that the original position must be
held at all costs. It meant that the German troops had to
turn about and continue the battle until their defence
was smashed. This hopeless effort, and useless sacrifice,
went far to ease Montgomery's subsequent advance to
Tripoli and Tunis, and paved the way for the eventual
capture of all the German and Italian forces in North
Africa.

The battle of El Alamein took place more than a month
before that greater disaster at Stalingrad. It is strange
that Hitler did not take heed of the warning, but stranger
still that he stuck to the same fatal policy as the years
passed and the lessons multiplied.

The General Staff were not allowed to order the construction of lines in rear, or even to discuss plans in case
of being driven back. They were forbidden to make any
preparatory plans for withdrawal. In 1943, however, they
managed to do a little preparatory work on the quiet, by

circulating instructions in discreetly worded leaflets.
These leaflets were distributed among the various armies,
but without any imprint to show that they emanated from
the General Staff.

It is very clear, as Dittmar remarked, that the policy
of clinging on at all costs in particular places repeatedly
changed the campaign for the worse. By putting too much
effort, and too large a proportion of the limited resources,
into closing one threatened breach in the general front,
fresh breaches repeatedly developed elsewhere. In the
end that proved fatal.

CHAPTER V

WAS NORMANDY A CERTAINTY?

To ALL appearance, the Anglo-American landing in Normandy progressed with supreme sureness from the start—on June 6, 1944. At no stage did it meet with any serious reverse. Indeed, the Germans never even succeeded in mounting a serious counterstroke. The Allied footholds were quickly extended into a large bridgehead, and then were gradually expanded until the German defence broke down under the pressure—two months after the landing. With that breakdown, the whole German position in France collapsed, and no effective opposition was met until the Allied armies approached the frontiers of Germany herself.

Was the success of the liberating invasion such a certainty as it appeared after the event? Investigation provides cause for doubting this now general assumption—and more cause than the Allied planners had reckoned with beforehand.

The crux of the problem was whether the Allied forces could establish themselves on the French shore, and create a bridgehead sufficiently wide and deep to build up

43

their strength on the far side of the English Channel. Once that could be achieved, it was fairly sure that, with their immense resources, they were bound to break through sooner or later. No dam would be strong enough to hold the flood in check if they gained enough space to pile up their massed power.

But, even with the utmost stretch of their landing-craft resources, they could only carry eight divisions in the first seaborne lift—besides dropping three airborne divisions—and a week would pass before they could double the total ashore. The completion of the build-up was a long way ahead. Rough seas would delay the process.

Everything turned on whether the Germans could check the invasion, or crush it, before its weight multiplied. There were nearly sixty German divisions in the West. That was a formidable total, even though many of them were low-grade or under-strength.

The Germans' primary handicap was that they had 3,000 miles of coastline to cover—from Holland to the Italian frontier. Of their available divisions, half were of a static kind, anchored to coast defence. But the other half were field divisions, of which ten were armoured and highly mobile. That offered them a fair chance of concentrating an overwhelming superiority to throw the invading force back into the sea before it grew too strong.

The chance was increased because the Allies did not make the headway anticipated in the first stage, when their landing had the advantage of partial surprise. Allied progress fell still further behind anticipation in the second stage, despite the opposition being much weaker than expected. These important facts are little known. This was not only obscured by the ultimate triumph but has also been covered up in subsequent accounts of the campaign.

It was hoped that the British would capture Caen on the first day of the landing. They failed to do so, and this key-point was not secured until over a month later. The intention was also to make an immediate armoured drive to Villers-Bocage, 20 miles inland, and thus cut the roads leading west and south-west from Caen. The drive was delayed, though opposition here was negligible. When it got going a week later Villers-Bocage was quickly reached, but then the appearance of enemy reinforcements caused a questionable decision to withdraw. Nearly two months passed before the place was finally gained.

To the westward, the advance inland from the American landing points was also much slower than the hopeful schedule—though the opposing forces were weaker than on the British sector. The idea had been that the whole of the Cherbourg peninsula might be secured in a fortnight, and the break-out achieved within three weeks—before the end of June. In the event, it did not come until the end of July. Not until late in August did the invasion catch up and outstrip the forecast, in reaching the Seine.

How was it that the Germans failed to profit by their extended opportunity of defeating the invasion?

Much was due to the paralyzing effect of the Allied air forces. By smashing most of the bridges over the Seine on the east and over the Loire on the south, they turned the Normandy battle-zone into a strategical isolation-zone. The German reserves had to make long detours and were so constantly harried on the march, that they suffered endless delays and only arrived in driblets.

But the Allies also owed much to disagreement and discord in the German Command. Before the event, Hitler's intuition proved better than his generals' calculation in gauging where the Allies would land. After the landing, however, his continual interference and rigid control deprived them of the chance of retrieving the situation, and eventually led to disaster.

Field-Marshal von Rundstedt, the Commander-in-Chief in the West, thought the invasion would come across the narrower part of the Channel, between Calais and Dieppe. His view was based on a conviction that this course was the more correct strategy for the Allies to follow. But it was fostered by a lack of information, as well as by our deception measures. Nothing important leaked out from the tight-lipped island where the invasion armies were assembling. Rundstedt's Chief of Staff, General Blumentritt, told me how badly baffled was the German Intelligence. "Very little reliable news came out of England. There were a small number of German agents there, who reported by radio transmitting sets what they observed. They gave us reports of where, broadly, the British and American forces were assembling in Southern England. But they found out scarcely anything beyond that. Nothing we learnt gave us a definite clue where the invasion was actually coming." That is a great tribute to the reticence of the British people, as well as to the thoroughness of the security measures. "Careless talk" must have been almost as scarce as "Fifth Columnists." Britain proved a barren isle for spies.

Hitler, however, had a "hunch" about Normandy, although most of his generals in the West continued to expect that the invasion would come nearer the Straits of Dover. From March onward he sent them repeated warnings about the possibility of a landing between Caen and Cherbourg. His conclusion was inspired by the general lay-out of the British and American forces and bases, coupled with his belief that the Allies would need to secure a big port so situated that it could be quickly pro-

tected by a fairly short front line—Cherbourg and the
Cotentin Peninsula fulfilled these conditions. The conclusion was strengthened by observers' reports of a big
invasion exercise in southern England where the troops
disembarked on a stretch of flat and open coastline similar to the intended area east of the Cotentin Peninsula.
Rommel, who was in executive charge of the forces on
the Channel coast, came round to the same view as Hitler. In the last few months he made feverish efforts to
hasten the construction of under-water obstacles, bomb-
proof bunkers and minefields, and by June they were
much denser than they had been in the spring. Fortunately for the Allies, he had neither the time nor the resources to develop the defences in Normandy to the
state he desired, or even to the state of those east of the
Seine.

Rommel also found himself in disagreement with
Rundstedt over the method of meeting an invasion. Rundstedt did not believe it was possible to prevent the Allies
achieving a landing, and relied on a plan of delivering a
powerful counter-offensive to throw them out before they
were firmly established. Rommel considered that this
would be too late, in face of the Allies' domination of the
air and their capacity to delay the German reserves in
concentrating for such a counter-offensive. He felt that
the best chance lay in defeating the invaders on the coast,
before they were properly ashore.

The actual plan became a compromise between these
different ideas—and "fell between two stools."

The Normandy coast itself was thinly held by a few
low-grade divisions, and behind them Rommel had only
one armoured division available for counter-attack in the
whole forward area. But for that division being on the
scene the British might have captured Caen on the first

day of the landing. Rommel had vainly begged for a second armoured division to be at hand near the mouth of
the Vire—which was the area where the Americans
landed.

While Rommel was restricted in his powers of immediate counter-attack, Rundstedt was even worse fettered in
trying to carry out a concentrated counter-offensive. That
was due to Hitler, and not only to the Allied air forces.
For Hitler insisted on trying to control the battle from
Berlin, and kept a tight hand on the reserves that were
supposed to be at Rundstedt's disposal. On D-day pre-
cious hours were wasted in argument on the German
side. The nearest available part of the general reserve
was the 1st S.S. Panzer Corps, which lay west of Paris,
but Rundstedt could not move it without permission from
Hitler's headquarters. As early as 4 a.m., soon after the
Allied parachute troops had begun dropping in Normandy, he telephoned Berlin and asked for the release
of this armoured corps—to back up Rommel. But his re-
quest was refused, as Hitler now doubted whether the
landing in Normandy was the main stroke. A "battle" of
argument went on until late in the afternoon before this
corps was released. Even then, its move was delayed. For
its artillery had been kept on the east bank of the Seine,
and the Allied air forces had destroyed the bridges. The
artillery had to make a long circuit south by way of Paris
before it could cross the river.

Thus instead of the massive punch that was to have
been delivered the morning after the Allied landing, the
effort dwindled into a piecemeal succession of taps,
spread over several days. As other reserves were still
slower to arrive, the armoured divisions became absorbed
in local fights to check the invaders pushing inland, instead of being used to drive them back into the sea. Three

weeks passed before another counterstroke was mounted, with a few fresh armoured divisions, and by then the invaders were so well consolidated that the attack broke down before it got going.

A feature of this critical period was that, although Hitler had correctly guessed the site of the invasion, once it had taken place he became obsessed with the idea that it was only a preliminary to a second and larger landing east of the Seine. That idea was based on the German Intelligence Service's large overestimate of the number of Allied divisions still available in England, and was fostered by the skilful way that the threat was kept up by the Allied cover plan and its "stage army" of wireless stations. Hence Hitler remained reluctant to let reserves be moved from that area to Normandy. At the same time, he was not willing to release them from other quarters.

Rundstedt wanted to evacuate the whole of Southern France, arguing that this was the only way left through which sufficient reserves could be collected for a big counter-offensive. But Hitler would not listen to such an idea. Nor would he agree to any withdrawal in Normandy. So the exhausted forces there were compelled to hold on until they collapsed beyond recovery.

In these circumstances, the Germans' ultimate collapse seems less surprising than the fact that they managed to check the invaders for so long. Even with all the help received from divided counsels on the enemy side, the Allies had a very tough fight before they could break out. Save for the split mind of the German Command, the Allies would have run a much more serious risk of defeat—before they had got their balance on shore. Even their command of the air might not have covered them against this risk.

These reflections raise the question whether Normandy was the best place for the Allied invasion. Another possible site was the west coast of France, in the Bay of Biscay, where the defence was negligible and the interior more open. When I asked Rundstedt about this in one of our talks, his reply was: "If the Allies had landed there, they could have succeeded very easily—both in establishing a large enough bridgehead and then driving inland. I could not have moved a single division there in time to stop them." Blumentritt added: "Such a landing would have met practically no opposition. There were only three divisions covering 300 miles of coast south of the Loire, and two of them were training divisions composed of raw recruits."

Experience of previous Allied landings, in the Mediterranean, had convinced the enemy that the Allies would only attempt an invasion where they could count on close-range air cover, so that he felt safe in discounting the chance of an invasion near the Loire. He would have been thrown off his balance even more than he was if the Allies had done anything so completely unexpected.

It seems clear that a landing could have been made, and quickly expanded, without any trouble. The Allies might thus have been able to secure ample room for airfields on French soil much sooner than they did in Normandy. While the greater length of the sea passage from England would have been a drawback at first, ports might have been quickly gained—before they could be blocked—for the inflow of supplies and reinforcements coming direct from America. As it was, the Germans' continued retention of the big ports on the French Atlantic coast was a handicap to the Allies for many months, long after they had reached the frontier of Germany.

Another potential advantage of the Loire area was that,

once a wide footing had been secured there, the invaders could hardly have been penned in for long, as they were in the constricted area and difficult country of the Normandy "bocage"—aptly called the "Norman Switzerland." The wide spaces of France would have lain open to them. Mobile columns driving up the Loire eastward —as Patton eventually did after his break-out from Normandy—could have found ample room for manœuvre in any direction. They might also have produced such a leverage on the rear of the defenders of the Channel coast as to ease the way for a second landing there.

A key-factor in the whole situation was that a great part of the German reserves were anchored to the north coast, not only because of the persistent fear of a landing there, but because of the need to cover the V-weapon sites. That accounts for much that seems puzzling in the campaign. By clinging on so long to that coast, Hitler caused a German collapse that could have been avoided. But his obstinacy is understandable. As long as he kept the fly-bomb launching sites in operation he still had a chance of breaking Britain's will to victory, if he could gain enough time to maintain and develop the bombardment. He was bound to forfeit it if he adopted the otherwise sounder strategy of a timely withdrawal to the Siegfried Line. That could only prolong the end, not do more.

His gamble failed, and hastened the end, but it had a better basis of calculation than is commonly imagined. His worst mistake was to hang on too long in Normandy instead of falling back to the Seine while his forces remained strong enough to hold that barrier. There, he could still have covered and continued the V1 bombardment of London.

CHAPTER VI

TWO WORDS—THE WAR'S GREATEST BLUNDER

H ISTORY may say that "Unconditional Surrender" was the most expensive of all phrases—and of all policies. That two-word formula was produced at the Casablanca meeting between President Roosevelt and Mr. Churchill early in 1943. It sounded so simple and neat, ruling out all argument by the losing side, but proved a source of worse complications than any it was intended to avoid.

It prolonged the war far beyond its likely end, thus leading to the sacrifice of countless lives that could have been saved. It jeopardized the chances of Europe's recovery, as the long drawn-out process of liberation entailed immense devastation on the Continent as well as the undue exhaustion of Britain. Another ominous sequel has been the conflict between the victors that resulted, naturally, from the complete disappearance of any European balance. War to the bitter end was bound to make Russia "top dog" on the Continent, to leave the countries of Western Europe gravely weakened, and to destroy any buffer. The "Iron Curtain" is not a safety curtain.

52

How did unconditional surrender come to be the platform of Anglo-American policy? It is a strange story. The manner of its adoption showed traces of light-heartedness and thoughtlessness such as too often mark the steps of statesmen in making decisions that are fateful for their nations, and for the world.

In advocating the formula, President Roosevelt drew his inspiration from the American Civil War of 1861-65. According to American accounts of the Casablanca meeting, he backed up his argument by telling a story how, when the Confederate army yielded, its commander pleaded that his troops might be allowed to retain their horses and sidearms, and how General Grant rebuffed the plea by insisting on unconditional surrender.

Statesmen are apt to be fond of pithy stories. But this one got history confused. For, as a matter of fact, it was General Grant himself who softened the sting of defeat by inserting unasked, a clause allowing the Confederates to retain their horses and sidearms. He made no reference to "Unconditional Surrender" at this time.

The phrase actually dated back to an earlier episode in Grant's career. The Civil War had opened with reverses for the Union armies, but a break in the clouds came with Grant's capture of Fort Donelson, in Tennessee. Here, in reply to the garrison's appeal for terms, he brusquely demanded "unconditional surrender." The news of this small victory thrilled the Northern public. They saw a happy omen in the triple coincidence that Grant's initials, "U.S.," were the same as those of the United States, which they were fighting to maintain, and also stood for "unconditional surrender." This term became a popular slogan.

Even if Roosevelt's U.S. Civil War parable had been a good parallel in the historical sense, it would have been a

bad one in common sense. It is absurd to apply to a war
of nations the terms that may fit the garrison of a fortress.
A nation cannot be kept permanently interned. It is foolish even to treat a war between nations like a war within
a nation—unless you are prepared to remain in permanent
occupation of the conquered country. Short-sighted as a
long term policy, such an outlook is self-obstructive as
strategy.

All deep-thinking strategists in the past have realized
the value of leaving a loophole of escape to cornered opponents, so encouraging a tendency to retreat. In that
way, opposition starts to trickle away; the trickle develops into a stream, and the stream into a flood. If, on
the other hand, no line of retreat is left, the most reluctant fighters tend to be stiffened with the courage of desperation. When, in war, the opponents are beginning to
wilt, a rigid demand for unconditional surrender has a
natural tendency to stiffen their resistance, and may even
cement an incipient crack. This elementary truth was
pointed out in the first classic work on the art of war,
that of the Chinese master-strategist Sun Tzu, in 500
B.C.

While the post-war complications of "unconditional
surrender" are only now becoming plain, the effect in
extending the length of the war and increasing its cost
soon became apparent.

The first ill-effect was seen in Italy. In July, 1943,
when Mussolini was forced out of office by a combination
of his old associates and the military leaders headed by
Marshal Badoglio, there was a good prospect of Italy
dropping out of the war immediately and thus upsetting
the Axis dispositions in general so far as to uncover
Germany. But the Allied statesmen, and their slogan,
came to Hitler's rescue.

The overthrow of Mussolini provided the clearest evidence of the Italians' desire for peace and to be quit of the German alliance. At that moment the German forces in Italy were still relatively small. Badoglio's coup caught them off their balance. Such a situation offered the Allies a great opportunity, if they were capable of grasping it. But the reiterated demand for unconditional surrender was naturally an uninviting formula, and a delaying factor. In so far as it checked the Italians' peace-seeking impulse at the most favourable moment it acted as a check on the Allies' prospects that operated in favour of the Germans. A psychological deterrent thus became a strategical brake.

Six weeks passed before this clear expression of the Italian desire to break away from Germany was translated into the conclusion of an armistice with the Allies. In that long interval, the Germans were able to push into Italy sufficient troops to dominate the Italian forces and seize the focal points, thus immeasurably increasing the difficulty of the problem that now confronted us. The gradualness of their arrival, however, showed the measure of our missed opportunity.

The stern and inflexible demands of the Allies obviously failed to provide the Italians with any adequate incentive and encouragement to withstand the Germans, or to make fresh sacrifices for that purpose. It was natural that they should feel themselves caught in the proverbial dilemma "between the devil and the deep sea." An ironical side of the resulting situation was that the Italian delegates did not sign the armistice agreement until they had been given a broad idea of the ultimate peace terms —the political, economic and financial conditions which the Allies proposed to apply. This implied that, in reality, their surrender was *conditional* on such a reassurance, even though the unconditional formula was preserved on the surface.

The Allied statesmen's care to preserve "face" cost time that could never be regained. The extent of the forfeit became clear during the next two years as the Allied armies slowly fought their way up the length of Italy's "leg," from the toe to the thigh, suffering repeatedly from cramp in that constricted zone.

The ill-effects of the "unconditional" policy were demonstrated again, and even more clearly, when the Allies came to tackling Germany itself. "Unconditional Surrender" multiplied the obstacles in the way of surrender. By ruling out any consideration of peace offers from the Nazi regime, it blocked the usual channel by which the psychological pressure of a nation's war-weariness can produce an appeal for peace. Faced with such a forbidding "condition," the Nazi leaders were bound to make the German people fight to the last gasp rather than put their own heads in the Allied hangman's noose. It became equally certain that they would take care to cut off any other head that might be inclined to bow to the Allies' demand.

At the same time, this demand offered the Army leaders no inducement to overthrow the Nazi regime. It became almost certain that any attempted *coup d'état* would be half-hearted, and receive only partial support in the army or outside. Thus the first effect of the Casablanca formula was to diminish the chances of any revolt in Germany.

It was of great help to Nazi propaganda, also, in convincing the German people that they had no alternative but to sink or swim with the Nazi regime. Without any assurance as to their future treatment, they were driven to rally behind a regime, tyranny though it was, which at least organized their immediate defence. The Allied policy tended to check even individual Germans from surrendering readily and in decisive numbers.

The complete blankness of the Allies' demand was given the appearance of utter blackness by all the anticipatory talk of what should be done to Germany after defeat. Responsible and irresponsible spokesmen alike indulged in this game of supplying godsends to Goebbels. In their fondness for such advance public planning of Germany's punishment and partition they failed to take account of their responsibility for needless loss of their own fighting men's lives.

When the Allied armies broke out from the Normandy bridgehead in early August, 1944, the over-extended German front collapsed like a punctured balloon, and there seemed little chance of Hitler organizing a fresh front to protect Germany. But the Allies' anticipations of victory before autumn were refuted by events. The way that the Allied advance became stuck was due, not only to the autumn mud and the supply problem, but to the much stiffened resistance of a much weaker German Army. Many of the prisoners taken looked poor specimens, and ardent Nazis were rare among them. But these low-grade troops fought harder than high-grade troops had done earlier. They were stiffened by the courage of desperation. That desperation was due to the absence of any gleam of hope in the Allies' ominously bare demand for unconditional surrender.

This meant that the Germans must throw themselves on the mercy of the conquerors, without any assurance that the latter would not prove completely merciless. Such a fear was reinforced by the evidence of past experience that the vengeful passions are uppermost in the hour of victory, that the extremists are apt to prevail in

any victorious nation, and that in any combination of
allied nations the most extreme tend to call the tune of
the peace settlement. Every German had been made
aware by now of the hatred which his rulers and their
tools had aroused in the surrounding peoples, and thus
felt that surrender without any safeguard would expose
Germans as a whole to unlimited vengeance. It seemed
better to fight on with the dimmest hope than to submit
to such a fate.

The German generals with whom I talked after the
war all said that, but for the unconditional surrender
policy, both they and their troops would have yielded
sooner, either collectively or separately. They gave de-
tails of many discussions in high military headquarters,
throughout the summer of 1944 and the following winter,
about the possibility of getting in touch with the Allies
and arranging an armistice behind Hitler's back. But
their intentions suffered a double check—from the Allied
Governments' forbidding attitude as well as from the
Gestapo's activity. The generals could hardly order their
troops to lay down their arms, and disobey Hitler, unless
they could promise them some security against Allied
vengeance.

Blumentritt, who was Rundstedt's Chief of Staff in the
West, said: "Nazi propaganda impressed on the troops
and people that all Germans were 'in the soup' together,
and it was able to quote many Allied speeches and broad-
casts to reinforce this impression. Allied propaganda, so
far as I know, never directly contradicted the Nazi statements of the dire fate that would befall Germany if defeated. It tended to blame the German people—not, as in
1918, their rulers. At the same time, the foreign embassies
tended to confirm the Nazi argument that the Allies were
determined on the total destruction of Germany." "Even

before 1944, many officers in the German High Command had wanted to sue for peace, but there was no encouragement from the Allied side—it was all the other way."

The dumbness of Allied propaganda has been explained by Mr. Allen Welsh Dulles, of the U.S. political warfare service, who, working from Switzerland, was in contact with the German underground movement against Hitler—"The Goebbelses and Bormans were able to use 'unconditional surrender' to prolong a totally hopeless war for many months. We were tongue-tied by the fear that any explanation of what unconditional surrender meant might be construed by the Germans as a promise some future Hitler could say had been broken."

The chance—almost a certainty—of early victory and a good peace was thrown away because of a rather fantastic fear. Moreover, in this fear of another Hitler in the remote future, the problems of the immediate future were forgotten—not least, that of Russia.

Albrecht von Kessel's diary records that some of the German underground were convinced that the unconditional surrender formula "jeopardized and possibly destroyed" six years of work by the anti-Nazi opposition. Abundant evidence has come out since the war which shows how large and widespread was the German underground movement against Hitler. The Allied Governments had evidence of this during the war, but gave it too little attention, and still less encouragement.

As far back as the spring of 1942, the Bishop of Chichester, when on a visit to Sweden, was met there by representatives of the German churches, who told him about the preparations for a coup to overthrow Hitler, and trusted him with the names of the principal generals and other leaders concerned. All they wanted was an as-

surance that, if the coup came off, the Allied peace terms
would not be vindictive. The Bishop brought this message back to Mr. Eden, who was then Foreign Minister.
It received consideration but nothing more. The British
Government was not willing to give any assurance.

If Mr. Churchill and his colleagues had done so, the
war might have ended three years earlier than it did. Instead, nine months after this peace approach, Mr.
Churchill joined with President Roosevelt in giving birth
to the "Unconditional Surrender" formula, which helped
Hitler to hold out for over two years longer.

No abstruse calculation is required to show what the
occupied countries suffered in those further years of war,
and how the protracted occupation impaired their prospects of recovering stability. Even plainer are the dire
effects of the prolonged devastation of Germany, and its
damaging reaction on all her neighbours in Europe. It
has greatly increased the Allies' burden in occupying
Germany and trying to restore order out of the chaos
created. The wholesale bombing of Germany has proved
the biggest of boomerangs. At the same time, those needless extra years of war undermined the position of Britain. Having withstood Hitler successfully she was too
impoverished at the end of the war to benefit from victory.

Britain's prospects of recovery have been impaired
by the disappearance of that very balance of Europe
which in the past she fought so many times to maintain.
The result of knocking out Germany so completely has
been that she now finds herself clinging precariously to
the low end of a see-saw plank, with Russia facing her
astride the top end—a war partner changed into a peace
menace.

While America has not suffered similar impoverishment, the price of pursuing victory regardless of consequences has been to leave her suspended under the threat of another war of incalculable effects. Seeking security by compelling the opponent's unconditional surrender has merely resulted in a worse state of insecurity in face of a fresh opponent.

This ironical, and perilous, outcome could have been foreseen by any statesmen not blinded by the fury of the fight.

CHAPTER VII

WERE WE WISE TO FOSTER "RESISTANCE MOVEMENTS"?

IN NO great war of modern times has there been such a widespread guerrilla warfare as in the last one. In the struggle against Napoleon's attempt to dominate the continent of Europe guerrilla warfare only became a serious factor in the area of one of the conquered nations—Spain. In the 1914-18 war it was quite insignificant in Europe, though it exerted an important influence on the outlying campaign against Turkey in the Middle East, under the inspiration of Lawrence of Arabia. But in the struggle against Hitler it broke out in every country that was occupied by the Germans. The flames were fanned by Britain as a part of her war policy. Applying Lawrence's conception on a much wider scale, and with much larger resources, special branches of her planning organization were devoted to the purpose of instigating and fostering "Resistance" movements wherever Hitler tried to impose his "New Order." When the U.S.A. entered the struggle, the policy was pursued with increased vigour.

In the occupied countries, this resistance took two forms. One was non-violent; a stubborn refusal to co-operate with the conquerors, and a passive obstruction of their administrative machinery. The other was an active campaign of sabotage, raids and ambushes designed to disorganize and demoralize the occupying forces. The British and Americans gave most attention to the development of the second form. They themselves were fighting, and felt that the people of German-occupied Europe should also be fighting, so far as they were able.

Was it a wise policy on a long-term reckoning—taking account not only of winning the war but of securing the peace that should follow victory? Was its contribution to victory outweighed by its legacy of disorder? These may seem startling questions. But they are underlined by all too much evidence that the foundations of peace have been undermined by the spirit of violence that is rampant in many of the liberated countries.

At the time, the policy was adopted with great enthusiasm and little question. Once the German tide of conquest had spread over most of Europe, it seemed the obvious course to pursue in the effort to loosen Hitler's grip. It was just the sort of course that appealed to Mr. Churchill's mind and temperament. Besides his instinctive pugnacity and complete intentness on beating Hitler —regardless of what might happen afterwards—he had been a close associate and admirer of Lawrence. He now saw the chance to practise on the largest scale in Europe what the latter had demonstrated in a relatively limited part of the Arab zone.

To question its desirability was to appear lacking in resolution, and almost unpatriotic. Few dared to risk such an imputation, even if they felt doubts about the ultimate effects of the policy on the recovery of Europe.

War is always a matter of doing evil in the hope that good may come of it, and it is very difficult to show discrimination without failing in determination. Moreover, the cautious line is usually a mistake in battle, where it is too commonly followed, so that it rarely receives credit on the higher plane of war policy, where it is more often wise but usually unpopular. In the fever of war, public opinion craves for the most drastic measures, regardless of where they may lead.

What were the results? The armed Resistance forces undoubtedly imposed a considerable strain on the Germans. In the West, their most marked effect was in France. They also proved a serious menace to the German communications in Eastern Europe and the Balkans. The best tribute to their effect comes from the evidence of the German commanders. Like the British commanders in Ireland during "the troubles" they were acutely conscious of the worry and burden of coping with guerrilla foes who struck out of the blue and were shielded by the population.

General Blumentritt, Chief of Staff to Field-Marshal von Rundstedt in the West, told me how the operations of the Maquis interfered with the switching of the German forces to meet the Allied invasion. Headquarters had to be strongly guarded and generals accompanied by armed escorts when driving about. Others told me of the way that the German Army was reduced to the use of only a few main roads as routes of supply in White Russia and Poland, because so many of the bridges were blown up by the partisans.

But when these back area campaigns are analyzed, it would seem that their effect was largely in proportion to the extent to which they were combined with the operations of a strong regular army that was engaging the enemy's front, and drawing off his reserves. They rarely became more than a nuisance unless they coincided with the fact, or imminent threat, of a powerful offensive that absorbed the enemy's main attention.

At other times they were less effective than widespread passive resistance—and brought far more harm to the people of their own country. They provoked reprisals much severer than the injury inflicted on the enemy. They afforded his troops the opportunity for violent action that is always a relief to the nerves of a garrison in an unfriendly country. The material damage that the guerrillas produced directly, and indirectly in the course of reprisals, caused much suffering among their own people, and ultimately became a handicap on recovery after liberation.

But the heaviest handicap of all, and the most lasting one, was of a moral kind. The armed Resistance movement attracted not only the high-spirited lovers of freedom but also many "bad hats." It gave the latter licence to indulge their vices and work off their grudges under the cloak of patriotism—thus giving fresh point to Dr. Johnson's historic remark that "patriotism is the last refuge of a scoundrel." Worse still was its wider amoral effect on the younger generation as a whole. It taught them to defy authority and break the rules of civic morality in the fight against the occupying forces. This left a disrespect for "law and order" that inevitably continued after the invaders had gone.

The habit of violence takes much deeper root in irregular warfare than it does in regular warfare. In the latter it is counteracted by the habit of obedience to constituted authority, whereas the former makes a virtue of defying authority and violating rules. It becomes very difficult to rebuild a country, and a stable state, on such an undermined foundation.

Passive resistance has such effects in much lesser degree. It may foster a continuing habit of evasion, but it does not sow the seeds of civil war, nor breed terrorists.

A realization of the dangerous aftermath of guerrilla warfare came to me in reflection on Lawrence's campaigns in Arabia, and our discussions on the subject. My book on those campaigns, and exposition of the theory of guerrilla warfare, was taken as a guide by numerous leaders of commando units and resistance movements in the late war. Wingate, then only a captain serving in Palestine, came to see me shortly before it started, and was obviously filled with the idea of giving the theory a fresh and wider application. But I was beginning to have doubts—not of its immediate efficacy, but of its long-term effects. It seemed that they could be traced, like a thread, running through the persisting troubles that the British, as the Turks' successors, were suffering in the same area where Lawrence had spread the Arab Revolt.

Looking back further, doubts were deepened by seeing how the irregular forces that France had armed to meet the German invasion of 1870 had turned into a boomerang. They had been merely a nuisance to the invaders, but they had developed into the agency of that appalling fratricidal struggle known as the Commune. Moreover, the legacy of "illegitimate" action has been a continuing source of weakness in the subsequent history of France.

Earlier still was the ominous example of the Peninsular War, when Napoleon's defeat of the Spanish regular armies was counterbalanced by the success of the guerrilla bands that replaced them. As a popular uprising against a foreign conqueror, this was one of the most effective on record. It did more than Wellington's victories to loosen Napoleon's grip on Spain, and undermine his power. But it did not bring peace to liberated Spain. For it was followed by an epidemic of armed revolutions that continued in quick succession for half a century—and have broken out again in this century.

These lessons of history were too lightly disregarded by those who planned to promote violent insurrections as part of Allied war policy. It is only too probable that the reverberations will continue in Europe as well as in the Middle East. Significantly, some of the most courageous members of the French Resistance now admit that the military effect of the Maquis, or guerrilla element, was outweighed by their cumulative ill-effects, and wish that the movement had been confined to the organization of non-violent resistance.

There is increasing evidence of the unmixed value of this form of resistance, as practised in Norway, Denmark and Holland—and of the Nazis' inability to cope with it. They were experts in violence, and knew how to meet it. But subtler forms of opposition baffled them.

PART TWO

TOMORROW

Riddles of the Immediate Future

CHAPTER VIII

WHAT WOULD ANOTHER WAR BE LIKE?

L IKE a dark pall of cloud, the shadow
of another war has spread over the world. In America
the press and people's talk resounds with the rumblings
of its thunder. On the Continent the subject is less openly
discussed, but only because people want to banish the
thought from their minds—feeling that the countries of
Western Europe would again be the first to suffer, and
that the next time there would be no recovery. Deep
down, they pessimistically regard another war as almost
inevitable. In England, the atmosphere is more tranquil
and the outlook relatively more optimistic. That is good
in so far as it arises from a will for peace, and a resolve
to curb emotions that make for war. But it is dangerous
in so far as it arises from a disinclination to face realities.

The British were "ostriches" from 1919 to 1938—and
when their heads were jerked out of the sand in 1939 their
eyes became too angrily bloodshot to keep a clear sight
of the strategy best suited to deal with the situation. They
survived the danger and in the end came through to victory, but are paying heavily now for the blindness before

71

and during the war. Not the least part of the price is that "victory" has brought so little prospect of peace.

Widely as ideas may differ about what exactly would happen in another war, there is general agreement that the effects would be even more ruinous than in the last. So it is vital not to shirk the question and the exploration of the problem—lest we miss any chance either of avoiding or of surviving such a war. "Ostrichism" is suicidal.

In exploring the question it is important to distinguish between the form that a war may take at the outset, and the way it may develop later. To confuse these stages of growth has been a common mistake in the past. Between World Wars I and II many prophets declared that another war would begin with the wholesale destruction of cities by air attack. Public opinion became so obsessed with this lurid picture as to neglect other possibilities as well as more immediate dangers. When air attack fell short of expectation, complacency spread. Yet in the end cities were being wiped out progressively from the air. The prophets were justified, though their vision had leapt too far ahead.

The defence of the West suffered badly in 1940 from the cleavage between two extremes of opinion: the new school which thought only of bombing, and the old school which prepared for a repetition of 1918. But Germany suffered still worse in the long run for relying too much on attack, while neglecting to disperse its industries and put its plants underground until too late.

In the same way there is a danger today in the cleft impression that Hiroshima has left. Public opinion has tended to assume that no weapon other than the atom bomb is worth bothering about, and that this weapon is so certain to be overwhelming as to make any form of defence useless. Such fatalism breeds a fatal inertia.

On the other hand, a major section of the military profession feels so out of its depth in an atom age that it tends to cling to old habits of thought, and prepare for the kind of war to which it is accustomed—a war like the last one, prior to Hiroshima. Faced with a new menace, it dreams of tackling the problem by the eventual mobilization of big conscript armies and their transportation overseas to seize the enemy's atom bomb bases. Wedded to the idea that "attack is the best defence," it pins its faith to such a deferred offensive in the old style. It even re-practises the Normandy landing, with little regard to what might happen to its own home-base in the long interval. Such mobilization schemes are out of date.

The ordinary citizen, with sounder instinct, feels that this sort of military planning is too much like children's play-acting. The kind of questions he is asking are more basic ones. "Can cities, or even nations, survive a war fought with atom bombs?" "How many atom bombs would be needed to decide the issue?" "Would ultimate victory in such a war be of any avail?" "Is it certain that atom bombs will be used?" "Can anything be done to minimize the menace?" "Do armies or navies matter any longer?"

The answer to most of these questions can be compressed in a sentence—"It all depends on circumstances." That is not such a vague answer as it appears. If a small country like Belgium or Holland were opposed to a power possessing atom bombs, its forces would be more useless and resistance more hopeless than was the case in 1940. If it came to a conflict it is likely that two or three atom bombs would suffice to decide the issue. But in the case of a vast country like Russia several hundred atom bombs might not be decisive—even if such a country were unable to retort in kind. China might be as difficult, or more difficult, to subdue by such weapons.

Chances of survival in another war do not depend on the same factors as the chances of victory. The more highly civilized countries, with more highly developed industrial and scientific resources, have a better chance of gaining a superiority in the new forms of weapon-power. Yet they stand at a corresponding disadvantage in surviving a bombardment of this kind. For they are extremely vulnerable by comparison with more primitive countries where cities and ports are less important, social organization less elaborate, standards of life lower, and the people more inured to hardship.

It was the continued backwardness of Russia, coupled with her immense spaces, that enabled her to survive Hitler's *blitzkrieg* in 1941. Similar factors helped China in withstanding Japan's fifteen-year effort to conquer her.

As in nature, the more complex organism is the more delicate, and less fitted to endure violent dislocation. Higher forms of civilization depend for survival not on their toughness but on applying their brains to devise new means of defence. They must rely on mental rather than on physical adaptability. That is a lesson we should remember when inclined to boast that we "can take it." Whether it be a matter of meeting the threats of future warfare or the present economic crisis, a spirit of go-and-get-it is more vital than a spirit of grin-and-bear-it.

These basic differences in the circumstances of nations are too often forgotten in discussing the problems of future warfare.

Before we can really begin to consider what another war would be like, we must come down from the abstract to the concrete—in order to get a firm footing. That means discussing how and where war might break out.

There are three ways in which another world war might be detonated. One is a direct clash between the U.S.A. and the U.S.S.R. Another is a conflict arising between the U.S.S.R. and states other than the U.S.A. but within the latter's sphere of interest—while the most obvious example is a Russian threat to European members of the Atlantic Pact, it is far from being the only one, for there is hardly any state remaining outside the Russian sphere that the Americans can afford to see succumb. A third way is from a conflict arising between states that the two giant powers respectively support—a duel that the "seconds" begin and the principals join in. Thus the three cases virtually amount to one. Their form, however, might differ considerably—according to the site of the initial outbreak.

The Pacific is the most likely area where a direct clash between the U.S.A. and the U.S.S.R. might arise. A war breaking out in that direction would probably be the slowest to reach a catastrophic pitch, and might be a lightning conductor for the much-battered countries of Western Europe.

The second and third cases might arise anywhere in Europe, the Middle East or South-East Asia. If the outbreak came in the Middle East, Britain's interests and forces would bear the shock. But her interests there, though important, are not *so* vital to her security as habit has accustomed us to assume, while an outbreak in that quarter might conceivably divert the lightning from quarters nearer home. Moreover, the campaign would probably be waged on relatively familiar lines. A similar reflection applies to the risk of an outbreak in South-East Asia.

An outbreak in Europe would be the most dangerous both in its form and for the future of Western civilization.

The European countries would suffer terribly both in the short run and in the long run. In the course of the struggle, the afflictions of the older and newer styles of warfare would probably be combined. Contrary to the belief generally held, however, the older style would be likely to predominate at the outset—at any rate if war should come before long, during the period when the pace of new weapon development is still more or less calculable.

War might come any time—even though no government desired or designed it. Taking account of the rivalries, fears and suspicions fomented by the friction of the "Iron Curtain" which divides Europe, we should be foolish to discount the risks of an unpremeditated outbreak. The atmosphere is perilously inflammable.

In such *circumstances*, complacency is almost as dangerous as passion. The acute crisis of 1948 provided an ironical echo to Mr. Bevin's 1947 assurance that so far as he could see there was "no chance of war in this generation." Any relaxation of tension, however, is too apt to bring a relapse into a mistaken complacency. Almost on the eve of war in 1914, and again shortly before its outbreak in 1939, British Foreign Office authorities entertained the view that any danger of war was subsiding.

In 1914, two pistol-shots fired by a young and fanatical Slav nationalist, who was the tool of a secret society of Serbian officers, had immeasurable consequences. They detonated the First World War, which in turn laid the powder-trail for the Second. Another incident of this kind, in the present explosive circumstances of Europe, might produce a Third World War. When relations are strained an ill-judged step on one side may all too easily lead to a precipitate step on the other side, and to neither drawing back for fear of losing face, at home and abroad.

That is the way wars break out, more often than by deliberate intention.

If war were detonated in Europe, what course would it take? Russia may not yet possess many atom bombs, but her army is far stronger than any available to oppose her in Europe. The Americans and the British have only small contingents left there, the armies of the liberated countries are only in process of reconstruction, and the German army has disappeared. We have thus to reckon with the probability of a Russian tidal wave surging forward to the Mediterranean or the Atlantic coast of Europe, or to both. Supply difficulties might check the Red Army's momentum, more perhaps than direct resistance could, but it is experienced in living on the countries it occupies. It might also count on dissident elements in other countries for help in clearing the path.

It would be unwise to assume that atom bombs would check its progress. Their radius of destructive effect is limited, and so is America's stock of them. At present they are not a tactical weapon, suitable against land forces—especially forces so fluid as the Russian.

The prospect of atom bombs dropping on Moscow and Leningrad might be a deterrent to a decision for war, but would hardly be decisive of the issue once war broke out. It is dubious whether America's stock of them would suffice to cripple Russia's war potential, even if her bombers could attain their objectives. The prospect is hedged with uncertainties, and dependent on a large element of chance. Russia's circumstances make her the least accessible and susceptible of targets for atomic warfare. The deeper her forces advanced in Europe the more shelter they would gain both for themselves and their homeland. Moreover, in so far as Russia has already begun to develop the new kind of weapons, she might be able to harass the cities of the West to a distressing if not fatal degree, coincidently with her forward march.

Later, as the war went on, the forecast would have to be revised as the outlook became different—more adverse to Russia's situation. But that prospective change would not carry much consolation for the peoples of Western Europe. They would be likely to suffer far worse in the initial conquest and occupation than in 1940, and again more frightfully in the process of liberation. Nor is the prospect much better for the principals.

By the later stages of an early war, or the earlier stages of a deferred war, destructive menaces far exceeding the original atom bomb would be developed. In the first place is an improvement in the atom bomb itself whereby the explosive effect and area of devastation would be greatly increased. The atom bomb used against Japan's cities should in theory have had an effect equal to 20,000 tons of T.N.T., but in practice only proved equal to a tenth of that amount. That deficiency can probably be remedied.

Moreover, humanity is now faced with the potential menace of the hydrogen bomb. Such a bomb, if successfully developed, could have an immensely greater devastating power than the present atom bomb. Leading scientists have estimated the blast as over 1,000 times more powerful, and the likely area of devastation as at least 100 times greater. While there are wide differences of opinion among them as to some of its effects, such as whether it would have any prolonged radioactivity, there seems to be general agreement that a single bomb of this kind could wipe out the largest of cities—if it could be delivered to the target. On the other hand, it is even less suitable than the atom bomb as a weapon against invading forces.

Another new weapon is a toxin mixed in a dust-spray, and it is said to be capable of infecting the whole population of a large city. Bacteriological weapons, however, have not fulfilled predictions as yet, and if they did might carry a liability to recoil on the user. Because of that "boomerang" risk, research is now being directed to ways of producing localized and temporary effects, rather than a spreading epidemic.

A further new weapon is a radioactive spray, combining extreme deadliness with the least possible chance of being counteracted by defensive precautions. This may prove the most effective of all the new "agents." But the problem of protecting the user against the effects of radioactivity is a difficult one, and particularly complex in the case of aircraft crews. It may be easier to profit by it for multiplying the delaying powers of river-barriers, as a check to an invader.

For conveying any of these new "agents" to their target, ordinary aircraft may eventually be superseded by developments of V1 and V2. How soon it will be, is difficult to estimate. While the range of guided missiles has already been greatly extended, the problem of combining long range with precision has still to be solved. It is wise to bear in mind, however, that although accuracy tends to lessen as the range lengthens, the new "agents" have so wide a lethal radius that accuracy in the aim of the missile becomes less important.

The limitations of range—with accuracy—might also be overcome in other ways. Thus seapower might find fresh offensive scope through the development of new types of vessels designed as floating platforms for guided missiles, which could be launched to their target from points close to the enemy's coast.

What is the chance that nations possessing these new

weapons of mass destruction may refrain from employing them if another war comes? Here again the answer is
likely to depend on circumstances.

In the light of past experience—of the way minds and
moods move in war—it is probable that if one side alone
has such an overwhelming weapon it will be used. This
is more probable still if it happens that the other side
has gained the initial advantage and cannot be easily
ejected from the conquests it has made. An aggressor is
apt to be more chary of unloosing novel forms of destruction if he thinks he can prevail on older lines and secure his booty undamaged.

But if both sides possess the same weapon—or even
imagine that the other has it ready—there is a fair chance
that both may hesitate to unloose it, from mutual fear of
the common consequences. That has happened before in
war, the latest example being the non-use of poison gas
in World War II, despite its great and increasing effect
in World War I. Mankind, and even its governments, can
show uncommon sense and restraint when they see
clearly enough that it is a matter of mutual preservation.
The trouble is that they easily become too optimistic
about their own chances of an advantage compared with
the other side's.

If they do not refrain, however, one can predict the
result with reasonable certainty—that whichever side
emerges as the nominal victor will find the fruits of victory more poisonous than ever. And civilization itself will
be the greatest loser.

CHAPTER IX

COULD EUROPE SURVIVE ANOTHER WAR?

T HE chances of peace and war are
closely balanced—almost on a knife edge. One may doubt
whether any Government wants another war, but it is
hard to see how it can be avoided if the present tension
persists. The "iron curtain" that now divides the world
fulfils its name all too well in preventing peaceful communication, but it is only a tin curtain in other respects.
A large extent of it has no strength as a military barrier,
and it is not sound-proof against the roaring on either
side of it. If anything, it tends to make the roars sound
worse, and sharpens their reverberation.

On this side of the curtain, the language used about
Soviet policy is stronger than was ever addressed to Hitler before war came, but what even Americans say is
mild compared with the abusive terms the Russians hurl
at American policy. In the light of history, it hardly
seems that such intense friction and mutual suspicion can
go on indefinitely without resulting in an explosion. It is
true that, last century, the "Balance of Power" several
times sufficed to tide over critical situations, at least when

81

rival power was really well-balanced, but it never had to
stand such strains as present methods of diplomacy impose.

Everyone who realizes what another war would involve must hope to see mutual restraint maintained, but
it would be unrealistic to count on peace being preserved
unless there is a relaxation of the present *hostilities*. The
world is again in a state of "camouflaged war" such as
went on from 1936 until it broke out into the open in
1939. We paid heavily then for the statesmen's slowness
to recognize the realities and meet the needs of the situation. The devastation of many countries in Europe and
the impoverishment of all has been the price of that
blindness or inertia.

This time the consequences are likely to be much
worse. Statesmen who are responsible for their people's
security ought to pin on their office walls a representative
selection of the warnings given by many of the scientists
who were concerned in the development of the atom
bomb and kindred weapons. They are grim enough, if
taken seriously, to make anyone who is not an invincible
optimist feel he might as well save time by putting his
head in a gas oven *unless* something *effective* can be
done to forestall the fate predicted. These warnings do
not seem to be taken seriously. At any rate there is little
sign anywhere that they are producing an adequate practical effect.

The statesmen do not behave as if the main thing that
mattered was to avert such a war. They do not even
show a real sense of urgency about protective preparations. Meanwhile too many of their official military advisers are apt to talk as if another war would be of the
same style as the last except for some fresh trimmings.

The extent of apparent unconcern with the prospect suggests an amazing lack of vision and understanding.

That prospect would be much worse for Britain and the other countries in Western Europe than for the two giant rivals, the U.S.A. and the U.S.S.R. Russia has shown her capacity to absorb and survive blows that would have pulverized more concentrated and complicated organisms like the states of Western Europe. America is much further out of range than these, besides being vaster. Space helps to make a country less sensitive—in a double sense.

Ultimate victory in another war would bring little consolation to the countries of Western Europe if they were to be first submerged by a fresh tide of invasion, and then liberated in a long drawn-out struggle waged with atom bombs and other new weapons of mass destruction. They are already suffering badly enough from the pains of the last "liberation," but these are mild compared with what they might suffer another time.

For them, prevention is more important than redemption—and this reflection now applies with almost equal force to Britain's case. She is a little further out of reach than her Continental neighbours, and her sea-moat is still a protection against invasion, but if they were overrun she would be exposed to a close-range bombardment beginning where Hitler's left off. Britain remains a concentrated island target, faced with weapons that can spread destruction more widely than did any of those immature ones which Hitler used.

In the realm of foreign policy, Mr. Attlee and Mr. Bevin have bound her closely to America, faithfully following Mr. Churchill's line. Economic stress has pulled the knots tighter. Strategically, however, she is on the other side of the Atlantic from America and uncomfortably close to any conflagration on the mainland of Europe —where the results of the Roosevelt-Churchill policy of "unconditional surrender" have completely removed the only possible fireproof safety-curtain. This was pointed out when the policy was formulated, but was not heeded by the responsible statesmen. It is no use to indulge in regrets now, but the effects on the present situation of Western Europe, including Britain, need to be clearly recognized.

Shortly after the first atom bomb exploded, and World War II ended, General Marshall, then the U.S. Chief of Staff, declared—"The only effective defence a nation can now maintain is the power of attack." In drawing this conclusion he was not thinking mainly in terms of an atomic offensive. For he went on to argue that the advent of this new weapon required the U.S. to have a larger army. (Admirals, with Mr. Churchill's support, have similarly argued that it makes battleships more necessary.) Accordingly, General Marshall propounded a plan of universal military training aimed to produce an army of 4,000,000 men within *one* year of the outbreak of war —in order to attack and capture the enemy's atom bomb and rocket bases. For he pictured war starting with a deluge of these new missiles. But he did not discuss the fate of the cities, and productive centres, before this vast army could be mobilized, transported overseas, and brought into action. This military "Marshall Plan" seemed a dangerously deferred insurance policy against the dangers he pictured.

As Mr. Marshall, U.S. Secretary of State, he subsequently guided America's policy in relation to Europe. While he was a most admirable representative of the old school in both fields, the limitations of his outlook raise a doubt whether his "realistic" policy took sufficient account of near risks and deeper realities. It also suffered from overlooking the time-factor. That same risk has been apparent in the economic "Marshall Plan."

Even if America's faith in the theory that "attack is the best defence" were conceived in more modern terms, it would hardly fit the circumstances of Britain and the other countries of Western Europe. It is all very well for the giants to rely on offensive or counter-offensive power, but Britain and her neighbours would be foolish to repose much trust in it in so far as they are involved. In themselves they have little power of this kind, and if they are to become merely an advanced base for the mounting of America's atomic and rocket weapons their lot will be disastrous whatever the ultimate issue. For an advanced base is always an exposed spot. With ruthless candour, American defence memoranda have described Britain as America's shock-absorber in another war. The position of a shock-absorber in the atomic and rocket age is a fatal one.

While the giant powers talk in offensive terms, the basic problem of Britain and her neighbours in the West is that of *defence*—in the real sense of the term. There is no longer any ground for them to hope that the results of initial defeat can be restored in the end by a victorious offensive. Their problem of defence has two facets—prevention and protection.

There is a lesson from the immediate past. From the moment Hitler gained power in Germany, his belief in the offensive spurred him to develop new offensive means, and the Western democracies' neglect to develop adequate defensive means opened the way for his initial success. That neglect was based on the failure of his opponents to see clearly that their initial problem was bound to be one of defence, since he, not they, would

take the lead in making war. In the later stage of the war
Hitler's continued belief in the offensive made him
neglectful of defensive precautions—and that mistake
proved fatal. But we should not forget how nearly fatal
was the initial mistake of the Western democracies. All
went down like ninepins save Britain, and her margin of
salvation was very narrow.

What can be done towards preventing such an initial
collapse if another war came? The only serious risk on
the present horizon lies in becoming involved, directly or
indirectly, in a clash with Russia. Viewing the shape of
it as traced in the previous chapter, the first-stage problem is that of checking an overland surge into Western
Europe, or into other territory that is of vital importance
to our security.

The primary need is to build up a strong barrier, in
place of a tin curtain—while taking care to avoid wasting
such strength as the Western Powers have in bolstering
up positions that are really indefensible. Neither atom
bombs nor the prospect of eventual reinforcement by
troops shipped from America forms a solution for this
problem. Conscription, too, is not an effective contribution. A large conscript army is slow to mobilize its
strength, and is not a suitable means to meet sudden invasion. It is particularly unsuitable for Britain, as she would
first have to transport it overseas, and the larger the army
the longer the delay. Britain's best contribution is in the
form of high-quality forces, such as armoured and airborne divisions, that are either on the scene or can be
quickly rushed there. That calls for a professional army,
and one that is as strong as possible. The same reflections
apply to American military aid. Plans for building up another great national army as in World War II carry no
promise of preserving Europe. Even a small increase in

the American forces now serving in Europe would count for more.

The Continental countries, too, would be wiser to develop the professional armies that provide ever-ready cover than to rely on conscript armies that are larger on paper. As shown elsewhere in this book the experience of 1940 exploded the illusion of strength which "numbers" produced—and there may be less warning another time.

Moreover, any army that depends on rail and road transport is inviting a paralytic stroke in the future. All transport should be capable of moving across country, and, better still, across rivers—by swimming instead of by bridges. But it is hardly conceivable that such new types of transport could be provided on the vast scale required by conscript armies and only Russians are capable of operating without transport and supplies. With élite professional forces, the problem of mobility would be simpler.

The military problem of a strong barrier is linked to the political problem of a strong base. In themselves, none of the European states on this side of the tin curtain have either the strength or the depth needed to ensure their chances of defence. Britain herself is small, and the extent of her scattered empire adds more to her liabilities than to her insurance against immediate risks. But it would be a different picture if these European states, including Britain, were combined in a solid block, with its forces and resources integrated, and the great land-mass of Africa behind it to provide strategic depth. Their interests have become increasingly a common interest, and by good fortune they alone have possessions in the adjoining African continent. In scale and potential such a Union would be comparable with the U.S.A. and the U.S.S.R. It could be developed into a formidable deter-

rent to aggression. Mr. Winston Churchill, belatedly rec-
ognizing the consequences of his own wartime policy,
has come out strongly in favour of such a Union, and of
it including the Germans. His advocacy may be unfortunate in view of the prejudices he cherishes and arouses.
But the idea is greater, and more essential, than any of
its sponsors. The Labour Government in Britain has
shown extreme caution over the project. Caution, like
patriotism, is not enough. It will not nearly suffice to meet
—economically, politically, or militarily—the critical situations that now face us. Vision is needed, and the moral
courage to follow it through.

It is worth emphasizing that the two problems of prevention coincide—those of putting a check on war, and
on penetration in case of war. For successful encroach-
ment may easily develop into invasion, and war. The two
solutions also coincide. For strengthening the base would
help to strengthen the barrier.

I pass now to the problem of protection against atom
bombs and rockets. For reasons already explained, this
danger might not be as acute at the start of war as is
generally imagined. But it might become acute later—and
would be overhanging the scene all the time. In any case,
it is so frightful a danger that no complacency is justified,
nor any delay in developing the fullest possible measures
of protection.

The soldiers' idea of "marshalling" a great expeditionary force to go overseas, drive the enemy back, and thus
capture his launching sites is so slow as to be hopeless. It
took three years last time, when the new weapons were
in infancy. The airmen's idea of bombing the sites was of
very limited effect in 1944, and is likely to be more futile
as the range lengthens. Those who talk of using airborne
armies to capture the sites show a better sense of the

time-factor, but overlook the difficulty of maintaining these at long range and overcoming an enemy who is strong on the ground—his own ground.

Compared with such offensive counters, there may be more hope in new means of defence. But much depends on the pace of development; at present it is not fast enough, compared with the growth of danger, to inspire confidence. While every new menace may have its antidote, there is always a time-lag in perfecting this, and a war may be decided in the interval. Progress has been made in developing radar-guided rockets for use from the ground against jet-bombers, as well as rockets that can be employed by fighter aircraft—missile "defenders" of supersonic speed that will "home" onto the attacking bombers, and explode by proximity fuse. But to develop such antidotes sufficiently to deal with the long-range rocket itself is more difficult. Even if radar or other devices be produced to intercept the missile, or, better still, discover and annul it before it is launched, they will need to attain something approaching 100 per cent accuracy —because of the terrific damage that even one atomic missile can cause. We ought to do our utmost in such defensive research—more than we are doing—but it would be rash to repose all our trust in it.

Civil defence, protection in the most direct sense, has become more vital than ever. Yet it seems to have dropped out of mind. In the first place the Western countries ought to develop a pattern of dispersion—not merely an emergency evacuation, but a planned dispersion of industry and population, beginning without delay. That, however, is not nearly enough. Essential industries and services must go underground in another war. That means they must have the underground sites prepared in advance. Nor will it suffice for plants and offices to be thus protected. The workers would need to be provided with quarters of a kind where they could live in conditions adequate for health.

Under the great cities, a series of air-conditioned honeycomb towns might radiate from the underground railways, which could serve their present purpose of intercommunication. Provincial centres would also be provided with a low-level layer where work and life could carry on. Surface buildings, including houses, might be connected by underground passages to the central subways. Pipelines might be developed more widely, and in new ways, for the transit of supplies.

All this may seem elaborate to the point of being fantastic, yet to plan anything less would be trifling with the problem of national survival in an atomic war. A nation that tackled the problem early would gain more in security than by increasing its conventional armed forces, and be immensely strengthened in foreign relations. To be a step ahead of possible aggressor nations in protection would be a long step not only towards self-preservation of peace. A nation that neglects such protective measures is living in a fool's haven.

CHAPTER X

"GLOBAL WAR"

THE phrases "global war" and "global strategy" have come much into vogue in recent years. What do these phrases mean?

There is, first, the generalized meaning of a world-wide conflict in which all the principal powers are engaged. That idea is not really fresh, since we have already been through the "First World War" and the "Second World War" within a span of thirty years. Naturally, a reorientation of the idea must result from changing factors—the decline of all the West European powers, the collapse of Germany and of Japan, the expansion and industrialization of the U.S.S.R., the preponderant position gained by the U.S.A. as a consequence of the two world wars, the immense developments of war-applied science which these terrific struggles produced, and the sweeping social changes which they also produced. The sum effect is to make it foolish for any people on this earth to consider their own problem except in relation to a world view.

The term "global" is used, however, in a second and more specific sense—to impress on us new aspects of the

91

fact that the world is round and not flat. We are now urged to study our strategic problems on a globe, instead of on a map. The impulse has come from the possibilities of flying, and the potentialities of firing projectiles, over Polar regions—the North Pole in particular.

Globes are to be found in schoolrooms, but they receive far less attention than wall-maps or atlases. They have been rarer, and more rarely studied, in Government offices and military headquarters. The habit of viewing the world from school-days onward on the flat surface of a map is apt to engrave impressions that are not easily corrected.

How different appears the relative size and situation of many countries and areas. On the flat map, the northerly lands become vastly exaggerated in proportion to those in the temperate and tropical zones. Canada and even Greenland bulk larger than China, while Scandinavia looks as big as India. Russia appears more than double the size of the whole of Africa, whereas it is actually somewhat smaller. On the other hand, the United States of America is made to appear more diminutive than it is in reality.

Such false comparisons, continually impressed from childhood, are bound to have misleading effects—of greater consequence than has ever been recognized. In reflection, we may begin to realize their subconscious influence on Russian minds. The British, for example, have suffered from the inflated idea of the British Empire's strength that was fostered by the extent of territory coloured red on maps of the world based on Mercator's Projection.

Such a map also distorts the geographical situation of some of the principal countries in relation to one another. Russia and North America have been thought of as standing in the right and left halves of the world, and at the right and left ends of the same lateral line. Politically, that picture has today become more apt than ever, though right and left are reversed, but geographically it is no longer fitting. The comfortable feeling induced by the broad Atlantic sea-belt has been dispelled by an Arctic wind—the freezing thought that bombers and rockets may soon be hurtling to and fro over the North Pole.

For on a globe Russia and North America are seen to be facing one another on their northern borders. In that nose-end view each looks closer and more threatening to the other than in the usual easterly-westerly side view. That appearance is intensified by the different contour they take—like two crouching wrestlers or gorillas with arms stretched out to grip one another in a strangling embrace.

This new global aspect is impressive. It has stimulated a flow of activity northwards. The Russians showed a growing interest in this direction soon after the Soviet regime was installed. In 1928 they claimed possession of all land lying between their continental coast and the North Pole. Within ten years they had made the "North-East Passage" from the Atlantic to the Pacific a regular traffic-route, with a chain of ports along their whole northern coast. They had also occupied the most northerly island of the Francis Joseph group, which lies nearer the Pole than Norwegian-owned Spitsbergen. What they have done since is a matter of speculation.

American activity has been a post-war rush, following the increasing friction with Russia, and the greatly lengthened range of bombing aircraft together with the development of guided missiles. The keynote was sounded by General Spaatz, the former U.S. Air Force Chief of Staff, when he declared in 1947: "If our de-

fences are to be between us and the enemy, they must be
on the Arctic frontier." That conclusion is of still closer,
if not more vital, concern to Canada—which has become
a buffer-state on that route. The point was rubbed in by
Admiral Jones, her late Chief of Naval Staff, who star-
tlingly announced that she would be "in the nutcracker
in the atom war against major American cities." There
has also been alarming talk of airborne invading forces
coming over the Pole, and, still more, of combined air
and land invasion from Eastern Siberia, across the Behring Straits, and through Alaska.

Most people have forgotten, but not the respective
Governments, that Alaska was "Russian America" until
1867, when this vast bridgehead on the American continent was ceded to the U.S.A. for a mere seven million
dollars—an infinitesimal fraction of what she has spent
in developing its defences and strategic communications
in the last few years. Airfields have been multiplying
there, and on a smaller scale in the northern parts of
Canada. There is a chain of meteorological stations,
which now have a strategic bearing, along and within the
Arctic Circle from Greenland to Point Barrow, the north-
west corner of Alaska. Both Canadian and American
forces have been carrying out experimental tests with
special equipment in mechanized operations on the Arctic frontier. All this has served to draw people's eyes up-
ward.

Yet the impressiveness of this new aspect exceeds its
importance. We ought not to overlook it, but would be
unwise to overrate it—lest it diverts attention from more
immediate risks. The effect has been too much like a
rush of blood to the head. For the novelty of this Polar
bearing has tended to blind people to limitations in real-

ity which prevail at present, and may continue longer than is imagined.

The shortening of range possible by flying or firing over the Pole, in a Russo-American conflict, is not much. From the most northerly point in Russia, New York is over 4,000 miles distant. It is considerably nearer the Russian airfields in the Russian-occupied zone of Germany. Even if airfields or missile launching-sites could be built in the Arctic islands of the Francis Joseph group they would be no nearer to New York than those available on the Baltic.

The cities on the west coast of the U.S.A. are slightly more exposed to attack from Russian territory, but such attack would come over the north Pacific, not over the Arctic. Even so, San Francisco is over 3,000 miles distant from airfields in Eastern Siberia.

Now look at the problem the other way round. The U.S.A. would gain nothing from attempting to attack Russia over the Polar route. Moscow is over 4,000 miles from her airfields in Alaska, and Russia's new industrial centres behind the Ural mountains are almost as far. The distance to Moscow is hardly any further over the Atlantic, from the American bases in New England. From the airfields in Newfoundland it is considerably less— about 3,500. From Iceland it is a bare 1,800 miles. But even that is further from Moscow than the airfields in Western Europe, where suitable bases are more plentiful.

Those who talk glibly about over-the-Pole attack are too inclined to overlook some of the basic factors, and handicaps. Besides the special difficulties of flying, navigation, and maintenance in such icy conditions, there is the problem of constructing suitable bases from which the bombers or missiles are to be launched, and the still

greater problem of keeping up supplies to them on an
adequate scale. The further north they are pushed, the
more remote they will be from the sources of supply, and
the more precarious their lines of communication.

But *range* itself—the distance that bomb-loaded aircraft can fly and projectiles travel—is the biggest handicap of all. The U.S. Navy's new Lockheed Neptune has
covered over 11,000 miles in one non-stop flight. This
would suggest to the ordinary man that it might be able
to bomb a target 5,500 miles distant and return to its
base. But in reality it could not attain anything approaching such an operational range when loaded with bombs.
The larger the bomb-load, the more its fuel-load would
have to be cut down.

A graphic illustration of how this handicap multiplies
is provided by the new B-36 that is now being produced
in the United States. This 124-ton giant is designed to
carry a bomb-load of 36 tons, but it would have to be cut
down to a mere 5 tons if the machine is to reach a target
5,000 miles distant. But that calculation does not reckon
with tactical conditions and deviations. Its operational
range with the minimum bomb-load worth carrying may
prove to be no more than 3,000 miles, if that.

Besides the B-36, the new B-50 is being produced in
quantity to replace the B-29, the "Superfortress"—which
was the only wartime aircraft capable of carrying the
atom bomb. The B-50 was designed to carry a bomb-
load of 10 tons, but at an operational range of 3,000 miles
its bomb-load is barely 5 tons. Both these new bombers
could be much more effective if used at shorter range.

The cost and complexity of manufacturing such giant
machines as the B-36, maintaining them, and providing
adequate airfields for their operation are further limitations. Relatively slow (300-400 m.p.h.) they may prove

vulnerable to the stings of the new jet-engined fighters unless themselves protected by a fighter escort. It is difficult to gauge to what extent their high "ceiling" (40,000 feet) would really secure them against interception. The need for an escort would be a most serious limitation on their *effective* range. While the new jet-bombers, such as the XB-47, are much faster (500-600 m.p.h.), their operational range is much shorter—hardly 1,000 miles.

As for "robot" missiles, their effective range is very limited at present, and may continue to be so. That of the German V1, the "flying bomb," was barely 150 miles, and that of the V2, the rocket, was only about 220 miles. Intensive post-war experiment makes it likely that this range may soon be extended to over 500 miles, and perhaps not far short of 1,000 miles, but whether adequate accuracy can be attained at the longer range remains doubtful. The prospect of a 3,000-mile rocket has become more remote than it seemed a few years ago. Moreover, the problem of guiding such missiles, by radar and other means, becomes more complicated as the range lengthens. We are still far from solving many of the problems associated with "push-button warfare."

The V2 weighed 14 tons, yet the explosive war-head it carried was only one ton. Subsequent advances in extending the range of such rockets would be offset if they were fitted with an atomic war-head. Indeed, the prospect of attaining the power of effective bombardment at super-long range may be less than that of developing new means of "closing the range"—such as submersible warships designed to mount rockets or other missiles, and capable of approaching near enough to the enemy's coast to bombard his vital points.

In sum, should another war come soon it is not likely that the world will see, as the curtain rises, American and

Russian fighting one another by long-range bombardment across the Arctic Ocean, nor across the Atlantic
Ocean. That popular picture is still a vision of the future,
not a near probability—and could be a dangerous dis-
traction from more vital realities. If the Russians were to
overrun Western Europe, the continuation of the war
with America might eventually develop into a trans-
ocean bombardment by long-range weapons of mass destruction, with spreading devastation in both continents.
But the Americans, if only to forestall any such ultimate
possibility, would have to fight on this side of the Atlantic
from the outset. No other strategy could as yet be effective, even for bombing action.

Moscow is barely 1,100 miles distant from some of the
present American air bases in Germany. It is only 800
miles from Swedish airfields. But even if the bases in
Germany had to be abandoned, and Sweden could not be
utilized, Moscow would still be only 1,500 miles from
bases in England. Even from Spain, which is now
receiving much attention from the American military
authorities as a potential bridgehead to maintain in Continental Europe, Moscow is no further than from Iceland.
From North Africa it is a shade closer—about 1,700 miles
—while the Caucasian oilfields, on which Russia's forces
primarily depend for their fuel supply, are little more
than 1,200 miles distant from African air bases. The Rumanian oilfields are within 1,000 miles range. Indeed, all
the main centres of Russia's war-making power are less
than half—and some much less than half—the distance
from North Africa than they are from North America
over the Pole.

In any plan of defence for the West, Africa is of vital
importance. Geographically and strategically that continent forms a pivotal position. It provides the forces of

Western Union with the possibility of strategic defence in depth, and with wide scope for developing counter-offensive action. It also offers one of the greatest sources of raw material in the world which has as yet hardly been tapped. Even today the U.S.A. is almost wholly dependent on African sources for three of the most important new war-making materials—cobalt, columbite, and uranium. The first two are needed for hardening steel, and become more important still with the introduction of the jet-engine. The third is the raw material for the atomic bomb. The world's largest known deposit of pitchblende, from which uranium is extracted, lies in the Belgian Congo.

With Africa securely held and its potentialities adequately developed, the U.S.A. and her allies would be assured of the strategic resources to outlast and outclass Russia's in the case of another prolonged World War. The strategic potentialities would be increased if Turkey were available as a forward position in front of the main one, since most of Russia's strategic-economic keypoints are accessible from there.

For a long time, British policy has magnified the importance of the "Middle East"—Iraq, Syria, and Palestine in particular—and devoted inordinate efforts to its sustenance, with poor results. More recently, the U.S.A. has interested itself in that area, in a still more confused way. But this "Middle East" is far more vulnerable, both to military invasion and political infiltration, than Turkey—a mountain-and-sea girdled country, with a more stable and martial people. The Turks, too, have more reason to make common cause with the West so long as they are assured of adequate and timely support.

Meanwhile, in Cyprus Britain already possesses a sea-girt advanced post, with big possibilities as an air base, that shortens the range by several hundred miles compared with the air bases on the North African coast.

It is doubtful whether the potential importance of these points, for a reorientated global strategy, have been fully grasped by the Western Powers. There have been too many signs of stop-gap policy, instead of clear-cut policy. They waver between distant visions and pettifogging adjustments of old habits. That can only carry them deeper into danger, without creating practical safeguards.

There is a danger, too, in America's preoccupation with the Pacific angle of a global view. It tends to distract too much of her attention and effort to a quarter which can have no decisive bearing on present issues. A sober estimate of the immense difficulties imposed by scanty communications and barren conditions would discount the idea that a powerful attack can be carried out and maintained across the Behring Straits, either way—from Siberia into America, or Alaska into Russia. Still more thought and effort has been devoted by the U.S.A. to the strengthening of her girdle of bases further south. While these are of regional importance, for America's security and influence in the Far East, no military effort which she mounted there, if war broke out, would seriously affect the main struggle in the West. Even the U.S.A.'s vast resources do not justify her in disregarding the strategic law of economy of force.

A true view of global strategy would emphasize the need of concentrating the maximum possible effort where it can have the closest possible bearing on the main issue. The earlier the concentration in this direction, the more effective it may prove—not merely in assuring the issue of a war but in averting war. For another war, with the weapons now in development, could be fatal to the world as a whole. It has become truer than ever that prevention is better than cure.

Two world wars have seen the aggressor being beaten in the long run. But that did not suffice to prevent the first being repeated, nor even the renewed threat of a third. A surer way of prevention would be to make it plain that an aggressor cannot even count on victory in the short run.

CHAPTER XI

THE DEFENCE OF WESTERN EUROPE

IT WAS remarked in World War I that many French generals had a habit of assuming that the formulation of a plan was equivalent to its fulfilment. They took great care to ensure that their instructions were drafted in correct form, and in accordance with the prevailing staff doctrine, but showed little concern as to whether the instructions fitted the actual circumstances, or whether they were, in fact, carried out. Subsequent exploration of the history of that war revealed many occasions on which their orders, though serving as evidence of their intentions, had no effect on the course of events. Often the orders were so obviously unrelated to the situation of the moment, or to the resources available at the moment, that the subordinate headquarters merely ignored them. Plans and events tended to pursue their way on two separate planes.

World War I was of such a slow-moving nature that the discrepancy had no catastrophic results. But the persistence of this High Command habit into World War II, with its much accelerated tempo, was a vital factor in

102

precipitating the French Army's breakdown in face of the *blitzkrieg*. The orders from above were repeatedly misplaced and mistimed—having been framed for a situation different from reality or one that changed. Thus they deepened the confusion of the executants and frustrated any remedy that might have provided a chance of recovery.

It is worth dwelling on the "French case" because, in its tragic consequences, it embodied the clearest warning of a disease that is becoming pandemic—bureaucratic schizophrenia. This might well be termed the characteristic mental disease of the modern state—as prevalent in the civil as in the military sphere, though even more dangerous in the latter. It produces the hallucination that planning is identical with performance. A common initial symptom is a tendency to devise an elaborate planning organization to deal with a problem and then to lapse into a satisfied feeling that the problem itself has been solved.

In September, 1948, the Defence Ministers of Britain, France, Belgium, Holland and Luxembourg met and decided to form a permanent defence organization for the five countries. Within a month this was designed and set up. At the top came the "Western Union Defence Committee" of the five ministers, assisted by a Permanent Commission which was established in London. Under it came the "Western Union Chiefs of Staff," to provide military advice and issue its *directives;* this body was composed by appointing one member from each of the existing Chiefs of Staff of the various countries—the Belgian member representing Luxembourg as well. The "Western Union Chiefs of Staff" meet in London, and are assisted by a "Military Committee," a large inter-national and inter-service organ which has to study the situation and furnish the data for reaching a judgment. It includes a "Supply and Resources Board."

The *directives* of the Western Union Chiefs of Staff go to the actual directing organ, the "Western Europe Commanders-in-Chief Committee," of which Field-Marshal Montgomery is chairman. This has its main headquarters in London, but has established an advanced headquarters at Fontainebleau, near Paris. The "Commander-in-Chief of the Land Forces" is French—General de Lattre de Tassigny. The "Commander-in-Chief of the Air Forces" is Air Marshal Sir James Robb. There is no Commander-in-Chief of the Naval Forces, but the empty chair at the Committee table is filled by the French Vice-Admiral Jaujard as Naval Representative.

With the subsequent formulation of the Atlantic Pact, under America's leadership, the planning organization is being still further expanded to deal with the problems of this wider defensive alliance and insurance scheme.

The actual defences of Western Europe, however, are very weak. Little has been done to develop them since the statesmen of the nations concerned agreed on the need for a joint solution of the problem. The actual measures appear insignificant compared with the volume of discussion, and show no such sense of urgency as their opening declarations conveyed.

The primary problem that has to be solved is that of Western Europe's ability to withstand an *overland* invasion—and prevent the Continent being overrun before America could make her weight felt. In that respect, it is the forces on the scene which count, not a prospective reinforcement from overseas, however great this might ultimately become. The opening stage is crucial. For that reason a realistic examination must concentrate mainly on the question of the land forces which are available, or could be made available.

A roof was put on the defence structure of Western Europe before the state of the walls in the different sections had been thoroughly examined. The present structure suffers from the fact that most of the "walls" were razed to the ground by the German conquest in 1940, and have had to be built up completely afresh—which has been a slow process under post-war conditions. The British section was an exception, but that was largely demolished by demobilization. Few people have any clear idea of the state of the various national forces. The majority are still inclined to think in terms of pre-war figures, and the veil of secrecy has mercifully hidden from them how much slighter the present effective strengths are than what were regarded as necessary before the war—though they did not prove adequate then.

On any manpower calculation, as well as on other grounds, France is the principal component of the continental part of the Western Union forces. She has a population of just over forty million. Holland has only nine million; Belgium, eight million; and Luxembourg little more than a quarter of a million.

In 1939 France had a peacetime army of 500,000 men, and trained reserves amounting to 5,000,000, though she lacked sufficient modern equipment to make effective use of them. After mobilization she expanded her 30 peacetime divisions to 90 by the time the German invasion came. France had then an Air Force of 1,730 first-line machines, nominally about equal to Britain's, but of the 260 bombers a large proportion were obsolete.

The French Army now is nominally as strong as before the war. But its operational strength (the number of formations organized for action) is much smaller, and not even as well equipped as in 1940 relative to the standards of the time. There are only 6 divisions in France and the French zone of Germany. Two of these are armoured divisions, equipped with wartime American tanks that are now obsolete. There are two more infantry divisions in North Africa—where General Juin has been reorganizing the local forces in such time as he could spare from the cares of reconstructing the civil administration.

At the same time the prolonged trouble in Indo-China has been a serious drain on the home army, especially in regard to trained officers and N.C.O.s. The total force there is still over 100,000, and distance cancels them out as a potential reserve in case of an emergency in the West.

But the heaviest drain has come from the combination of short service with the handicap of having to rebuild a military system which had been demolished. With only one year's service, the main effort has been put into the training of the individual soldier, rather than to the creation of operational formations.

Embryonically, the post-war system of training that General de Lattre introduced has better promise than the old. Before the war, the French Army was depressingly hidebound, and its chiefs were the least inclined of all to think that they could learn anything from anybody else. So it went on perpetuating the methods of World War I until it crashed on meeting different methods in World War II. Its new chiefs have been more ready to profit by other people's experience, and in their training system at least they have made use of good points from all quarters. Instead of being kept in barracks, the young recruits are mostly trained in small open-air camps under a system designed to toughen them physically, harden their

nerve, foster their initiative, and develop versatility. It
is the most advanced system of *primary* training in any
army, and one that is designed to produce troops of high
quality—the decisive factor in modern warfare. The
period of service is short, however, for developing the
technical skill required by modern weapons, and for the
extensive tactical practice required to develop manœuvring power in large formations.

But the heaviest handicap of all is the French Army's
continued lack of modern weapons, especially of the
heavier types—tanks, artillery and aircraft. The material
it has is largely obsolescent, if not obsolete. That applies
also to the other types of equipment needed for modern operations. Post-war munitions production has been
paltry, and the slow rate imposed by national poverty
has been made slower by poor planning.

The Air Force has had even less chance than the Army
to recover lost ground. In numbers of men its strength is
only about 70,000, but even that lowly figure gives an
exaggerated impression of its operational strength in
squadrons.

We come now to the "Benelux" countries. Of these,
Belgium had the best army before the war, both in
efficiency and equipment, although this was not up to
first-class standards. Its peacetime strength was 65,000,
of whom nearly a third were professional soldiers, and
was organized in 6 skeleton infantry divisions and 2
motorized cavalry divisions. It could mobilize 600,000
men for war, and managed to put 23 divisions into the
field. Holland had more of a militia-type army, with an
average peacetime strength of less than 30,000. When
war came she mobilized about 400,000, organized in 10
divisions and the equivalent of as many in smaller units,
but their equipment and training were of a low standard.

When the *blitzkrieg* burst on them, they were no match for the smaller but more highly trained and equipped German forces that led the invasion.

Both armies have profited from that hard experience in reconstructing their systems of training. But their present peacetime strength is even lower than pre-war, their trained reserves are fewer, and they are still very short of modern equipment. Belgium's annual contingent of recruits is 37,000, and they serve for only twelve months. She has three divisions in cadre form, which would have to be filled up with reservists after mobilization. She is in process of building an air force of fifteen fighter squadrons. Holland also has the framework of three divisions, but it is even more of a skeleton than Belgium's, owing to the need of maintaining her forces in the East Indies. Her scanty air strength is also drained away to that troubled area.

In these two countries, as in France, the training problem has absorbed most of the resources, and it is unlikely that they could bring any operationally fit divisions into action in a sudden emergency. Here is the crux of the problem, for the pace of modern invasion may be too fast for a defence that depends on a complicated process of mobilization in the threatened countries.

To avoid a disrespectful omission of the other member of the Benelux, it may be mentioned that Luxembourg's pre-war army amounted to 250 men, whereas she now has two battalions and a plan to produce 15,000 men on mobilization.

French official representatives have told the Americans that 60 to 80 modernly equipped divisions—thirty of them armoured and the rest motorized—are required to defend the front between the North Sea and the Alps. It can be seen what a huge gap exists between such planning and the means of fulfilling it.

What could Britain contribute to the immediate defence of Western Europe. The Army numbers approximately 375,000—of whom 185,000 are Regulars, the remainder being conscripts under the eighteen-month National Service scheme. The Air Force numbers just over 200,000, of whom two-fifths are National Service men. The composition and distribution of the Services is officially concealed from the public, though it would not be difficult for any foreign Intelligence service to arrive at a close estimate of the lay-out.

In 1939 the R.A.F. had 55 bomber squadrons and 39 fighter squadrons, exclusive of those that were stationed in the Middle East, India, and the Far East. Of the total at home, 37 bomber squadrons and 34 fighter squadrons were ready for action at the outbreak of war. It has been stated that the number of fighter squadrons is now appreciably more than before the war, and that the majority of them have now been re-equipped with jet-engined machines. The number of bomber squadrons is certainly much less than in 1939—and some critics have hinted that it is barely a third of the pre-war number. On the other hand it must be remembered that the machines are much larger, and it is probable that the total bomber-load of the present bombing force is much greater than that of the pre-war force. But its striking value suffers from the fact that it is still equipped with machines of the types that were produced in the war, and has yet no jet-engined bombers.

The facts about the composition of the British Army are rather more definite. It has been stated that there is one infantry division and one armoured division in Germany, while a second infantry division is stationed in

North-East Africa. It has frequently been said, without contradiction, that there are no divisions at home. In any case, the dispatch of the Guards to deal with the troubles in Malaya made it plain that the cupboard was bare—of organized formations. Even Mother Hubbard's dog would be able to draw that conclusion, let alone an intelligent Intelligence Service. The British Government could not have found a clearer way of disclosing what the Army Estimates conceal.

Three divisions is a very poor operational strength for an Army of 375,000 men. Before the war the Army was only half the size, yet produced seven divisions at home, available to help the defence of Western Europe, and three in Egypt and Palestine. Three of the ten were armoured divisions. That was the result of the reorganization which Mr. Hore-Belisha initiated in 1937-38. As his personal adviser at that time I was closely concerned with solving the problem of getting the maximum number of operational formations out of a limited scale of man-power. The harder problem was to get the equipment produced, owing to earlier neglect to develop armament factories. The divisions also required to have their administrative services increased after mobilization, before they were ready for major operations. But those that we had overseas were capable at any moment of dealing with disturbances and checking the kind of hostile infiltration that has given so much trouble since the war.

The present low capacity, and scarcity of divisions, is due to two factors. First, to swollen establishments of non-fighting troops—a universal legacy of wasteful wartime organization, which in all armies tends to develop too much top-hamper and too large a "tail." Second, and still more seriously, to the unwise post-war policy of mixing conscription with the professional system. This entails a vast proportion of the long-service Regulars being diverted to help in training the short-service conscripts—which greatly reduces the Army's readiness to meet a sudden emergency.

It would thus appear that, unless and until the system is reorganized, to produce more divisions, the British contribution to the defence of Western Europe will be limited to the small force of two divisions that is already present in Germany. The American combat force there is likewise small—barely the equivalent of two divisions. These additions do not go far to augment the forces of the Continental countries already enumerated.

As for the countries "on the flanks," Italy has eight incomplete infantry divisions and aims to raise four more, as well as one armoured and one Alpine division. But all are meagrely equipped—with surplus British and American wartime equipment that is now becoming out of date. Denmark has plans for creating two small divisions, and Norway might be able to produce the equivalent of two in brigades, but they would only be skeletons until mobilization took place.

Given time to mobilize, the total forces of Western Europe might be much increased. There are plenty of reservists who could be called up, if not plenty of equipment for them—a handicap which would heavily diminish their mobilizable strength. Some estimates put this at nearly a hundred divisions, but such a figure seems theoretical rather than practical. Beyond this is the question of whether there would be time to mobilize.

For the Russians are estimated to have about 30 divisions in their zone of Germany. They are reported to include the equivalent of 8 armoured divisions, with tanks that are more powerful than any in Europe except the latest British type, and 6-8 motorized divisions. This constitutes a formidable spearhead for an opening thrust. It is much stronger than the forces hitherto available to guard the West.

The total strength of the Red Army is vastly larger, even on the present "peacetime" basis. Estimates range from 3,000,000 to 4,000,000 in men serving, and in organized divisions from 170 to 200. On mobilization, these might be raised to between 250 and 300, and within a year could be doubled—which would almost equal its last war figure of 550.

As the Russians have not been able to carry the motorization of their forces nearly as far as in Western armies, there would be delay in bringing their huge weight to bear so far West, because of the difficulties of movement and supply—although one must reckon with the toughness of the Russian troops, and their ability to live where others would starve, and the way they can "live on the country" where they are operating.

Delay would give the Western countries a chance to mobilize their reserves—which are so much larger than the forces they have ready for action. If they could check any attempt to overrun them quickly, and forestall their reinforcement from overseas, the prospect would be more hopeful than it looks at present. But there is obviously a big gap between the strength available and the strength required as a minimum insurance.

A sense of this gap, and doubts as to how far it can be filled, have given fresh force to a differing current of opinion—particularly in England. This has been under the surface for some time. It was brought out in a recent House of Lords debate that was initiated by Lord Templewood and Lord Trenchard, and was endorsed by Lord Portal. Since the first had been both Air Minister and Foreign Minister, while the others were the two most famous past Chiefs of the Air Staff, their arguments made a deep impression.

The thesis was put in a sentence, by Lord Templewood: "I am convinced that for the years immediately before us a dominant Allied Air Force can hold up and disorganize any Russian advance."

He went on to put his proposal in concrete terms—

"I contemplate an Allied Air Force, to operate at the very beginning of a war, of at least 100 jet fighter squadrons, 150 latest type long-range bomber squadrons, 50 pilotless rocket units and 150 transport squadrons. With a fully equipped and manned force of this kind I am convinced that the Allies could stop and disorganize any attempted advance across the Continent."

Significantly, he did not even mention the need for land forces, but emphasized that besides "the immediate organization of the necessary bases"—

"It needs also a determined effort to convince the countries of Western Europe, and particularly France (who for years past has ignored the teachings of air strategy), that air force is the most effective defence against Russian military aggression. Most of all, it needs the closest possible co-operation with the United States Air Force, now the predominant air power in the world, and the constant inter-change of ideas, machines, and personnel between the British and American Air Forces. By these means, provided they are adopted with resolution and without delay, we can most effectively prevent war in the years before us and give European civilization the breathing space that it needs to recover its strength for beating off the attacks that now threaten it."

Lord Trenchard expressed complete agreement, except that he proposed an Anglo-American air force of 550 squadrons—adding "150 squadrons of long-range fighters to protect our long-range bombers," but omitting the 50 pilotless rocket units.

He expressed equally strong disbelief that the Russians could be stopped in any other way—

"With her vast army of millions of men, and masses of equipment and aeroplanes, she would overwhelm any garrison that we might maintain, or are maintaining, in Berlin, or on the Elbe. They would come pouring through, right into France and across France to the coast. . . . Could we stop them with 1,000,000 men on the Elbe? Is it practical, politically or economically, for ourselves or our Allies to put 1,000,000 men on the Elbe? As we know, it is not."

But Trenchard, like Templewood, was sure that the Russians could be stopped by air power, if the Allied air force was of the scale they proposed. He declared that the war had shown "beyond a shadow of doubt" that "no formed bodies of troops can advance any distance by road or rail without air superiority." No body over a division strong could advance more than a short distance "in the face of superior air power."

The issues involved are so vital that it is essential to enquire whether the contentions of this influential school of thought are justified by such experience as we have for guidance. It is evident that Lords Trenchard and Templewood were basing themselves on the evidence of the Western Campaigns. Contrary to this assumption is the fact that on the Eastern Front both the Germans and the Russians repeatedly made long advances without having air supremacy, or anything approaching it. In North Africa, too, Rommel several times succeeded in defeating the British forces, and advancing dangerously far towards Egypt, without such an advantage in the air.

It is dangerous to draw conclusions from the disabilities suffered by the German forces in Normandy, where the Allies had an overwhelming mastery of the air—to dominate a relatively defined area, with limited routes of approach. Even there, under these extreme disabilities, the German forces managed to move about to an extent which is apt to be overlooked by comparison with the hindrances they suffered.

From the evidence I have gathered in my discussions with the German Commanders, it has become clear that the Russian forces, particularly their striking spearheads, are much better fitted than those of any Western Army to carry out such an advance in face of a strong opposing Air Force—because of their lesser dependence upon supply, their troops' greater capacity to do without what other armies regard as necessities (in food and equipment), and the skill they have developed in moving dispersed.

Moreover, the single-minded "air" school of thought do not seem to take due account of the effect of the Russian Air Force in hindering such Allied air attack on the advancing Russian armies, and their communications. At the start of a war, this interference would be much more marked than German interference was in the latter stages of the last war—another reason why it may be dangerous to draw conclusions from experience in the Western Campaign of 1944-45.

While it seems important to correct excessive assumptions in the argument of the air school of thought, I agree with its basic thesis—so long as this is not carried too far. When the British rearmament programme was being planned in 1935-36, I argued that it would be wise to concentrate primarily on a powerful air force, backed by a small but highly mobile army. Mr. Chamberlain was convinced by that argument, as he told me early in 1937, just before he became Prime Minister. A few months after, the principle was adopted by the Cabinet as the basis of British military policy. It was abandoned in 1939, under pressure of the mass army advocates and the French. Yet in the light of all the evidence now available from the enemy side, it is very clear how easily the German drive could have been paralyzed by a combination of air bombing and armoured counterstroke—whereas the immobile mass of the hundred Franco-British foot-marching divisions proved helpless. Their action was always too late.

Likewise, with the present problem, a large army with little air support would weigh less than a powerful air force coupled with a smaller army. The problem is, basically, where to strike the balance.

From my own reflection on the problem, it seems to me that the primary need under present conditions is to develop a highly mobile land force of the *minimum* scale *necessary* to check the Russian *spearheads* that could infiltrate in face of air attack—the Western Union is far from possessing that minimum insurance at present. Having determined what the scale of this "ground-check" should be, the preponderant effort should be concentrated on developing air strength—to paralyze the follow-up advance of the Russian masses.

If Western Union had available even twenty high-quality divisions, modernly equipped and ready for action on the spot like a fire-brigade, the whole situation would be changed for the better. But that scale is the minimum necessary—in the view of various authorities who have examined the problem.

Such a number is not an impossibility. But it could only be attained by a radical change in the present military systems. One way would be to extend the period of full-time conscript service to three years, in all the Western Union countries, despite its heavy economic and social drawbacks. The other way would be to concentrate on obtaining sufficient professional soldiers to form operational forces on the required scale. That would involve a remodelling of the present mixed system and also more attractive rates of pay, but the economic burden on the nations would be considerably less than that which would be caused by three years' conscript service. It would also be more sure to produce an army of expert skill and dependability in emergency.

If the scale of the "fire-brigade" could be doubled, the prospects of defence would be increased out of all proportion. But such a figure would hardly be attainable except at the cost of essential air strength. Even the manpower required for such a force—as distinct from a conscript force that can only be mobilized *after* the emergency has arrived—might only be possible in one of two ways: by incorporating the Germans in the Western Union forces, or by stationing a large American land force permanently in Europe.

On any basis, however, the equipment problem remains to be solved. At present, that is the worst deficiency of the continental members of Western Union, and it is even worse in the air sphere than on land. This need can only be met by large-scale and early provision from the U.S.A.

CHAPTER XII

BRITAIN'S MILITARY PROBLEM

FOR immediate support against invasion, the Continental countries have to rely largely on Britain. Her forces are the "local reserve" for the defence of the West while the U.S.A. forms the "general reserve." Since so much depends on immediate support it is important to examine in some detail Britain's capacity to provide it, and consider how far this can be increased.

In terms of money and manpower Britain is now contributing a greater share than any to the total military effort of the Western European countries. For several years past the annual expenditure on her forces has been over $2,100,000,000 * and for 1950-51 the sum of $2,184,-000,000 has been voted by Parliament. That is nearly double what was devoted to the forces the year before the war.

What defence value was actually provided for these vast sums? The frank answer is: "Very little."

If an attack had come in 1948, or in 1949, the capacity

* Throughout this chapter, pounds have been converted to dollars at the ratio of $2.80 to the pound.

of the forces to meet it would have been much less than
in 1939—a time that the British people have come to regard, looking back, as one of perilously inadequate
preparedness.

Britain's weakness in 1939 was exposed by the test of
war. But the people were acquainted with the deficiency
of strength and equipment, though they did not fully
understand what it meant—as was evident from the
absurd degree of optimism that prevailed during the first
nine months of quiescent warfare, the period that was
called the phoney "war."

The present weakness, though worse, has been hidden
from the people and their Parliamentary representatives
by the dense cloak of official secrecy that has been kept
on since the war. Never has so much false "security"
covered such real insecurity. It is foolish to imagine that
the "situation" of the forces cannot be detected, at least
in outline, by foreign Intelligence services. But they are
unknown to the British people, who have no such facilities for discovering the facts.

All that the public and its Parliamentary representatives are told is the number of men in the forces, and the
amount they have to pay for the forces. They are informed there are 720,000 men in the forces compared
with 450,000 in 1939, and that twice as much money is
being spent on defence. It is thus natural for the public
to assume that the country is much stronger today. But
both these bare figures convey a false assurance about
what is really a poor insurance policy. For the operational strength—the effective fighting force ready for
emergencies—is far below the meagre scale of 1939.

Almost half the total number of men are short-term
conscripts, whose training is inadequate for modern
warfare. Beyond this, a large proportion of the Regulars

are occupied in helping to train and look after the conscripts, to the detriment of their own operational training. The maintenance of such nominally large numbers costs so much money that the rates of pay cannot be raised sufficiently to attract enough Regulars. But because of the larger proportion of the total defence outlay that is being absorbed by the mere upkeep of such numbers—their pay, food, clothing, housing, etc.—it becomes impossible to provide them with more than a small fraction of the new weapons required to make them effective.

In sum, never has so much been spent on so many for so little. These ill-effects become clearer in examining the state of the several Services. Such an examination is overdue. It is customary in England to take the Navy first. But it would be more reasonable to change the order and deal with the Army first, since this is the Service that will have to bear the first shock overseas if another war should come.

The sum devoted to the Army for 1950-51 is $840,000,-000, and has been maintained at that figure for the past three years.

What military insurance value is being obtained for such vast sums? There are 375,000 troops serving in the Army, apart from reservists and Territorials. That is double the pre-war number. On the figures it appears an impressive number of men "under arms," and all the more comforting because less than a quarter of them are serving in garrisons outside Europe. The year before the war half of them were serving outside Europe, over a quarter being tied up in India. That left little more than 100,000 available for emergencies in Europe, compared with nearly 300,000 now. On paper this looks a much better insurance for the security of the West.

The real strength of an Army, however, is represented not by gross numbers of men in the service, nor even by the number of trained men, but by the number of fighting formations that it can deploy. Until troops are organized in formations, and these are trained collectively, they cannot operate as an effective force. In this respect the present Army is largely a shadow force, and compares very badly with the nominally much smaller pre-war Army.

It was stated in 1948 by members of Parliament closely associated with the Army, and by other well-informed critics, that Britain had only two divisions altogether— one in Germany and one in North Africa. Also, that both of these were infantry divisions, and that the only armoured formation was a single brigade, widely scattered, in Germany. No Government spokesman disputed these statements. Since then it has been announced that an armoured division has been re-created, by mating a lorried infantry brigade to the solitary armoured brigade.

Even so, three divisions is an appallingly poor product for an Army of 375,000 men. At the British Army's lowest ebb between the first and second wars it had four— and although they lacked modern equipment they were at least being trained as formations and providing some practice for commanders in handling such bodies. When Mr. Hore-Belisha became Secretary of State for War in 1937 he saw the key importance of creating the largest possible number of operational formations, and tackled the problem with characteristic energy.

In barely two years, when war came, there were five Regular infantry divisions and one armoured division in England, while a second armoured division was being formed. In Egypt and Palestine two infantry divisions and one armoured division had been organized. That made ten in all.

Beyond this, seven anti-aircraft divisions were formed from the Territorial Army for the defence of Britain against air attack—in 1937 there had been only two. At the same time the rest of the Territorial Army had been reorganized before the end of 1938 to produce twelve infantry divisions (three of them motorized) and one armoured division. In 1939 these divisions were in process of being duplicated. In 1950 the Territorial Army is only a skeleton.

The pre-war re-equipment of the Army took more time than its reorganization, as hardly anything had been done before Mr. Hore-Belisha came into office and started to urge things on. The deficiencies had not been fully overcome by 1940. Even so, the amount of new equipment, and especially new weapons, provided for the Army before the war was far greater than it is receiving now.

That becomes evident from an examination of the Estimates for 1939 and 1950 respectively. In 1939 no less than $156,800,000 was devoted to fighting equipment—"warlike stores," to use the official phrase. In 1950 only $134,400,000 was allotted for it. When account is taken of the greatly increased cost of any piece of equipment today compared with that of 1939 it is obvious that the Army must be getting much less in the way of equipment than it did then.

Yet the sum required for the complete re-equipment of an Army of the pre-war scale would not be large compared with what is being spent yearly on the mere maintenance of the present numerically large Army, with its very few fighting formations. The nation is paying a prodigious price for an Army of "much fat and little muscle."

Why are there so few fighting formations, and why is there so little new equipment? The answer, in either case, can be put in one word—"Conscription."

When the National Service Bill was introduced in 1947, almost all the generals welcomed it and gave it their blessing. Now they are cursing it. The way that expert opinion has swung around is most remarkable. It was natural that they should favour it in principle, since it promised a larger army than could possibly be raised by the voluntary system, and seemed likely to remove many of the problems of recruiting and organization that had been a worry in the past. But experience of peace-time conscription has changed their views, and led them to see that it produces more problems than it solves—and worse ones. The now common note of condemnation is testimony to the commonsense of present-day generals.

Whatever the theoretical advantages of conscription, in practice it is ruining the efficiency of the Army, and proving fatal to its readiness to meet an emergency. The attempt to work a mixed system, combining short-term conscripts with long-term Regulars, is failing in both ways.

Conscripts cannot be trained in eighteen months, or two years, to the high grade of skill required for modern warfare. By the time they are trained even to an "employable" level, so little of their period of service remains that their employment is bad economy. It swells the bill for transportation out of all proportion to the service they render—the estimated cost of "movements" is $61,600,000 for 1950-51 compared with $5,600,000 before the war.

At the same time the mixture heavily handicaps the training of the Regulars and their effective utilization.

A very large proportion of them are absorbed directly or indirectly in the training machine for the conscripts, and in "caretaker" jobs at home and overseas. The enlarged size of the Army has much increased the scale of administrative duties, and Regulars are naturally called on to undertake these. In sum, far fewer than before the war are available for incorporation in fighting formations.

That means Britain has, in effect, a much smaller force available to meet an emergency than she had in 1939. With so few formations, commanders and staffs cannot get adequate practice in exercises with troops—so that even the force Britain has cannot be properly trained. Worse still, it cannot be adequately equipped—because the money that is needed for new weapons is swallowed up in paying for "useless mouths."

Pay alone absorbs $238,000,000 of the money that is being spent on the Army. In 1939 it absorbed only $33,-600,000, yet pay rates were proving more attractive to recruits than they are now.

As the value of money has depreciated, however, it is fairer to put the contrast in terms of percentages of the total cost of the Army. Pay now absorbs nearly 30 per cent of the Army's budget, compared with 8 per cent in 1939. But pay is only part of the ordinary cost of maintaining a soldier, irrespective of the Army's operative equipment and more permanent requirements. This mere man-maintenance cost (pay, food, clothing, carriage, and other supplies) absorbs nearly 60 per cent of the Army's budget, compared with 30 per cent before the war. On the other hand, scarcely more than 10 per cent is now given to the provision of "warlike" equipment, whereas in 1939 nearly 40 per cent was devoted to it.

These figures show how little security value Britain is getting for the present immense outlay. They make it clear that Britain is "maintaining" the most uneconomic kind of Army. If the number of men were cut down, a much larger percentage of the money could be devoted to military equipment *without* any increase in the budget. That would also release more manpower for industry, and thus help Britain's industrial effort. With a smaller number of men, if they were all Regulars, a larger number of fighting formations could be produced, ready for action. Conscription is a millstone round Britain's neck—threatening to sink her both militarily and economically.

While the Army would be likely to take the first shock if the Russians or their satellites started to advance, the Air Force would have to come into action immediately in support, and the prospects of defence might turn on its effect. It might also have to meet an immediate air threat to Britain herself. An examination of the state of the R.A.F. should thus come next.

The House of Commons voted $624,400,000 for the R.A.F. in 1950-51, and $579,600,000 was spent in the previous year. More security value was got for it than from the greater sum spent on the Army, but not really "value for money." The operational strength of the R.A.F. is far less than it was the year before the war. Yet, as with the Army, the scale of manpower is twice as large. Over 200,000 men are being "maintained" to maintain the much smaller force of aircraft.

Examination of the Estimates shows that, as with the Army, 25 per cent of the money is absorbed by the pay of personnel—compared with 7 per cent before the war —and on top of that comes the other man-maintenance costs. A little over 30 per cent is allotted for aircraft and their equipment. That is a much higher proportion than the Army devotes to "warlike stores," but a much lower proportion than the R.A.F. devoted in 1939, when about 75 per cent of its total money was spent on making it ready for action.

Here again we are confronted with the economic drawbacks, direct and indirect, that have resulted from reliance on conscription. The personnel of the R.A.F. now comprises just over 115,000 Regulars and 76,000 conscripts. The Air Marshals have come to see the ill-effects of the mixture as clearly as the generals. Lord Trenchard put the issue plainly in a House of Lords debate: "The National Service Act, as we know it today, is a handicap to the R.A.F. and not an advantage to it. . . . It may be that 20,000 or 30,000 National Service recruits will be useful for what may be called the ordinary domestic duties of the Service. . . . But nothing under three years is any good as a period of service in the R.A.F. It is no good for men who have to keep the machines in order, for a mechanic needs not only training but experience."

The "maintenance" of so many short-term conscripts, constantly turning over and absorbing many Regulars to train them, absorbs money that would be better spent on raising the pay-rates of the latter to a level that would compare more favourably with what skilled mechanics can earn in civil jobs—and thus enable the R.A.F. to recruit sufficient Regulars to dispense with the National Service men.

What is the situation as regards new equipment? The Regular fighter squadrons have all been re-equipped with jet-engined machines, and are being brought up to a strength of two flights instead of one—a flight consists of eight machines. Some eight of the twenty auxiliary squadrons have been re-equipped with jet-fighters. The delay here is due not so much to slowness in the rate of production as to the need for extending the runways of the airfields to the length required by jet-fighters—2,000 yards instead of the former 1,500 yards.

But there is still a lack of night jet-fighters in service—and that is a very serious lack. The way that the defences were penetrated in an exercise-test not long ago made the deficiency all too apparent.

As for Britain's bomber force, this is barely a tithe of its strength at the end of the war, while it is equipped entirely with wartime machines that are now obsolescent—Lancasters and Lincolns. While these big four-engined machines carry a bomb-load much greater than any bombers existing at the start of the last war, and this outweighs their much smaller numbers, their value as a force is discounted by other factors.

Their range was enough for bombing Germany, but is not enough for operating against Russia—if Russia were to launch an attack on the West. They might be used against the nearer communications of the invading armies, but are not really suitable for that role. They might also be used from airfields in the Middle East to operate against oilfield targets in the Caucasus and industrial targets in southern Russia. In either case such relatively slow 250 m.p.h. machines would run heavy risks if they met Russian fighters, especially jet-fighters.

Britain has no jet-bombers in service at present. The Air Ministry has been concentrating on the development of a long-range type with four jet-engines, but that is a long-term project. Meanwhile, it is starting to produce a twin-jet bomber. That will be an asset. But it would be wise to realize that there is no early prospect of Britain having a long-range striking force comparable, even in quality, to what she possessed in the last war.

In these circumstances it is absurd to talk, as many important people do, of the counter-offensive power of Britain's bomber force and its value as a deterrent to any aggressive move on Russia's part. Such notions are akin to the folly of those who, just before the 1939 war, wanted to restrict her fighter force in order to increase her bomber force—relying on the hoary and superficial argument that "attack is the best defence." If they had gained their way, Britain would have lost the "Battle of Britain." And their influence did go far enough to bring her perilously close to losing it, so narrow was the margin of her fighter strength. That should be a lesson now.

By comparison with the Army and the Air Force, the Navy appears to be of less immediate importance in the present situation, though remaining of basic significance—for any island country. Except for Russia's, all other navies that might be a potential threat have been swept off the board. The Russian Navy is small in numbers, except in submarines, and most of its surface fleet is obsolete. In dealing with any naval effort that Russia could attempt Britain can count on the backing of America's immense naval resources. Moreover, in all modern experience the Russian Navy has been a failure; its impotence even in its own Black Sea waters was a remarkable feature of the last war, and the more surprising because it had, on paper, such a large force of submarines.

Beyond all these limitations is the basic fact that Russia is in a naval sense strategically bottled up by force of geography. From her main naval bases, in the Baltic and Black Sea, her surface ships and submarines can only gain access to the open sea through two narrow channels. It should not be difficult to seal them up. Her few ports on the Arctic Sea are of limited capacity and remote from manufacturing centres; they would require much development before they could serve as bases for a strong and sustained submarine campaign. Similar reflections apply to her ports on the Pacific, which are also far more remote from the sea-routes that are vital to our security.

In view of all these favourable circumstances, it may seem curious that so much of Britain's resources should still be devoted to the maintenance of the Navy. Its allotment for 1950-51 amounts to $540,400,000. That is nearly as much as for the Air Force, which is obviously of much more urgent importance in present circumstances.

Examination of the Naval Estimates results in the impression that Admiralty administration is well directed, and that, speaking broadly, the money is laid out with a better sense of proportion than the other Service Estimates show. Less than 20 per cent of the money is absorbed by the pay of personnel while 40 per cent goes towards making the fighting elements of the Navy ready for action. This more economic proportion is not due to a lower scale of pay or amenities. The Navy since the war has recruited volunteers more easily than the other Services. It may also be remarked that the admirals, perhaps remembering the long-back lesson of the press-gang period, have never favoured conscription, and the Navy has only taken a tiny number of National Service men—amounting in 1949-50 to a mere 7 per cent of its own strength, and less than 8 per cent of the total call-up.

The basic question is whether the proportion of the whole defence budget that is given to the Navy shows a proper sense of proportion, and of current realities—in the Cabinet, and particularly in the mind of the Minister of Defence.

The British Government has committed itself, and the

country, to partnership in the "Western Union" of Europe. That has definitely put Britain's frontier forward, over the Channel, to a land line on the Continent. She has now taken the further step of joining in the "Atlantic Pact." That has extended the stretch of her Continental frontier. Furthermore, her earlier policy has committed her to the defence of positions in the continent of Asia. The sum effect leads her far from the strength-conserving "British way in warfare" that she followed in past centuries. It commits her to a defence on *land*, abroad, in which the primary role is necessarily played by the Army, in combination with the Air Force.

The location of the most likely threat—that of Russia —emphasizes this priority. Russia has immense land forces, and also immense scope on land for exerting their power. She has a large air force, which has long been accustomed to operate in close conjunction with her land forces. She may be tempted to develop a sea threat also, with new means, but she has little experience and much natural disadvantage in this sphere.

In these circumstances, is it sensible that 27 per cent of Britain's outlay on all three Services should be devoted to the Navy, and almost as much as is allotted to the Air Force—which has to help in guarding the sea as well as the land? Is she forgetting to "put first things first"?

It is wise to bear in mind that navies take even longer to build up than other forces, but it is also wise to remember how the shape of the Navy before the war failed to fit "the shape of things to come." Britain paid a heavy price in the war, and ran needlessly grave risks, for the way that the Sea Lords had clung to their faith in battleships, while tending to discount both the growing threat from the air and the revival of any threat from the submarine. An immense amount of money was misspent in consequence, to the neglect of urgent necessities.

The battle fleet remained an article of belief, defying all scientific examination. Admirals cherished their battleships in a religious spirit—looking upon them almost as bishops look upon cathedrals. The blindness of hardheaded sailors to realities that were obvious to any dispassionate observer is only explicable if we understand the place that battleships filled in their hearts.

Even now the idea of the battle fleet seems to linger, and the shape of the post-war Navy is still influenced by it—although there is no longer any battle fleet existing in the world that could oppose it. Britain maintains a "Home Fleet" and a "Mediterranean Fleet." Four battleships are retained on a training basis. There are also 3 large Fleet carriers, with 3 in reserve, and 2 more in construction; 5 Light Fleet carriers, with 7 more in construction; and 16 cruisers, with 10 in reserve and 3 partly built. It is an impressive total of powerful ships—but it seems rather a waste of money in the absence of any serious threat on the surface of the sea.

In contrast, we know that the Russians captured sixty or more of the snort-equipped Type XXI "electro-submarines" which the Germans were building at the end of the war. These can stay under water for weeks on end if necessary, and have double the under-water speed of earlier wartime types. The Russians also captured a quantity of component parts of the improved Walther Type XXVI, faster still, with hydrogen peroxide propulsion. Along with them they took a number of the best German designers and U-boat commanders, to help in developing the new-type submarines.

These are potentially a far more deadly menace to Britain's security than anything she met in the last war—

if the Russians develop them effectively. It may be hoped
that the Russians will do no better in this new naval field
than they have done in the past with more familiar
means. But it would be folly not to recognize that here
lies the one sea-danger that matters.

Yet the British Admiralty is maintaining in activity
only 25 frigates—the name now given to anti-submarine
vessels—with 19 more on a training basis, although 129
are laid up in reserve. The existing frigates, with their
speed of 20 knots, are hardly faster than the new-type
submarines. Yet only one new frigate is being built at
present. American experts think that the best answer to
the new-type submarine may be another submarine,
smaller and still faster. But Britain's outlay on such new
construction is too scanty.

There is clear need for a readjustment of Britain's naval
forces, and for a concentration of effort on the one real
threat. It is dangerous to disperse the limited resources
in "shadow-battling." Russia has no sea-communications
that matter to her, and is thus immune from the pressure
of sea-power—at least in any present form. If the offensive
effect of seapower is ever revived it is likely to be through
developing radically new types of warship, probably
submersible and mounting atomic missiles.

Meantime Britain needs to be ready to meet a more
immediate kind of threat to her own security. The Light
Fleet carriers may be useful in combating submarines,
but although in the last war half the submarines sunk
were destroyed from the air, the larger proportion of
these fell to shore-based aircraft.

That is a further pointer to the urgent need of recasting the distribution of the defence budget between the
three Services. The Air Force has to carry *four* major responsibilities—to guard the country against attack from

the air; to provide air cover for the land defence of the West; to carry out a counter-offensive (it is the only Service that could); to help the Navy in covering the sea-routes against a possible submarine offensive. Three of these responsibilities are more certain to be heavy, if war should come, than the one for which the Navy may be needed (in conjunction with the Air Force).

It is very doubtful whether the R.A.F. could effectively fulfil all of them, even if it were given a bigger proportion of the total outlay on defence. But it seems quite crazy that it should be receiving barely 30 per cent.

Yet in official quarters there is too little sign of any realization of the need for recasting the proportions. Modern defence is a scientific problem, which can only be solved by clear thinking, and clear-cut decision, not by mere compromise between conflicting interests. In trying to increase defensive strength a bit *everywhere*, there is a danger of not being strong enough *anywhere*.

What can be done? A further increase in the defence budget would improve the prospect, but on present lines it would have to be a very large increase to provide an adequate degree of security. That would entail back-breaking taxes, and be fatal to the chances of national recovery. Military security has to be reconciled with economic security.

Can better value be obtained from the present outlay? The answer is certainly: "Yes." *How* can better value be gained? The answers have emerged in examining the present feeble state of Britain's bulky forces, and the way the money is going, but may be emphasized and amplified.

The first, and most essential, step is to scrap conscription. Such a step would immediately provide an effective

land force much larger than exists at present. This may
seem an astonishing statement, since it would involve
discarding half the total number of men now serving in
the Army. But it is not difficult to prove.

Government spokesmen have already veered round on
the subject of conscription so far as to express the hope
that they will eventually be able to dispense with National Service men in the active forces. They still tend to
argue, however, that this will not be possible until the
number of Regulars has considerably increased—because
of the extent of Britain's "commitments." The argument
will not stand examination.

"Commitments" is an impressively vague term with
which Ministers are fond of making play. More precisely
defined, it means the territories which a nation has to
defend against external attack or where it has to maintain
internal order. The latter requirement, policing, always
subtracts from the number of troops who can be used for
defence.

By the post-war withdrawal from India, Egypt and
Palestine, Britain is now released from her heaviest pre-
war policing commitments. The evacuation of all her
footholds in China except Hong Kong is a further reduction. At the same time her defensive commitments in
Africa are diminished by the disappearance of the pre-
war menace of Mussolini's colonial empire and ambitions.
Her fresh commitments since the war involve small
policing requirements compared with those territories
she has evacuated. They are, now, mainly in the nature
of defensive commitments—and for these the best insurance would be to have more operational formations. If
Britain scrapped conscription, she could provide them
—even from her present resources.

The number of voluntarily enlisted Regular soldiers

has already risen to 185,000—which exceeds the pre-war figure, apart from the Army in India. As Britain's policing requirements are less than pre-war, it would be quite practicable to utilize a larger number of Regulars in operational formations than she could then.

If it would not be possible, because of the increased specialist and administrative elements, to produce quite so many divisions as she had in 1939, she should be able to get the equivalent of at least six out of 185,000 Regulars. That would be a much stronger force, to meet an emergency, than the mere three divisions that have been produced from 375,000 men under the National Service System.

So Britain could well afford to dispense with the conscript mixture, without delay.

From the big sum which would be saved on the pay and maintenance of the 182,000 National Service men, the Government should devote part to raising the pay of the Regulars. That would promise an early increase in the number of men enlisting, and thus make possible the creation of further divisions. According to the calculation given in the House of Commons by Brigadier Head, an increase of 25 per cent on the pay of Regulars would amount to a mere $42,000,000 a year. There would still be a large surplus even if the Regular Army rose to the desirable scale of 250,000. This large saving could be devoted to new equipment, on a more ample scale than is now planned.

A further advantage of returning to the pre-war system is that it would help to eliminate the internal waste of manpower that conscription has fostered. All experience has shown that once establishments swell, attempts to curtail them are always vain—and merely tend to petty reductions that cause more inefficiency. Effective reduction only comes through a complete reorganization. The adoption of a basically different system is the best way to produce it.

The abolition of conscription would be even more beneficial to the R.A.F. than to the Army, since short-term conscripts cannot be turned into efficient mechanics, and still less into air crews. The money saved would provide not only the means for raising pay-rates, to attract sufficient volunteers, but also an even larger surplus than in the case of the Army which could be devoted to new equipment.

At the same time the hard fact remains that the cost of completely re-equipping the R.A.F. with new machines on the scale required would far exceed its present allotment in the total defence budget.

It is likely that the new four-jet bombers now being developed will cost something like $700,000 apiece. Thus the initial outlay alone in providing a force of 500, half the wartime figure, with a mere one for one reserve, would amount to $700,000,000. Even for a small force of 200 bombers it would be $280,000,000. Moreover, the maintenance cost of such machines is extremely high. One can only wonder whether Ministers who airily talk of "Britain's new bomber force" have taken due account of the problem, and of the extent to which they will have to increase the defence budget. For while something might be saved on the naval side, as already indicated, it would not be large—especially if the Navy is to be provided with new anti-submarine craft. In sum, Britain can only provide herself with an up-to-date bomber force by a great increase in the budget, unless she neglects other urgent needs.

Facing the problem squarely, it would be wise to consider whether a better solution cannot be found in a distribution of roles between the members of the Atlantic Alliance—one that would fit their respective situations and capacities. The United States have already gone a long way in creating a large strategic bomber force composed of new-type machines. Could Britain not arrange to leave that role to them, instead of expending a large part of her limited resources on a delayed effort to produce a similar force? They are better able to carry out that role, and also have less need of defence against land, sea or air attack.

National pride and Service pride will naturally present obstacles to such a clean-cut solution, especially as it would mean relinquishing a share in the leading offensive role. But there are also some weighty reasons against its complete relinquishment. It would become difficult for the British Government and its Service advisers to exercise influence on bombing policy and strategy—and all the more difficult since they would lose knowledge of that sphere. They might be unable to obtain the application of long-range bomber action in some direction that appeared vital to them if American interests was focussed in another direction. The clean-cut solution would also cut out the possibility of experiment in that sphere, and remove the spur of competition that stimulates progress. The development of bombing technique in the last war owed much to the way that the British and American air forces pursued different trends of thought and practice, with the eventual result that each learnt a lot from the other, to the improvement of their joint performance. The existence and development of alternative courses always carries the best promise of attaining the object, in any field.

Yet the cumulative weight of these considerations cannot alter the fundamental condition—that Britain, if she

is to avoid bankruptcy, can only re-create a strategic
bombing force of the former scale at the sacrifice of minimum needs in more vital respects. The most that is possible without such crippling sacrifices is the creation of a
small force of the new four-jet bombers.

Thus, in any case, Britain will have to depend on the
U.S.A. for the major contribution in the sphere of strategic bombing. Britain's economic limitations make this
inevitable. The sooner the fact is recognized the sooner
Britain can hope to find the way out of the slough of inefficiency and insecurity in which her defence steps are
now bogged. For besides a redistribution of roles between the British and American forces there must be a
redistribution of money and roles within the British
forces. The Air Force today is all too clearly inadequate
by comparison with its multiple responsibilities. There
is urgent need for a stronger fighter force and tactical
bombing force, besides the case for creating the nucleus
of a new long-range bombing force. The existing strength
is far from sufficient to provide defence for Britain, cover
for her troops on the Continent, and a reinforcement for
the countries she is now pledged to defend—it is only too
evident that their own capacity to meet air attack is even
less than in 1940. At the same time the anti-submarine
forces, both air and naval, call for an increase. And the
field force of the Army needs not only reorganization but
new equipment.

The sum of these minimum requirements can only be
met by a radical reorganization of the Services separately
and as a whole, guided by a clear decision about priori-
ties. It means cutting out expenditure that does not produce effective fighting power. The largest possibility of
finding the money for new equipment lies in reducing

"gross" man-power by scrapping the present National
Service system. That would be real "economy of force."

Any such new plan calls for a clear and strong directing mind. The present Chiefs of Staff Committee is supposed to have the virtues of a trinity, but the theory has
never been fulfilled in practice—as the members are human. In war, the cracks are often cemented by the pressure of emergency, but in peacetime, when the total sum
for division is more limited, the cracks become cleavages.
The Chiefs of Staff Committee, being composed of the
professional heads of three separate Services, tends to
differ widely in view and interests. Their divergence
fosters the inclination of the Cabinet, as a committee of
democratic politicians, to seek a solution by equalitarian
compromise. That is not the way by which military problems are solved. Strategical planning may have a basic
element of compromise between conflicting risks but its
effectiveness depends on the right determination of pri-
orities.

The problem and the situation call for a Supreme Chief
of Staff, over the three Services. It will not be easy to
find the right man, and the creation of such a post will
carry risks—not only that he may be too inclined to favour his own service, but that he may be too hesitant to
give it priority where necessary, from fear of such an
accusation and excessive desire for conciliation. Nevertheless, the dangers of the present "drifting committee"
system are even more certain.

If the idea of a Supreme Chief of Staff is not acceptable, the only hopeful alternative is a strong and decisive-
minded Minister of Defence. But this almost inevitably
means that, where the three Chiefs of Staff differ, the
Minister will seek an outside adviser who is not attached
to any particular Service and can take a detached view.

The Services had better make up their minds which of the alternatives they prefer. For in fact, if not in theory, they share responsibility with the Cabinet for the confused state of Britain's defence planning since the war, as also for the pre-war haze that obscured vital needs.

CHAPTER XIII

"HOME DEFENCE" IN A NEW WAR

T HE problem of "Home Defence" nowadays is not so much to repel invasion as to prevent "atomization." There are other menaces for which we ought to be prepared, but it is essential to reckon with that of atomic destruction—the primary, and worst, case. Here, the main lessons of experience on which we can work are provided by the two atom bombs that were dropped on Japan in August, 1945—the only two that have hitherto been used in war.

The first bomb, dropped on the city of Hiroshima, was originally estimated to have killed about 60,000 people, but later calculations have put the total up to nearly 100,-000, including those who died subsequently from radiation. That was not far short of half the people in the city. The bomb was accurately aimed, exploding over the centre of the city. Most of the city disappeared—in the blast of the explosion or the terrific "fire storm" that followed.

The second bomb, at Nagasaki three days later, happened to explode over part of the city that lay in a valley some two miles from the centre, which was screened by high hills. This time just under 40,000 were killed. The apparently diminished results disappointed some of the experts, as it had been reckoned that the plutonium bomb used here would have a 15 per cent greater radius of destruction than the uranium bomb used at Hiroshima. But on later examination the blast effects were found to have been even greater than there, and there was total destruction of buildings over an area of 3 square miles.

An expert mission, sent out to Japan in 1946 to study the damage in the two cities, made an illuminating report on the comparative effects that such bombs would be likely to have on Western cities and buildings. It estimated that, with Western-type houses, all would be wrecked up to a radius of a mile, and be made uninhabitable up to 2-2½ miles, although steel-framed buildings might survive at half a mile distance from the centre of the damage. In an average Western city, that would mean about 30,000 houses demolished or damaged beyond repair, and three or four times as many made uninhabitable. In such a city, "the number of people expected to be killed by one atomic bomb is nearly 50,000."

So here we have the measure of the present problem of Civil Defence in the larger sense—except for two important qualifications: that we do not know how many bombs to expect, nor how much more destructive they may be than those used in 1945! But it is clear that the immensity of the problem calls for a proportionately "big" solution. The measures that carried Britain through the 1940-41 blitz and the 1944 V1 bombardment will not suffice.

To put plainly what needs saying, and driving home— the countries of the West, in their present state of "preparedness," would have small chance of surviving even a small number of atom bombs, placed with passable accuracy. The huge sum of money spent on "defence" in the last few years has provided them with no security in the most vital respect. Their Governments have gone on behaving as if the atomic danger was quite remote.

While five years have passed since Hiroshima, the Western nations have been strangely slow to begin applying its lessons—although tension with Russia has been increasing all the time, while it was obvious from the outset that her development of the atom bomb could only be a matter of time. Even the mere revival of Civil Defence services has been very tardy. It came a long time after the leaders of the Western nations had been dwelling on the fact that the world had again entered a state of "cold war."

A "cold war" implies the risk of changing into "hot war." In that case, the prospect for us has become much hotter since September, 1949—when President Truman announced, on the 23rd: "We have evidence that within recent weeks an atomic explosion has occurred in the U.S.S.R." The discreet phrasing of that announcement could not veil its significance—which sent a shudder through the Western world. The meaning it conveyed was that Russia had broken America's monopoly and was now able to use the awful devastation of atomic power as a weapon in war, as well as a threat in peace.

In the spring of 1949 Mr. Churchill, in his Boston oration, declared: "It is certain that Europe would have been Communized, and London under bombardment some time ago, but for the deterrent effect of the atomic bomb in the hands of the United States." Where is that security now? What protection would it be to the cities of Western Europe, and London, if a threat to "atomize"

Moscow could be answered by a threat to "atomize" them?

The comforting assurance of Mr. Churchill's Boston oration was conveyed to the public in the morning newspapers of April 1st, 1949. It could be recalled that on April 1st, 1939, they had carried the announcement of Mr. Chamberlain's guarantee to Poland—given in the belief that it would preserve peace in Europe. The parallel between those two April Fool's Day announcements, exactly ten years apart, was an uncomfortable coincidence.

In the months following Mr. Churchill's declaration numerous deterrent hints were given that, in the event of any aggressive move by Russia, it was the intention of America's strategists to deliver an immediate atomic attack on Russia with their long-range bombing force. As recently as July, 1949, General Bradley declared: "Should Western Europe be attacked, then the United States must fling the full force of its strategic air offensive against the enemy." But it was then still being reckoned that Russia would not have developed the atom bomb until 1952, and that during the interval there would be ample time to build up the defences of Western Europe, against both land and air attack, under the protective deterrent cloak of America's atomic monopoly.

Now that the monopoly has been broken, the deterrent has diminished in value while the protection has disappeared. The peoples of Western Europe can no longer find comfort in the thought that any advance of Russia's armies could be answered by the destruction of Russia's cities. Their own cities are now exposed to similar destruction by the same means. As their countries are smaller and more clustered with cities, they stand to suffer much worse by any competition in atomic bombing —*if such bombing once begins.*

Yet after the momentary "earthquake" caused by President Truman's announcement, and the brief outburst of speculation it produced as to the consequences to be expected, the subject faded out of press and public discussion. Britain's fresh economic crisis swamped it. But the devaluation of the British pound may not be as dangerous in consequences as the devaluation of the American atom bomb and its protective value for Western Europe. While it is natural that the Western statesmen should be largely occupied with current economic problems, it would be unfortunate if the atomic risk slipped too far to the back of their minds. That it is receiving due attention is very doubtful. If the present Civil Defence schemes are the measure of high-level plans to meet the tremendous risk they can best be described by the saying that "A mountain has been in labour, but brought forth only a mouse."

Instead of facing the stark problem, with its terrific potential consequences, the civil and military leaders of the Western nations behave like the proverbial ostrich, burying their heads in the sand, or else go on blindly trusting in America's power to win a competition in atomic bombing. Even now, there is still talk of starting it at the first hostile troop-move—regardless of the obvious fact that Russia's ultimate subjugation by such means would not redeem the obliteration of the densely crowded countries of Western Europe.

Listening to such talk is too much like listening in to a lunatic asylum, and living in these countries too much like the situation of sheep in a slaughter-house.

Marshal of the Royal Air Force Viscount Trenchard, the most famous of all Britain's air chiefs, expressed views recently that call for attention. Dealing with the possibility of an advance into the West by the Russian armies, he said:

"We must be prepared to say now that if this threat from the East materializes we will at once hit with the latest development in the possession of the Western Powers—the atom bomb. How many millions of a nation's men would have to be destroyed before peace could be assured? Is there any doubt whatever in any man's mind that the atom bomb today could probably destroy anything over 10,000,000 and up to 20,000,000 people in a month. I am not overestimating, nor am I trying to be unnecessarily brutal. I say that a nation which lost that amount of manpower in such a short period could not exist and would have to submit."

Lord Trenchard's estimate of the probable casualties was reasonable. His conclusion as to the effect in compelling a country's submission is questionable as applied to Russia. Even 20,000,000 dead would be a small fraction of her population. Her rulers showed in the last war that their resolution was unshaken by the loss of such a percentage of their people. Moreover, that figure might not be attained—as Russia's cities are relatively few and widely scattered. On the other hand, his conclusion applies only too clearly to the congested countries of Western Europe. A scale of 20,000,000 killed would wipe out half the population of England or France, or the whole population of Belgium and Holland combined.

In these awkward circumstances it seems a trifle muddle-headed, to put it mildly, for anyone to advocate that the Western Powers should start the throwing of atom bombs if war began in a more old-fashioned way. It would be the most madly up-to-date version of the proverb that "those who live in glasshouses shouldn't throw stones." If American leaders want to *start* "throwing atoms about" they are likely to meet objections from their allies in Europe even if they do not meet them at home.

It is a bad enough prospect that if the Russians were to drop atom bombs on Britain or her neighbours in Western Europe, the Americans would naturally reply in kind on their allies' behalf. That would not rebuild the cities of Western Europe, nor restore their population to life. Victory has no point if its purpose has disappeared —from the face of the earth. There is at least more hope for civilization in a mutual holding back of the atom bomb—as happened, and persisted to the end, with poison gas in the last war. Even without the atom bomb, a new war could be terribly damaging. To start using atom bombs on our side would be the most likely way to ensure that history's verdict on our vanished civilization would be "suicide while temporarily insane."

If atom bombing starts, on our initiative or otherwise, *how* would it come? The most obvious means of delivery is by bomber aircraft. This means would offer the best chance of intercepting it, with the new jet fighters. But it is not a very sure prospect—and against a weapon like the atom bomb anything less than a 100 per cent chance of interception may carry catastrophic consequences. The chances would be seriously diminished if the Russians employed jet bombers, and still more so if they could operate from bases in Western Europe.

Another possible means of delivery is by guided missile—pilotless plane or rocket. The Russians are known to have been developing the German V1 and V2 weapons, with the aid of the data and experts they captured in Germany, and to have been carrying out trials in the Baltic. But the experts doubt whether the wartime range of 150 miles with the former and 220 miles with the latter has been greatly extended—at any rate with equivalent accuracy. So this menace might not materialize for France and the Low Countries until the Russians overran Western Germany, and not for Britain until they had reached the coast and established launching sites there. It is not a likely danger to America within a measurable time.

A third means with which we must reckon, however, is that of guided missiles, with or without an atomic warhead, launched from submarines off the coast. The U.S. Navy has already carried out trials with submarines specially adapted to mount flying bombs and rockets. It would be wise to assume that the Russian Navy, which has been devoting most of its post-war effort to its submarine fleet, is likely to have grasped the possibilities of developing the underwater missile-carrier—which because of its mobility, invisibility and flexibility could give navies a more far-reaching offensive power than ever before. Submarines of this new type could be a formidable menace to all cities that lie near a coastline—and the majority of great cities in America, as well as in Britain and the countries of Western Europe, are within guided missile range from the sea.

A further means of delivering the atom bomb is by what are called "underground methods." This danger is likely to increase with the improvement of methods of bomb-construction. The atomic explosive might be smuggled into a country little by little in the baggage of agents —it is an ordinary-looking metal, out of which watch cases, cigarette lighters, keys, etc., can be made. The bomb itself might be built in a machine-shop owned and manned by ardent but discreet sympathizers with a regime opposed to their own country's. Alternative methods would be to carry the atom bomb complete into the country tucked away in the hold of an ordinary cargo-ship, or in a commercial plane—low-flying over cities is now such a common habit that an unexpected crash would not be difficult to stage. Such strokes would, of course, have to be timed while nominal peace still prevailed—as a new "Pearl Harbor" opening gambit. While it might not be practicable to deliver them on a scale requisite to decide a war, they could conceivably produce such chaos as to open the way for a knock-out to follow.

Leaving aside the possibility of such preliminary "underground" strokes—what are the prospects of defence against atom bomb attack in war? The honest answer is: "Very dim—at present." Much hope is pinned to the development of defence by rockets radar-guided or attracted to intercept the enemy's bombers, or even his long-range rockets—but these means of defence seem still a long way from maturity. Meantime we have to rely on interception by jet planes, which cannot deal with rockets, and have a very uncertain chance of effectively sealing off other types of atom bomb "carrier"—since so few of the latter have to slip through the defence to achieve immense destruction.

As for the much-lauded value of "defence by attack," this may be a deterrent to war, but has rarely availed to prevent a counter-bombardment—as was seen in the case of the V1 and V2 bombardments of Britain in 1944, where incessant attacks by the vast Anglo-American Air Force, both against the launching sites and the enemy's homeland, failed to do more than produce a partial reduction in the stream of incoming missiles. And now, in facing atom bombs, we are up against the grim fact that "so few can do so much" in the way of devastation.

So we are forced to recognize the vital necessity, and priority, of passive defence—to diminish a country's vulnerability to bombardment. That is the sphere of Civil Defence, but it needs to be greatly widened in scope, as

well as to receive a much bigger share of Governmental
attention and expenditure if the defence is to be at all
effective in averting mortal injury to the country.

What are the prospects that any extended scheme of
Civil Defence could prevent atomic bombardment proving fatally decisive? Here, some reasonably good ground
for hope has been found in studying the evidence of
Hiroshima and Nagasaki. An expert investigation reported that of the shelters "all survived except the very
poorest earth-covered shelters within a few hundred
yards of the centre of damage"—but few people had troubled to take refuge in them, since the attack seemed to
be on so slight a scale! "Deep shelters . . . would have
given complete protection."

These bombs, however, were exploded overhead. If
they had exploded on ground-level the blast effect would
probably have been more intense, though not so far-
reaching. If they had penetrated deep into the ground
before exploding, the effect is more problematical.

For a fraction of a second there was an intense flash
from the bomb, the radiated heat of which scorched objects fiercely, even at great distances. This flash burning,
or heat radiation, caused many deaths. Yet quite flimsy
intervening objects proved enough to save people from
injury by it—experts say that even a sheet of brown paper
might suffice.

Radiation proper, from the neutrons and gamma rays,
caused still more deaths—many of them lingering deaths
spread over the weeks that followed, which increased the
total by about 20 per cent. To give protection against
such deadly radiation is no easy problem, and it is still
surrounded by many uncertain factors. We do know
that a considerable thickness of resistant material is required, but what types of material will best suffice to ex-

clude this radiation has still to be satisfactorily determined. The exact persistence of dangerous radioactivity is also uncertain. But it calls for the provision of protective footwear and gloves, perhaps also of masks, if people in the attacked cities are to emerge from shelters and resume activity without excessive delay.

Radioactivity was found to be far more prolonged and widespread when the bomb was exploded under water—in the second Bikini test of 1946—than it had been when dropped over land. Thus a bomb that fell on a river or lake inside a city might carry more radioactive effect than if it dropped among buildings, while one that was dropped in the harbour or docks of a seaport city would have a much more serious effect. The great ports are likely to be primary targets for atom bombing.

That would be particularly dangerous to an island country like Britain, whose existence is largely dependent on the flow of food ships into its ports. It is thus not surprising that a pessimistic view of Britain's prospects is taken by many scientists and reflective observers here and abroad. A typical example was provided by the comments of Dr. D. F. Martyn, Chief of Radio Research to the Australian Council of Scientific Industrial Research, who declared on his return from conferences in Europe that "Britain could not be defended in an atomic war, because she would starve." He urged "the mass migration of 20 million people from Britain to the Dominions, and planning throughout the British Commonwealth to meet the threat of atomic warfare. Britain's ports, through which half her food must come, could easily be knocked out."

Such a hopeless view of the prospects is justified as things stand at present. But the prospect would not be hopeless if the necessary measures were taken. What is required? It is not only the people of the British Isles who need to face that question, and tackle the problem of protection, for with the new means of conveyance now being developed all peoples lie under the shadow of atomic bombardment. They ought to face the fact, and bestir themselves to do what is possible. "Ostrichism" is more fatal than pessimism.

We can see, unless we bury our heads in the sand, the outline and scope of the Civil Defence measures that are needed—and which ought to have been under way long ago.

There must be a large-scale development of deep shelters, beyond those remaining from the last war, or else of massive concrete towers such as the Germans built— one of these in Hamburg sheltered as many as 60,000 people. There must also be a widespread construction of small surface or sub-surface shelters, newly designed in the light of atomic data. In the gravity of present circumstances it is sheer folly not to treat such provision as more urgent than housing programmes. There should be public aid for improving the shelter value of cellars, and for linking them up from house to house by underground passages, so that if the exits from some demolished houses are blocked, escape may be possible from others—this step saved many lives in German towns where it was carried out.

There must be a calculated dispersion of vital industrial plants, and the key parts of these should be placed underground. The Germans put off such measures until very late, but benefited a lot when and where they attempted them. Before the end they had built eighty underground factories.

There must be a fresh concentration of scientific research and tactical thought on developing improved and more extensive means of concealing vital targets, as well as deflecting the attacker—to offset the advantage the latter has gained, through radar and infra-red photography, in overcoming protective camouflage, smoke-screens, and cloud.

There must be a decision, without further delay, on measures to provide the people in the big cities and industrial areas with protective shoes, gloves and masks against radioactivity—so as to forestall the state of civic paralysis that may otherwise be produced by the effects, and still more by natural fear, of such radioactivity.

There must be, not merely broad plans, but detailed arrangements ready for the evacuation of children, old people, and non-essential workers from the cities if war comes, and for the subsequent transfer of workers from completely demolished sectors to other sectors of the city, or areas elsewhere. This calls not only for comprehensive billeting arrangements but for the advance manufacture of large stocks of tents—to ensure greater flexibility and accommodation capacity in carrying out emergency evacuations. Such tents should be light and easily portable, while watertight and draught-proof, like those of the one-piece mountaineering type.

There must be a greater effort than has yet been attempted to widen the many dangerous transport bottlenecks—particularly in the exit roads from the great cities and ports.

There must be a concentration of engineering and other research on devising alternative channels of supply and methods of landing supplies if the big ports are disabled. The artificial harbour, the landing ship and the pipeline might be adapted from military offensive to civil defensive purposes, and their potentialities developed.

With advance preparation, the smaller ports could be more fully utilized in emergency.

There must be a more farsighted plan in building up national food reserves, and for their storage in more widely distributed places than at present, with better protection against atomic attack. New protective and purification arrangements for water supplies are equally vital. At the same time improved kinds of compact emergency ration should be prepared and distributed for keeping constantly available in shelters and cellars. The food problem may prove to be the biggest of all problems under future atomic attack. It will be vain to provide shelter adequate to preserve people from wholesale massacre if they perish from wholesale starvation.

In the case of island countries such as Britain there should also be adequate plans for the evacuation overseas of non-essential "mouths." The shipping that brings supplies and military reinforcements into the island should take people out of it, to the fullest extent possible. Wiser still would be the early development of a comprehensive Commonweath plan to stimulate and facilitate large-scale emigration, by families and groups, from Britain to the other countries of the Commonwealth —as a peacetime measure to meet changed economic conditions as well as future war conditions. The present tendency to regard emigration as desertion is absurd. It should be applauded as a public-spirited step to relieve the strain on overcrowded countries, as well as a revival of the adventurous spirit of the past that is needed to tackle the future.

These are some of the vital steps that must be taken— beyond the development of adequate fire, rescue, hospital, and warning services—if the Western nations are to have any reasonable degree of Civil Defence against atomic attack. They are minimum needs. If international control of atomic energy is not established, and the stockpiling of atomic bombs continues, it may become necessary to frame a much larger policy for transferring industry underground. We may have to provide cities and industrial centres with a bomb-tight "basement" for working and living, in atomic warfare, if we are to ensure against national extinction.

The reduction of national vulnerability should be the first concern of any scheme of defence framed to meet the modern conditions of war. A nation's security turns on the measure of its vulnerability to attack as much as on its forces.

Any intending aggressor will naturally ensure that he has a superiority of force, numerical or technical, before venturing on war—a superiority sufficient for him to reckon on being able to defeat the forces of his immediate opponents. He will aim to do so before other powers or distant allies can intervene. But an aggressor will not court a long war, and is likely to abstain if he has reason to think that the conquest of his immediate opponents will be a slow business—because of factors other than their actual forces. In these days of airpower, the most important of such factors is a country's capacity to stand air bombardment without being crippled. So the diminution of a country's vulnerability becomes the best deterrent to aggression—far better than a relatively feeble power of counter-attack.

Thus the conclusion is more hopeful than appeared after thinking halfway through the problem. Provided that adequate measures of Civil Defence are taken without losing time, the prospect of the nations' defence against "atomization" looks better than most scientists have recognized in their repeated declarations that "there is no defence against the atomic bomb." The prospect would be much better still if an infallible automatically controlled rocket can be developed to counter both the bombers and guided missiles of an attacker. But adequate Civil Defence could tide over the interval, and is needed to do so. Even without that hoped-for counter-weapon, adequate Civil Defence in combination with the threat of hitting back might well suffice to deter an enemy from atom bombing—so long as we restrain hot-heads on this side from starting it. The much-feared poison gas attack never came in the last war since both sides possessed good defence against it as well as deadly gases they could use.

PART THREE

TODAY

Russia's Forces

CHAPTER XIV

THE SHADOW OF WAR WITH RUSSIA

THE more carefully one weighs all factors, the more likely it appears that there could be no real victory in a war between the Western Powers and the Soviet Union, but only a common loss—with the ordinary people on either side suffering most, as usual. The main difference from the last war is that the mutual sacrifice would probably be even greater. It might also be more prolonged.

In the event of a conflict the first phase might see a rapid surge forward of the Russians in Europe and Asia. It would not decide the issue—any more than the German surge of 1940, but there would be a long interval before America could develop her resources sufficiently to turn the tide. The pursuit of final victory in Russia might prove longer still. Indeed, there are reasons to doubt whether it would ever be attained.

The best chance might lie in an internal split, starting near the top—since it is almost impossible to overthrow a totalitarian regime from below, by popular revolt. But cracks in the top storey of such a structure are slow to show, and easy to stop up by ruthless action, while they may be cemented by external pressure. Experience should have warned Western statesmen against pinning too much hope to the possibility of a split. Soviet Russia is a tougher and more firmly consolidated system than Nazi Germany—and that proved much tougher than any of its opponents anticipated.

The only certainty is that most of Europe as well as Russia would be devastated in the process—more ruthlessly than in the Second World War—bringing misery to myriads of people on either side. While America would escape such widespread devastation, it is quite possible that before the end her great cities might suffer even worse than those in the fighting zone.

When venturing this forecast I can hear readers exclaiming: "How can there be another protracted war in the atomic era? No nation could for long withstand bombardment of the kind that was seen at Hiroshima." There is a popular idea that a new war would be quickly ended by the atomic bomb. That is a doubtful assumption. After the First World War, a similar belief prevailed about the rapid decisiveness of an ordinary bombing onslaught. It proved a bubble-belief. Even when the bombing fleets and bomb-loads had been multiplied to a scale far beyond pre-war imagination, the effect continued to fall short of anticipation, and the war went on. In the long-drawn process the enemy's cities were gradually ground into dust, but the resistance of the people was slow to crumble.

The atomic bomb promises to speed up the pace of destruction, and make it more horrifying, but that does not assure a swift ending of the struggle. There are counter-balancing factors. A number of cities might be quickly demolished, but their fate would not necessarily spell a people's surrender. Some nations are less dependent on their cities than others, and all have learnt a lot about dispersing and "earthing" their vital resources in such ways as to maintain the power of resistance. It has been shown, too, that human beings have an indefinite capacity of adjusting themselves to the gradual degradation of their living conditions. The lower a people's standard of living the less adjustment is required, and the easier it can maintain its endurance. Here lies the Russians' greatest asset in any conflict with the Western nations.

Now that both sides possess such a devastating weapon there may well be a growing, and mutual, hesitation to unloose it—as happened with poison gas in the last war. A Western advantage in the quantity of such bombs would be offset by the drawback of greater vulnerability that attaches to the more highly industrialized countries, where the population is more densely concentrated in city areas.

Even as it is, events have shown the limitations of this tremendous new power. In theory, America should be able to decide every international argument as she wishes. In practice, she has not been able to get her own way—because those who oppose her policy shrewdly realize that she could only use the atomic bomb as a last resort. Opposing countries can thus feel reasonably safe in defiance over any political issue that is not a life-or-death matter to the atom-owner. They may be able to go a long way in pursuing their own aims, even aggressive aims, without deferring to her protests.

Even if open war developed, a nation that is superior in ground forces might still find ways of offsetting the apparently decisive power of the atom bomb. The deeper its armies penetrate into foreign territory the safer its own position may become, for a time at any rate. The nations on the other side would not be able to employ the atom bomb in driving out the invaders, for that would involve the utter destruction of the cities they were seeking to liberate. Their power to loosen the invader's grip indirectly, by striking at his own cities, would also be diminished by their increased air distance from such targets.

Moreover, the invader might find shelter for many of his essential government services and industries by moving these forward into the captured territory. He could make room for them by shifting part of the captive population back into his own cities—which would be a considerable deterrent to atom bomb attacks there. For example, if the Russians were to overrun Denmark, Holland and Belgium, they could start moving a proportion of the people of Copenhagen, Rotterdam, Amsterdam, Antwerp and Brussels back to Moscow and Leningrad. In such circumstances, the Western Powers might hesitate to attempt the obliteration of these Russian cities. Hesitation is most likely at the outset of a war, when democratic governments tend to be less callous than they become as it continues. The use of mass hostages may prove to be a human counter to unselective weapons— weapons of wholesale massacre—like the atom bomb.

All these reflections point to the conclusion that the atom bomb has not nullified the value of armies—especially the forces that are ready for action without a long process of mobilization. It will not be easy to wrest the advantage from the country whose army can start with a jump deep into other people's territory.

Here we are brought face to face with the facts of the present situation. Russia is the strongest military power in Europe, and the only one capable of starting with a jump.

The attainment of the Allied war-aim of disarming Germany automatically ensured Russia's predominance. (Churchill's post-war note of alarm on this score casts an ironical reflection on his fervent faith earlier in the value of enforcing Germany's unconditional surrender.) Once the American forces went home there was no possibility of maintaining a balance of power in the immediate sense. The only real counterbalance since then has lain in a sober reckoning of the ultimate prospect in a war to the bitter end.

Any comparison of the respective forces, now or in the near future, points to the possibility of a Russian wave of advance swamping the Anglo-American-French zones of occupation in Germany, and then pouring deep into the countries beyond. The Rhine might be no adequate barrier to forces that rapidly overcame so many great river-lines in Eastern Europe. River-lines require holding in strength to be secure, and this is lacking.

Whether a Russian wave could sweep as fast and as far as the German wave did in 1940 is problematical. On a purely military calculation that is more doubtful. *Sustained* momentum depends on supply organization—unless the resistance is very weak. The Russians' organization is not so highly developed as was the Germans'—and they would be starting from a line much farther east. On the other hand, their path might be smoothed by political factors. They might be helped by the co-operation of much larger sections of the people in the Western and Mediterranean countries than the Germans were. Communism has an international appeal such as Nazism never enjoyed, nor knew how to create.

Thus there is more than a possibility that Western Europe might soon be submerged, leaving Britain once again in the grim situation of 1940, with an even greater ex-

tent of the Continental coastline under hostile control
—this time extending beyond France into Spain and
Portugal.

Such a line of advance, however, is not the only one
on the board. Italy is an obvious possibility, and Greece
another—its vulnerability was demonstrated in 1941. The
mountain-obstacles which cover them in the north could
only be made secure barriers if they were occupied by
forces much larger than the British are capable of providing.

The Middle East forms another avenue, with wider
prospects. It is true that the mountainous approaches
from Azerbaijan, through western Persia, form a natural
cover to this zone against invasion from the north, but
the cementing of it would call for much larger defending
forces than are available. A Russian advance would be
handicapped by the long stretch of difficult country; but
it might profit by the political instability of the region
and its consequent susceptibility to preparatory infiltration. We should be unwise to discount the possibility of
the Russians soon arriving on the Persian Gulf.

The Soviet Union has sufficient forces under arms to
develop more than one of these lines of advance at the
same time. That is a point which should not be overlooked. Even if the clash itself arose in the Far East, out
of the incipient conflict of Russian and American interests there, the development of a state of war might
prompt the Russians to throw their surplus weight in any
of these directions. The Soviet Army in the Far East is
virtually separate, and the immense length of its communications with European Russia limits the extent to
which it can be reinforced, so there would be a very
large surplus.

It may be thought that, although the Western Powers

could provide only small reinforcements for Greece and the Middle East, the balance might be adjusted by the intervention of the Turkish Army. This obviously forms a potential flanking check to a Russian thrust in either of these directions. But whatever its capacity to defend its own territory in Asia Minor, Turkey can hardly be reckoned as capable of a riposte offensive, beyond its own borders, in its present stage of equipment.

In Western Europe, too, the counterbalance will be far from adequate so long as it depends mainly on the sparse British and American armies of occupation. It will turn on the rebuilding and re-equipment of the armies of France and her neighbours, together with the economic restoration and political stability of these countries.

For the present, the principal check on a Russian irruption lies in the Russian people's desire for a chance of peaceful recovery after the terrific war-strain they have undergone, and on the measure of their Government's realization that the immediate chances of military success would be outweighed by the adverse long-term prospects—once America's immense technical resources were again mobilized. A dramatic opening success is no compensation for the ruinous effects of a long war, more devastating than the last. The Soviet Government often seems ill-informed and defective in judgment about current matters, but it has usually shown a shrewd grasp of fundamental factors.

More danger may lie in the Western nations' tendency to superficial thinking, governed by emotion, and in a failure to realize what war with Russia would mean. When the emotions of the Western nations are stirred up they are apt to lose sight of the cost, and human consequences, of their impulsive decisions. That was shown in the Polish Guarantee—which now looks such a tragic fiasco; in the "unconditional surrender" demand—which merely prolonged Germany's resistance, producing the boomerang effects that now make "victory" look such a farce; in the unlimited bombing policy that uselessly destroyed the economic foundations of peace, to our own present cost.

There is a school of thought—more common in triumphant America than in war-weary Britain—which, regarding war with Russia as bound to come, is inclined to force the issue. It talks of the importance of being ready "to strike first," regardless of the basic fact that American comparative remoteness entails delay in exerting her weight, and of the risk that war might be needlessly precipitated in the attempt. It ignores the likelihood of initial Russian successes, the long road of recovery in consequence, and the irreparable damage that civilization would suffer in the process. It underrates the difficulties of gaining so-called "victory" over Russia even when the balance of strength has turned.

Both Napoleon and Hitler imagined that the conquest of Russia would be a simple matter. Hitler reckoned that he could succeed where Napoleon had failed by relying on the greatly increased effect of modern weapons. His calculation was justified to the extent that he went farther than Napoleon, and produced a longer struggle. But he failed as badly in the end, and merely brought more misery all round on the effort.

Those who speak lightly of conquering Russia ought to acquaint themselves with the experience of the German generals, and learn what the attempt meant to the German soldiers who were the living stake of Hitler's gamble. American equipment might be more capable of meeting the problem of Russia's vast spaces, but American troops, however determined, would hardly be as well fitted to bear the extreme rigours of such a struggle.

While "appeasement" never pays, the mutual friction of two "tough" policies generates a shower of sparks, and any of these are liable to detonate an explosion. The risks are increased by the way in which a course of appeasement on our side changed to the present tough policy. It is all too easy to precipitate war in a mood of exasperation.

Danger lies in producing a situation where the other side cannot draw back without "losing face." The atmosphere today is too tense to be safe. We can help the chances of it by keeping our head, and our temper.

The Russians have an extraordinary knack of stirring up opposition, and offending even their friends. But a realization of their sacrifices and suffering, together with the effects of their prolonged isolation, brings more understanding of their one-sided view of "security," and should lead us to curb our irritation at their suspicious and aggressive attitude. Despite such appearances, we should not discount the underlying desire for peace among a people who have suffered so much from war.

CHAPTER XV

HOW GOOD ARE RUSSIA'S FORCES?

Iт is usual to estimate the strength of Russia's forces in numbers of men, and to set it forth in rows of 0s that are aptly called "round numbers." According to a statement of Britain's Minister of Defence, Russia has between 3,500,000 and 4,000,000 men under arms on her present peacetime basis compared with 3,000,000 at the time when Hitler invaded Russia. Mr. A. V. Alexander's estimate corresponded with that published earlier by Mr. Hanson Baldwin, the eminent military correspondent of the *New York Times,* who, in more detail, put the number of existing divisions in the Red Army between 175 and 195. Authoritative quarters in France put it as 175 to 180. So there appears to be close agreement as to how big the forces of Russia are.

More important is the question: "How good are her forces?" On that vital question, views widely differ. A prevalent opinion in both British and American military quarters is that the quality of Russia's forces is very low, technically and tactically, compared with their quantity. It would seem that the Governments are inclined to ac-

168

cept that opinion, for otherwise they could hardly be content with the paltry defence measures they have set on foot.

It is essential to examine the question as thoroughly as possible. Before we can do that there are a lot of cobwebs to clear away. For only seven years ago authoritative military opinion, both in Britain and in America, was as mistaken as Hitler himself in estimating the chances of Russia's capacity to stand against an army of Western type. British generals who carried weight by their rank took the view that Russia would be beaten within six weeks, and American ones put it even shorter. That time their miscalculation had no worse effect than to make them look silly, but another time it might prove disastrous.

Post-war analysis of the 1941 Russian campaign shows that they were not quite so foolish in their judgment as events made them look at the time. For Russia's military power was badly cracked, and the Germans might have come nearer to definite victory but for their blunders and initial miscalculations. But the margin of error in top-level military judgment on both sides and in all quarters was big enough to be a general warning for the future. It demonstrated the military tendency to jump to assumptions, and the need for a more scientific exploration of the facts.

In the case of modern Russia, there have been two special factors which made for mistaken conclusions. One is her isolation, and the other is the prejudice that the word "Communism" created from the start. Nothing makes people jump to hasty assumptions like a label, particularly when it is a coloured label. On the whole, soldiers are less inclined than civilians to underrate the forces opposed to them, but in the case of the Russian

forces the label "Red" has acted on them like the proverbial "red rag to a bull," and as a result they have often
been led astray in their judgment of facts. They could not
imagine that the Red Army could have any discipline,
and they have always been apt to regard any particular
flaws or failings as proof of its general incapacity. Similarly, the Russians' judgment about other nations has
suffered from the deluding effect of the word "Capital-
ism," on a "White" label. It has several times misled her
leaders into assuming that they had only to push on and
their opponents would show the white flag.

Mutual delusions have been multiplied by Russia's
isolation, and the consequent lack of information. Even
during the war the Western powers knew far less about
the situation and forces of their Russian ally than they
did about their German foe. Whereas they were able to
discuss the detailed organization of the German forces,
and could pin-point the location of units with remarkable
accuracy, they were given only the vaguest outline of
how their allies were organized and disposed. Their military missions were kept in a gilded cage, with heaps of
entertainment but very little scope for observation.

It is thus natural that Western soldiers' ideas have been
largely coloured by the impressions that many of them
get from the glimpse they had of the Russian troops when
the armies came in contact at the end of the war, and
before the "iron curtain" descended. That was a chaotic
period, and one of relaxation after prolonged effort.

Impressions of disorderliness, untidiness, stupidity, and
primitiveness predominated. The crudity of much of the
Russian equipment caught the eye, and so did the
odd assortment of transport—tanks and high-powered
trucks mingled with one-horse farm-carts. The lavishly
equipped Westerners could not understand how an army

could have carried on without so many things they had
been accustomed to regard as necessary. They found it
hard to believe that such an army could be efficient in a
different way from their own. They felt that it would be
easy to brush aside what looked to them such an ill-
equipped rabble. The reaction was all the stronger because their own wartime propaganda had built up such
a high estimate of the Russian Army.

These superficial glimpses have greatly affected Anglo-
American military views, and largely account for the low
estimate of the effectiveness of the Russian forces. But
such a low estimate is hard to reconcile with their performance against the German Army, especially their
long-striding advances in 1944-45. For we had much
trouble in overcoming German forces even with a great
superiority of power in all forms, and while the Russians
had a larger superiority in manpower over the Germans,
they had not such a big superiority in firepower and
nothing like such immense superiority in airpower as we
did. It is not reasonable, and is dangerous, to explain
away the Russian successes as merely due to pure numbers of men. The truth lies somewhere between the low
and high estimates.

The only foreign soldiers who are really acquainted
with the Russian Army are the Germans—having come
to know it in four years at close grips. It is to them that
one must go for any first-hand evidence. I have done so—
in a long series of discussions since the war with German
generals and fighting men. By piecing together their
evidence one can build up a fairly clear and complete
picture of the equipment and tactics, the character and
quality of Russia's forces.

First, let us take the question of material. There have,
of course, been changes and developments since the war

—but an exact idea how good the weapons and other equipment were at the start of war, and how much they improved during it, may be a fair indication of likely improvement since the war.

The general testimony is that the Russian weapons of most types were remarkably good even in 1941, when the German invasion was launched. The Russian rifles were more modern than the German and had a higher rate of fire. Their machine-guns were equally good. Their mortars were so simple in construction and roughly finished that they looked like the product of a village blacksmith, yet they were most efficient, while their apparent crudeness was far outweighed by the advantage of rapid output. It was all the more advantage because their artillery, though excellent, was not so abundant as had been expected, and when a large part of it was overrun and captured in the first few months the Russians filled the gap by using large quantities of mortars, mounted on trucks, as a substitute until the enlarged production of artillery pieces from the new factories in the unoccupied areas began to make up the shortage.

It was in tanks that the Russians enjoyed their greatest advantage. This asset was the one of which they had the most need—since the invader's hopes of victory were mainly based on the decisive effect of his tank forces. Unfortunately for the Russians this technical advantage came into operation just too late to make a difference in the early battles. That is a hitherto unrevealed story which is of great significance as a clue to what happened in 1941.

When the German invasion came, in June that year, the Russian tanks were still of types that had been produced under the second Five-Year Plan. They were becoming out of date—though not more so than those the

Germans were using (which were mostly of 1933-37 vintage). The Russian tanks also outnumbered the German ones. But the Red Army forfeited that numerical advantage by the way it dispersed its tanks, instead of concentrating them as the Germans did, and by clumsy handling of them. As a result, they were destroyed piecemeal by the skilfully manœuvred German panzer divisions, and the Red Army was left stripped of most of its tanks by the end of the summer.

But new models, designed while Germany was overrunning the West, were just coming into production—the T34 medium tank and the KVI heavy tank. They proved superior to anything the invader had, and cramped his manœuvring style. The T34 began to appear late in the summer, as the Germans completed the last bound before the advance on Moscow, and those that were available were used as strategic reserves to block the back end of holes that were made in the front. By 1942 the new types were being turned out in large quantities.

Here it is worth tracing the evolution of the Russian tanks. In the 1920s the earliest Russian-built tanks followed French patterns, with some modifications. Next, they bought Vickers models under licence from England, and developed these. The ten-ton T26 (based on the Vickers six-tonner but armed with a 45 mm. gun) became their main light tank—although its limitations, especially its inadequate armour, were shown up in the Spanish Civil War, large numbers were still in use in 1941.

The Russians were also quick to copy promising features of any foreign model even where they could not buy it. Thus the lay-out of the T28, a medium-heavy tank of 30 tons with a 76 mm. gun which they produced in

1933, was inspired by the British experimental "sixteen-tonner." The T35 heavy tank, of 49 tons, was modelled on the still earlier British "Independent" tank of 1925. Whereas the British Army, restricted for money, was trying to evolve smaller types of tank that would cost less, and could only produce a few experimental models of each, the Russians made theirs on a larger pattern and with a heavier gun, while also building them in quantity.

Some of the later pre-war types took points from German tank design. Before Hitler defied the Versailles treaty restrictions on building tanks the Soviet Government had given the Germans facilities for establishing experimental tank centres in Russia, at Kazan and Voronezh. This did not prove of great advantage to the Germans, as the models they developed in Russia, like those of the Russians, were not designed for wireless control on the battlefield; according to Guderian, the Germans' first standard light tank, the Panzer I, was developed in Germany itself from 1932 onward, and as an adaptation of the British Carden-Loyd. The Russians profited more from the mutual arrangement. They not only learnt some useful ideas but were able to buy the latest German aircraft engines, which they adapted to tank propulsion. That helped them to make their tanks bigger, and to mount a larger gun, while keeping up their speed.

The experience of the Finnish War, however, showed them that the armour protection of their tanks was inadequate, confirming earlier evidence from the Spanish Civil War that had been disregarded. They made hasty efforts to thicken the armour on their existing machines, particularly the T28, though at the cost of their mobility and efficiency in proportion to weight. But the margin of time before the German invasion came proved just too short for the production in quantity of really new designs.

Thus in June, 1941, the Russians consisted largely of thin-skinned T26 and BT light-medium tanks, backed up by the T28. The latter was about to be replaced by the new 43-ton KVI—which showed a number of German features in its design, and was twice as heavy as the Panzer III and IV, the heaviest German tanks then in use. When it came into action, however, the KVI forfeited its advantage through its clumsiness, and from various mechanical defects which required remedy. Much more effective was the new medium tank, the T34. This went far to turn the scales.

The T34 can be traced back to an American source. A private designer, Walter Christie, had there developed by the early 1930s a very fast tank of novel design which showed high promise. The Russians bought a sample, improved on it, and produced a medium (cruiser) tank, the BT, which they produced in quantity by 1936 as the main machine of their tank forces. It was much more reliable than its imported prototype, but its armour was thin—and for that the Russians had to pay a heavy price in the 1941 battles. From it, however, they developed the T34, which had thicker armour (52 mm.), a more powerful gun (76 mm.), and was faster (34 m.p.h.) than any tank the German or any other army in the world had at the time. Other assets of this 28-ton machine were its low build and unusually broad tracks. The Russians designed their tanks for Russian ground—sandy soil that so often turned into deep mud after rain—and that gave them a further advantage.

The production of the T34 mounted steadily during 1942, despite all the upsets caused by the renewed German advances. Even while the months-long battle of

Stalingrad raged, a tank factory in the city was turning
out ten to fifteen T34s a day. The German besiegers, operating far ahead of their bases and nearly two thousand
miles from their factories, could not make up the wastage
in the constant tank fights. Their twenty-ton 20 m.p.h.
medium tanks, the Panzer III and IV, were outclassed—
as the German generals ruefully admitted. That was bad
for the morale of the German troops at a crucial time.

By 1943 the Germans had produced the 60-ton Tiger
tank, with its 100 mm. of armour in front and its great
88 mm. gun. This took heavy toll of the more lightly
armed and armoured British and American tanks in the
enclosed country of Sicily, Italy and Normandy. But in
the open spaces of Russia the relatively slow Tiger was
more handicapped in dealing with the speedy T34s. The
German tankmen derisively called their Tiger a "furni-
ture van."

Then in 1944 the Russians introduced their new heavy
tank, the Stalin, developed from the KV. This had a 122
mm. gun and 150 mm. of armour in front, yet was lower
in build and thus less of a target than the Tiger. Only
by skill in tactics could the Germans combat the superiority of the Stalin tanks. Moreover, the Russians produced these in large quantities, whereas the German
output of their improved heavy tanks, the Panther and
Royal Tiger, was comparatively small—due partly to the
effect of the Anglo-American bombing campaign.

In sum, the Red Army has proved over a whole decade
its capacity to keep abreast or even a step ahead of other
armies. This story of the "tank race" is worth telling in
detail, as a warning, because it shows how the Russians
concentrated on the development of the arm that mattered most, while also turning out well-designed and reliable weapons of other kinds. They seem particularly

good at making weapons that are especially "fool-proof." That may reflect an especial need on their part, due to a lower average level of education among the users, but it is a very desirable asset anywhere in view of hard-testing war conditions.

Since the war they have had the experience of German technicians to combine with their own, and a knowledge of the many new weapons and improved types that were being evolved in Germany. So it would be wise to reckon that the Russians are at least keeping their former rate of progress in design.

Evidence of this has already been seen in the air—the sphere where it is most difficult to hide things. In the war, the Red Air Force was not so striking as the Red tank force—though certainly not to be despised. It had concentrated on close support of the troops on the ground, especially by low-flying attack, to the virtual exclusion of longer-range and more complex operations. In that limited role the Russians were quite effective, if not up to the highest Western standards. Their Yak fighters, Lavotchkin fighter-bombers, and Tupolev (TU2) twin-engined bombers had a good performance. Western critics have been rather too inclined to base their opinions on the Red Air Force's obvious defects—technical and operational—where it went outside the limits on which it had mainly focussed. Its standard of navigation is poor and its methods are primitive. It is not equipped with the instruments for blind-flying and direction by radar. But the pilots often show a natural skill, and any amount of daring.

The output of machines is far larger than in any other country since the war, but they are mostly of light ground co-operation or training types. Quantity production is helped by simplicity of construction, and the majority still have wooden frames. A greater handicap is in engine-design, which has been backward by comparison with Western progress.

That is one reason why the Russians have embraced jet-propulsion with great eagerness. Their development of this new line has been helped by the fact that they bought a considerable number of the Rolls-Royce Nene and other jet-engines before such arrangements were checked. Several new jet-engine types of fighter have been seen, by foreign observers, and one of them has been timed to be travelling at well over 600 m.p.h.

As jet-engined fighters and fighter-bombers are too fast to be suitable for co-operation in ground operations, it would seem that the Russians are now concentrating on the problem of intercepting "atom-bombers." There has also been a significant development of new long-range bombers similar to the B29, or Superfortress, while a promising four-engined jet bomber has been appearing. All this suggests an increased interest in strategic bombing on the Russians' part.

Likewise, the production of new long-range transport aircraft may be a hint of contemplated airborne operations. One of the mysteries of the last war is why the Russians, who were the pioneers of parachute forces, never tried to use theirs during the war—in contrast to the Western countries, who were late-comers in this new sphere. But while they had a far greater number of trained parachute-jumpers than any other country, they were short of transport aircraft as well as backward in navigational technique. Here are two obvious reasons—though there may be others—for that blank page in the record of Russia's achievements in the war. In studying the problems of another struggle, starting further west, it is not likely that her strategists can have failed to see how a strong airborne arm might serve them as a "tin-opener" if they were to take the offensive initiative at a suitably chosen moment. The clearest of all lessons of the last war was that Hitler's advance, which came so near achieving the conquest of the West, broke down on two rocks—first, his inability and unreadiness to throw a land force over the sea into the island of Britain; second, his failure to capture the rock-keys of the Mediterranean.

While the Red Air Force hitherto has been a less impressive force than the Red Army, the Red Navy has been by far the least effective of the Services—no better than in Tzarist times. It failed even to dominate the Black Sea during the last war, still less the Baltic. It has three battleships, some nine cruisers and perhaps sixty destroyers, but most of them are obsolete. It has recently built its first two aircraft-carriers, ships of 22,000 tons capable of carrying sixty planes. Its main strength lies in its submarine force, the largest in the world—its total is stated to be about 250. Such numbers convey a false impression, as the bulk are of out-of-date types.

Important developments are to be expected, however, from the fact that the Russians are now in possession of a number of the latest type German U-boats and the component parts for building a lot more, as well as the experts in their design. A large submarine force of this type—which does not have to come to the surface and combines speed with an immensely long radius—could be of great potential effect in another war, especially for a renewed and tighter blockade of Britain, and as an invisible "iron curtain" to stop supplies and troop-shipments from America to Europe.

Beyond that is the possibility of developing submersible troop-carriers. These could be an epoch-making contribution to the solution of the problem of overseas invasion by a land-power which does not enjoy command of the sea, particularly for the invasion of a relatively small objective. It is the problem to which a farsighted strategic planning staff, of a power with large resources, would long since have directed its efforts. While "airborne" is one possible way of solution, "undersea" is another. It would seem, however, the more remote one—taking account of the technical difficulties, especially for a country that is inexperienced in amphibious operations.

While it would be wise not to discount the possibility of the Russians' embarking on wider forms of action than they attempted in the last war, it is reasonable to reckon that lack of practical war experience in unfamiliar techniques may diminish the potential threat.

On a present reckoning, the power of Russia's forces rests mainly in her Army—and, in that, on her armoured arm. This is her spearhead.

It is a very formidable arm, and anyone would be foolish to underrate its menace. At the same time, it has limitations that should be noted in assessing its powers. The Russian tank force—though the best element in all Russia's forces—did not prove as potent as the inherent superiority of its machines. That was due partly to technical, and partly to tactical, limitations. These are worth study because they bring out the curiously mixed quality of the Russian forces in general—that mingling of contrasts which makes one observer jump to the conclusion that they are inefficient and another to the conclusion that they are super-efficient. The eye of the one is caught by obvious blemishes and deficiencies, so that he overlooks the excellence of the basic elements. The mind of the other is so impressed by these basic elements that it fails to note the restrictions on their effectiveness.

The two sides of the case come out in examination of the Russian tank arm.

The machines were rough inside and out—they were not even painted. Their design showed little regard for the comfort of the crew. They lacked the refinements and instruments that Western tank experts considered necessary as aids to driving, shooting and control. Until 1943 they had radio only in the commanders' tanks.

On the other hand, they had a good thickness and shape of armour, a powerful gun, high speed, and reliability—the four essential elements. The comfort of their crew was of less importance, especially as Russian soldiers were tougher than others. Regard for comfort and the desire for more instrumental aids involve added weight and complications of manufacture. Such desires have repeatedly delayed the development and spoilt the performance of British and American tanks. So they did with the Germans, whose production suffered from the search for technical perfection.

The principles on which the Russians worked in their mechanization programme can be clearly discerned. They picked up ideas from many different tank types abroad, and picked out features which they thought worth incorporating in their own tanks, and then developed the amalgam in a model on their own lines. They concentrated on the mass production of only one or two types. They tried to make these as simple as possible in construction. This was of great help to rapid output in quantity. In 1942 the Russian armoured corps mostly had only two types of vehicle, the T34 tank and the Ford lorry, whereas the German panzer divisions had a dozen different types of armoured vehicles and twenty of unarmoured vehicles—a great complication of the problem of repair and spare parts.

Thus the balance of advantage would seem to rest with the tank policy that the Russians followed. But it also carried handicaps that reduced the advantages provided by the basic superiority of their tanks. While the crews might be able to stand more discomfort than Westerners could, that power of endurance did not prevent them being hampered in action when in a tank that had a cramped body. The deficiency of their optical instruments lowered the chances of hitting the target when they opened fire. Lack of other "gadgets" was a handicap on movement. Until all tanks were fitted with radio, the sub-units could not manœuvre quickly—and so forfeited much of the advantage offered by the speed of the machines.

Western armies are apt to lose mobility and flexibility through their abundance of means, their variety of specialities, and their elaborate organization—they become tangled up in the many strings to their bow. But the Russians are apt to be cramped in their action through having too few. Over-complexity and over-simplicity both make for inelasticity, though in opposite ways.

CHAPTER XVI

THE CHARACTER OF THE RED ARMY

THE Red Army is an embodiment of contrasts. Its strange mingling of new and old, of scientific method and primitive habit, of rigidity and flexibility, is even more marked on the tactical than on the material side. That is natural—for the machines are the product of men, and handled by them. The apparent incongruities which baffle casual observers, and lead them to widely different conclusions, become more understandable and easier to reconcile when set against the background of the Red Army's development.

German soldiers are the only ones in the West who have had experience, or even close observation, of the Red Army in action—and they have seen it during successive stages of development under the hardest test. Two essential points emerge from their accounts. The Red Army is two in one—there is an "army of quality" within the "army of quantity," and although even the former is of curiously mixed quality it has been developing at a much faster pace than the mass which encloses it.

The other point is that any judgment on the Red Army

should be accompanied by the date of its vintage, just as we know a wine by its year. An expert who has only tasted "Red Army 1941" may be quite misleading about "Red Army 1943," and so on. While the difference of vintage is likely to be less marked since the war ended, it is not safe to assume that the present quality is the same as that of 1945. But a knowledge of certain basic tendencies may be a guide to the question whether it is likely to have improved or otherwise.

In examining the wartime record, it is natural to begin with the leadership. When I asked Field-Marshal von Rundstedt which were the best generals he met, his verdict was terse: "None were any good in 1941." Rundstedt's chief opponent, on the Southern front, was the famous cavalryman, Marshal Budenny, one of the legendary heroes of the Civil War. Rundstedt remarked that the aptest description of Budenny was provided by a captured Russian officer who said: "He is a man with an immense moustache, but a very small brain." Budenny had been an imposing member of the "military court" called to sit in judgment on the generals who were arraigned for treason in 1937, and it is clear that this wholesale *political* purge had very damaging effects on the capacity of the Red Army to meet the test of war. The 1941 invasion showed that incompetence was preponderant in all levels of command.

But the subsequent *military* purge had better results, opening the way for the rise of talented commanders who could prove their case in the more realistic "trial by battle." The combination of practical test with wider opportunity produced a remarkable change. By 1942 the level of leadership was rising, and it went on rising year by year, while the war lasted.

All the German generals to whom I talked expressed

high admiration for the ability of Marshal Zhukov, whom they regarded as outstanding. Next to him they placed Marshal Koniev, praising him as a clever tactician though not regarding him as on Zhukov's level. They considered that quite a number of the other higher commanders had become skilled in the art of manœuvring large forces, but that the proportion of able leaders tended to decrease on the lower levels of the high command, where less scope was allowed for initiative.

The run of opinion was that the top and bottom of the Russian ladder of command became the strongest sections, while the middle piece was shaky. The top rungs were filled by men who had proved themselves so able that they were allowed to exercise their own judgment, and could safely insist on doing things in their own way. The bottom rungs were filled by junior officers who, within their limited sphere, tended to develop a good tactical sense, because the incompetent soon became casualties in a field that was ruled by the hard realities of the enemy's bullets and shells. But the intermediate commanders, even more than in most armies, were concerned with other factors. Their superiors' orders and judgments were more to be feared than the enemy.

Tactically, the best troops were the so-called armoured corps—here the level of intelligence among officers and men was much above the average. I use the term "so-called" because in fact the actual armoured element was only a small part of them—they had about 200 tanks, and no other armoured vehicles. The composition of these corps varied—here the Russians had a strong sense of flexibility—but averaged about three armoured brigades, and one motorized infantry brigade. There were also "mechanized corps," which usually comprised one ar-

moured brigade and three motorized infantry brigades,
each including one tank battalion.

The battalions were small by western standards, and
German officers have remarked to me that the Russians
profited much in tactical effectiveness by having such
handier-sized units. The corps itself was little larger than
one of our divisions. In the case of these armoured corps
there were no divisional headquarters interposed; by
cutting out this extra link in the chain of command and
letting the corps commander handle direct as many as
half a dozen brigades time was saved and flexibility
gained. (See Chapter XX.)

The Russian high command rarely placed these
armoured corps under the control of the ordinary armies,
but grouped two to six of them in what were called
"armoured armies," and kept them for special striking
roles. That was wiser than our normal habit of putting
armoured divisions under an infantry commander, who
is apt to be pedestrianly minded, and accustomed to slow-
motion warfare. The Russians were careful not only to
keep their "army of quality" distinct, but to ensure that
it was treated as such.

When the battle-front became static after one of the
big bounds that the Russians periodically made, these
"armoured armies" were withdrawn into reserve. There
was then usually an interval of several months before the
Russians had repaired the communications and brought
up supplies, accumulated large stocks of ammunition,
and were ready to launch a fresh offensive. The cracking
of the enemy's new defence-line was left to the ordinary
infantry armies, helped by a special reinforcement of
artillery and also tank units from the higher command's
general reserve.

In a detailed account that was given me of a typical

Russian offensive in the later stages of the war, the methods pursued were made very clear. The assault was delivered by three armies, with some 30 infantry divisions, concentrated on a sector 25 miles wide—similar attacks were simultaneously launched on other sectors of the entire front. An armoured army was waiting in readiness behind. Its advanced units lay twelve miles behind the front.

The infantry assault was preceded by a bombardment lasting two hours, by some 1,200 guns, and the infantry then pushed forward, eating gradually into the German defensive position. By the third day, after fresh divisions had been put into action, the position was broken through. The armoured army moved forward just before the break-through had actually been achieved, completed it, and then pushed forward as fast as possible "into the depths" of open country beyond. Similar break-throughs had been made in other sectors, and the loose-linked chain of exploiting armoured armies swept on nearly 300 miles, penetrating successive rear positions where the Germans attempted a stand, before the surge was brought to a halt.

The Russian infantry assaults usually suffered heavy losses in achieving their breaching purpose, being planned and executed in battering-ram style. It often happened that assault after assault was shattered by the defenders' fire. On the other hand, the small infantry units often showed skill and cunning in the way they went on "trickling through" after the formal assault had failed. Thereby they redeemed the failure, and turned the scales. With shrewd instinct, junior leaders often chose to advance over ground, such as a marsh, that appeared to be a barrier to advance. If a handful of men trickled through in this way in the evening, they might swell to a thousand or more by daylight—and the threat played on the Germans' nerves.

Russian tank tactics also showed a mixture of formality and ingenuity. In 1941 the Russians had tied their fast tanks down to the service of the infantry—the same mistake that the French had made to a large extent in 1940. But even when they learned to concentrate their tanks in armoured corps, and to handle these operationally, they still went back to the "penny packet" method when assaulting an enemy position.

Their tank tactics were of a drill pattern, with each step carefully planned in advance. Before an attack, the subordinate commanders were given maps on which their routes and objectives were marked by coloured lines. Such extremely detailed planning suggests that the executants were not highly intelligent, or that it was a policy not to allow much scope for individual judgment and initiative.

Attacks ran much on World War I lines—"tramlines" they might be called—with the tanks closely backed up by the infantry. The assault was delivered by a long chain of mixed packets, with a company of tanks leading a company of infantry. The Russian companies were small, ten tanks or eighty infantrymen, which allowed some degree of local flexibility. Once the enemy position had been broken through, the tanks would concentrate and continue the advance in a large body until another defensive position was reached. The Russian tank forces became with experience skilled in manœuvring in mass during these intermediate stages, but assault methods remained more stereotyped than in other armies.

Their tactical limitations were accentuated by the extreme simplicity of their equipment. The mechanized formations had only two kinds of vehicle, the tank and the lorry—no reconnaissance machines, staff cars or motorcycles. If they wanted to send a written message or an order, they had to send it in a tank—and that was the more frequent because their habit of giving very detailed instructions was unsuitable for radio communication. Late in the war, however, enough American jeeps became available to provide a few for each tank battalion.

The quick support of tanks by infantry elements, and mobile combination between the two, was hindered by the lack of any armoured carriers or other cross-country vehicles. That meant waiting until infantry brigades or divisions could be brought up in lorries—and these might be stuck far behind when the sandy roads turned into mud. But the Russians partly filled the gap by mounting infantrymen on the tanks, and carrying them forward in that manner until the enemy's fire compelled them to dismount. This was typical of the Russians' way of improvisation to overcome their handicaps.

The mass of the army was much worse equipped. Even the volume of American supplies did not go far to make up the shortage of lorries and most of them were needed to carry the infantry parts of the armoured corps, or for the rear services. The ordinary infantry division had to scrape along with a makeshift collection of horse-transport—and little of that.

What it meant was vividly explained to me by General von Manteuffel, who led many tank raids behind the Russian front. "The advance of a Russian Army is something that Westerners can't imagine. Behind the tank spearheads rolls on a vast horde, largely mounted on horses. The soldier carries a sack on his back, with dry crusts of bread and raw vegetables collected on the march from the fields and villages. The horses eat the straw from the house roofs—they get very little else. The

Russians are accustomed to carry on for as long as three weeks in this primitive way, when advancing. You can't stop them, like an ordinary army, by cutting their communications, for you rarely find any supply columns to strike."

The tactical standard of the ordinary divisions was not high, and in many cases rather poor. Their handling, by the commanders, was often unskilful and unimaginative, while reckless of losses. The view of their opponents was expressed in the comment that one of the German army commanders made to me: "The Russians were always very bull-headed in their offensive methods, repeating their attacks again and again. This was due to the way their leaders lived in fear of being considered lacking in determination if they broke off their attacks." The Germans many times overheard wireless orders that threatened commanders with the direst penalties if they hesitated to launch their troops into a renewed assault—and the troops in their turn were pushed forward with the threat of being shot in the back if they faltered.

Such bull-headed attacks failed far more often than they succeeded, while piling up the losses—into millions. But they had a psychological effect on the defender even where they failed. They gave him the feeling that no matter how many waves he shot down, more would come on. That "got him down." It made him more susceptible to the flank threats that arose whenever the Russian armoured spearheads pierced some weak point in his extended line.

But it would be a mistake to assume that fear was the main cause of the Russians' amazing fortitude and disregard for losses. Besides it there was fanaticism, for a Communistic idea, which Soviet indoctrination had grafted on to a deep-rooted patriotism. And beyond that there was a fatalism natural to the Slav-Asiatic character of the people, but given a more automaton-like effect by the new combination of a mechanistic age with a deterministic view of human life.

When Russian troops were attacking, an unexpected counterstroke often succeeded in driving them back—by shaking their confidence and throwing them off their balance. But when they were on the defence, it proved very hard to make an impression on them. That diminishes the chances of dislodging them by air attack or by a threat to their flanks—to which most armies are acutely sensitive. On the other hand, it gives an opponent more chance of getting right round their flanks before they have realized the danger, and cutting them off—though it may still prove very hard to make them surrender even when their situation is hopeless.

Here we may find the reason why the Germans took such an immense total of prisoners in their great pincermanœuvres, yet also had to pay a heavy price themselves, in life and delay, before they could actually put the encircled Russians "in the bag." It is significant that the younger German soldiers who were in the fighting line tend to be even more emphatic in their testimony to Russian toughness than the higher generals who planned these vast encirclements—for it was the former who had to "finish the job." Even so, it was not so hard to force the surrender of such large masses as it was to overcome the small parties that were cut off and surrounded in the course of battle. These commonly held out until they were all killed or crippled.

The "unimpressionability" of the Russians, as well as their exceptional capacity for endurance, needs to be taken into account when considering the claims made for air power as the decisive answer to a Russian threat in the West.

While preserving the military asset of this primitive toughness, the Russians have added to it a technical ability which they did not formerly show. This is an unusual combination, and it is still underrated in the West, particularly by the exponents of Western air power. For example, Lord Trenchard has discounted the interference of the Red Air Force by arguing that while the Russians may have plenty of machines, and can make good ones, they are inefficient in operating and maintaining them. He went on to declare that the same applies to mechanical vehicles on the ground—"they cannot maintain them and they never have been able to maintain them." That represents a very prevalent view in the West.

Is it a safe assumption? Germans who fought on the Eastern Front say that the Russians had improved greatly in mechanical sense and skill by 1944-45 compared with 1941. The bigger repairs were not carried out as quickly as in the German Army, but their normal maintenance service was good, and they had plenty of well-trained mechanics. In fact the German tank officers told me that, in the later part of the war, their own maintenance companies were manned almost entirely by Russians, and these proved as good as their own men. From this, it seems that the Western powers may be in danger of clinging, and pinning their hopes, to an out-of-date idea.

There is a danger, also, in the tendency to dwell on the Red Army as one of quantity without quality, or of uniformly low quality, and to talk as if the problem was that of stopping such a mass-produced army. Trenchard implied this when declaring: "I cannot believe that 500,000,

1,000,000, or even 2,000,000 men could advance without being stopped by the power of the Royal Air Force, backed by the power of the American Air Force."

In reality, the initial problem is that of stopping a much smaller but skilled force composed of mechanized spearheads. In the later stages of the Eastern Front campaign, it was these fast-moving spearheads which carried out the decisive penetrations, while the mass army walked on behind. It may be more of a problem to stop 200,000 of such troops than to stop the 2,000,000 mass.

To meet that problem a large air force is not enough. While a large army with little air support would be an even less safe insurance, there is need for a fair-sized land force of a highly mobile kind to check the Russian spearheads that might infiltrate in face of air attack. The Western allies are at present far from possessing that minimum insurance on the ground. When it is attained, then it may be wise to put the preponderant effort into developing air strength—to check the mobilized masses of Russia on their long walk to the West.

Those masses *are* backward, in skill and equipment, by Western standards. But the leaven is increasing, and rising in both skill and equipment. The post-war disbandment of many divisions and the reduction of the total numbers under arms, has made it possible to give a higher scale of modern equipment to those that remain, especially the spearhead divisions. With the aid of rebuilt factories, and the acquiring of new centres of production in the satellite and occupied countries, it has become possible to improve the quality as well as the scale of mechanized equipment. The proportion of long-service professional soldiers in the peacetime Army is very high—American estimates put it at one out of every three men now serving—and that is an aid towards constituting the spearhead divisions from men of high skill and training, mechanized and tactical.

It is notable, too, that the increasing technical efficiency of the Russians goes along with a continued talent for improvisation. This has not been weakened but rather strengthened by their technology. The effect was aptly expressed by a German general who remarked: "Their technical and mechanical *sense* is great, much greater than anticipated by us. They can construct a house out of some tree trunks with an axe, and have only to buy the glass for the windows. The same is true—mutatis mutandis—for their motor-vehicles. Give the Russian some scrap of old cars and he will build you an automobile!"

This capacity for simple but ingenious expedients was repeatedly demonstrated in their bridging methods. Until late in the war they lacked the special equipment on which other armies depended, or anything comparable to the Bailey bridge, yet proved able to get across the exceptionally broad rivers of Russia with little delay—by felling trees near the river bank and turning them into well-built wooden bridges in astonishingly quick time. For tracked vehicles they often used "stick" bridges, composed of closely spaced trestles without any road-bearers. At Stalingrad they sprang a surprise on the Germans by building an under-water bridge, by which they moved reinforcements of infantry and tanks across the Volga each night. As the bridge could not be detected from the air the Germans were puzzled, for a long time, by the way that day after day the constantly battered and apparently isolated defenders of the west bank seemed to remain as numerous as ever. During the Russians' later advances they made continued use of such under-water bridges as a means of surprise.

In sum, Russia's forces present, and represent, a collection of contrasts that confuses the Western observer who tries to place them as a whole in a specific grade. They defy such classification—like Russia itself. So many people ask: "What is the truth about Russia?" The extreme variation of the attempted answers shows the impossibility of a definite one. There was deeper understanding in the man who, from closer experience, replied: "Everything you hear about Russia is true. All the good things you hear are true, and all the bad things are true."

Likewise with Russia's forces, these have the characteristics both of the primitive horde and of the mechanized robot. While some parts show one characteristic more than the other, all parts show traces of both, in varying degree. Thus it comes about that a "mechanistic" human tendency towards centralized rigidity is still accompanied by a remarkable knack of improvisation, while on the other hand the flexibility that the mechanized vehicle itself offers is restricted by old habits of pedestrian action, even where the new regime favours a dynamic mobility.

A crucial question remains—is it probable that the Red Army has continued to make steady progress since the war? While it may be wise to reckon with the possibility, there are reasons for doubting the probability of an all-round continuance of its progress. The Soviet regime does not foster a critical attitude, and the Soviet Russian is not usually self-critical. In the military sphere it would seem that only the test of war itself arouses in the leadership a sense of reality. The natural peacetime relapse, together with renewed political suspicion of the more able officers, may well have been operating as a check on progress since the war.

There have, in fact, been several indications of a tendency to eliminate war-proved leaders of energy and ambition, and to bring back into favour those who are regarded as more politically sound. Thus "Red Army 1949," instead of being four years more advanced than "Red Army 1945," may actually be somewhat retrograde in comparison.

CHAPTER XVII

THE RIDDLE OF RUSSIA'S AIRBORNE FORCES

Warfare is taking new forms. Events since the end of World War II have shown us how war can continue in so-called peace, and how conquest can proceed without open conflict—through a combination of infiltrating propaganda, political pressure, and underground forces. More than twenty years ago I wrote about the prospective part that such "masked invasion" was likely to play in future campaigns, and my 1945 book *The Revolution in Warfare* sounded a fresh warning about the probability of its intensive and extensive development. It seemed a very obvious forecast. But the Western Powers were slow to perceive it, and slower still to counter it.

If the present "camouflaged war" or "cold war" should turn into "shooting war," it is to be hoped that they shall not again be caught off guard by other new developments which have not been officially foreseen. The possibilities of the unexpected are not yet exhausted. Besides the prospect of *surprise weapons,* they include that of *surprise moves.*

197

The prevailing view seems to be that the worst case with which Atlantic policy would have to reckon in the early stages is that of being thrown back to the position of 1940—with England as an isolated island on the edge of an occupied continent. There is a general assumption that, even if the countries of Western Europe were overrun, England would be in no immediate danger. Is that assumption justified? It is not a safe assumption. One dangerous and early possibility has been ignored in public discussion of what might happen in case of another war.

This possibility is related to a "missing factor" of the last war that remains veiled in mystery. One of the greatest puzzles of World War II is why the Russians made no use of parachute forces. The Germans seized the keys of Holland and Belgium with such forces in 1940, and in 1941 captured Crete by the same means. Later in the war the Western Allies used them on a still larger scale in the invasion of Normandy, the drive for the Rhine, and the crossing of the Rhine. The Russians had been pioneers in this new field. As far back as 1935 they had carried out mass parachute drops in their Army Manœuvres, and had moved a whole division by air from Moscow to Vladivostok. They had developed methods of carrying guns and tanks along with infantry in these airborne moves. Parachute-jumping had become a widespread practice in the Red Army, and by the time the war came it was reported that over a million men had carried it out. Even if this figure was exaggerated, the number of men then trained was certainly much larger than in any other country. Yet in the war the Russians never employed them in any large operation. The most they did was to drop small parties of saboteurs behind the German lines.

This "missing factor" has been overlooked in most

studies of the war. It has not received the attention it deserves, nor has any adequate explanation come to light. The suggestion that lack of training was the cause is hard to reconcile with the fact that such training was under way in Russia long before it started anywhere else. The suggestion that shortage of air transport was the cause does not explain why no operations at all were carried out. In the later stages of the war, when the Russian air forces far outnumbered the German, there was opportunity to carry out airborne strokes with little risk. But the Russians refrained from attempting them, even on a limited scale.

Such complete abstention is very puzzling. The bare fact remains that the Russians, helped by the wide spaces in the East and their great superiority on the ground, were able to decide the issue without bringing their airborne arm into play.

There is, however, another possible reason for their restraint—that they were already working on the long-term calculation that the fight against Germany was likely to lead on to a struggle with America and Britain, for the control of Western Europe. In that case why disclose the card which they had been keeping up their sleeve when it was not essential to winning the first round? Such reasoning would be natural in a long-sighted mind of super-secretive disposition.

The struggle for the control of Western Europe has duly developed since the overthrow of Germany—as the almost inevitable consequence of the disappearance of that buffer. It has become more intense month by month, and the margin between political pressure and military action has become perilously narrow. The Russians may reckon that, if the present "cold war" should turn into actual war, there would be little to stop them from overrunning most of Western Europe with their armies. But they would still be faced with the obstacle which frustrated Hitler—and Napoleon before him. This time it would be more than an obstacle. It would be the obvious base, from an early moment, of America's counter-offensive air power. This lesson is equally plain.

Hitler lost his war because, after conquering Western Europe, he could not cross the English Channel. That anti-tank "ditch" baulked his all-conquering armies. They were not prepared for an attempt at oversea invasion. His belated effort to organize an armada was outpaced by the growth of the island defences, and by the approach of the autumn gales, while his admirals were scared of the British Navy. His best chance would have been to throw a force over the Channel in the weeks immediately following the collapse in France, when the British Army was disorganized and almost disarmed after the evacuation from Dunkirk. But Hitler was then hoping that the British would accept his peace offer, while such an improvised invasion attempt was too much for the methodical Germans. So the chance was forfeited.

Blocked by the English Channel, Hitler turned eastward like Napoleon—to a quarter where he could effectively exert the strength of his land forces. He left the problem of England's continued resistance to be tackled by the more gradual method of submarine blockade. This did not fulfil his anticipations, though its pressure more than once became uncomfortably close to a stranglehold on England's supplies. Meanwhile, however, he exhausted Germany's strength in the effort to conquer Russia. That sealed his doom, and Germany's.

The basic lesson of World War II is that Hitler forfeited the immense advantage he gained in 1940 through failure to subdue "the island on the edge of the Continent"—the island which became the base of America's bombing forces and the springboard for the liberating invasion of Europe from the West. That lesson can hardly have been overlooked by Stalin and his military advisers.

It is the job of General Staffs to explore all the problems of any future conflict that may arise and the ways of solving these. They would be failing in their professional duty if they did not do so. That does not necessarily imply an aggressive intent—though the legal experts of Nuremberg have chosen to construe it as such, applying to the military profession a different standard from what they practise in their own. Soldiers have to think out offensive as well as defensive moves just as lawyers conduct cases for their clients whether they think them innocent or guilty.

It would be only natural that the Russians, viewing America's power as a threat to their position in Europe, should have been working out plans to forestall it, not only in the political but also in the military field. They must have had particularly in mind the position of England as the "aircraft-carrier" island anchored off the Continent—the closest-range launching platform available for America's air and land forces. As a reasonable part of their job, Russia's strategists must have been considering ever since 1945 the ways and means of succeeding where Hitler failed, if war should come. It must be clear to them that his downfall arose from his failure to solve this particular problem. If they are strategists of real foresight they will have had it in mind even earlier—while they were still fighting Germany.

It is not an easy problem to solve. Their Navy is even less adequate than Hitler's to dispute the command of the sea, while initially at least they would be worse placed geographically to undertake a submarine blockade—

which is, in any case, slow to take effect. Submarine troop-carriers might be a means, but that would spell a very big development, not easy to achieve within a few years, while invested with many complications. It is more likely that they would try the alternative which Hitler neglected—of carrying troops *over* the sea, through the air. They have long possessed forces of this nature, and could have done much to develop their means of transport and escort during the post-war years.

If Germany had possessed a large force of airborne troops in 1940, and thrown them into England at the time of Dunkirk, the effect would have been very serious, and perhaps decisive. But she had then barely 5,000 parachute troops backed by one air-transportable division (about 12,000 men) and these had been depleted by their efforts in the conquest of Holland. Even so, General Student, the Commander-in-Chief of Germany's airborne forces, told me after the war that he had favoured the idea of dropping all the available parachute troops on the chief ports in southern England before her troops had been evacuated from Dunkirk. But he was knocked out by a sniper's bullet at Rotterdam, and was unable to press his project on Hitler.

Russia has a vastly larger number of parachute-trained troops than Germany had in 1940. Her strategists may reckon that England, after the years of peace and demobilization, is less prepared for emergencies than she was even in 1940. That combination of factors might seem to offer big possibilities for bold action, if no peaceful solution were reached in the present political deadlock. The Russian leaders do not mind large sacrifices in playing for high stakes. Their troops are schooled to run big risks, and to be used in "suicide" operations. They are also accustomed to carry on for weeks without the supplies that Western armies deem essential—foraging for themselves in the country where they are fighting. Thus the Red Army is inherently "prepared" for ventures that more orthodox strategists would hesitate to undertake unless fairly sure of maintaining their communications.

The effect of airborne forces turns largely on the degree of surprise. At a time when nations are not mobilized, or only just beginning to mobilize, a widespread descent of fiercely determined paratroops might have a much greater effect than it ever did in the last war. It could produce chaos.

The degree of surprise would be increased by any tendency in the Western countries to discount the strength or value of Russia's airborne forces—merely because of their non-use in the last war. That would fit in all too well with the calculation that deferment of their use then might produce a bigger dividend later. If the Russian strategists were working on any such calculation they must have been encouraged by the way that the existence of their airborne forces has been ignored in most of the post-war commentaries on the Red Army that have appeared in the British and American Press.

It is not enough that Western defence chiefs should be awake to the risk, and have their measures ready to meet it. A clear indication that the possibility is recognized on this side might prove a deterrent to it—since its chances would depend so much on its unexpectedness. It is important, also, that the public should be forewarned of the possibility, for that is the way to minimize the confusion that might be produced by such a stroke, if attempted.

PART FOUR

THE TIME FACTOR

Some Current Military Problems

CHAPTER XVIII

SOLDIER, SAILOR, AIRMAN—OR SINGLE SERVICEMAN?

Most of the main operations in the Second World War were combined operations in the biggest sense. Events bore the most striking testimony to the *multiplied* effect of action in combination. They have thus given fresh impetus to the long-discussed idea of creating a joint staff—a single organ of higher direction. Have they also brought in sight the possibility of combining the three fighting services into one, to form a Single Service?

The more we study the course of the war, and analyze the lessons of the campaigns in North Africa, Italy, and France successively, the clearer it becomes that they were much more than military victories, in the soldier sense. The battles on land were largely decided by wider factors, and forces. Hard fighting had less effect on the issue than the hard conditions under which the losers had to fight—as in most of the really decisive victories of history. And although the operations of the Allied land forces played the most prominent part, especially in the final

207

phase, the basic conditions that ensured success were produced elsewhere—overhead and offshore.

This conclusion is even more true of the war in the Pacific, but that was so obviously and fundamentally an oceanic campaign as to cause it to be regarded as a special case, where conditions differed from the normal conditions of continental warfare. It is thus of more general significance to deal with the course of events in the Western theatres, where the land masses filled most of the space, and the intervals of water were narrow. While seapower and airpower were essential to success in the final stage of the war, following the Allied landing in Normandy, the most illumination on the need for the closest combination can be gained earlier, from the crucial period of the campaign in the Mediterranean theatre.

The vital importance of air superiority was a factor that no observer could miss. The equally vital, and, in a sense, primary importance of seapower was a factor that becomes increasingly clear in retrospect, and in analysis.

Everyone knows the description of the navy as the "silent service." A more apt name would be the "unseen service." Compared with the others, it operates in a sphere that is out of sight, and in a way that is hard to trace. There is no *blitzkrieg* possible in naval warfare— no lightning flash over the seas, striking down an opponent. Seapower acts more like radium—beneficial to those who use it, and are shielded, it destroys the tissues of those who are exposed to it.

But in the Mediterranean campaign its influence was more perceptible than usual. For the Axis armies that threatened the British position in Egypt and hindered the Allies' clearance of the African continent were operating across the sea from the European continent. With their short lines of communication, much shorter than those of the Allies, they were theoretically capable of massing in Africa land and air forces outweighing the Anglo-American forces. Their failure to do so, at any time after 1940, was visible proof of the practical effect of sea-air power. It was this that decisively limited the enemy's land power, by restricting the use of his lines of supply. Beyond all, it dried up the springs of his mechanized mobility.

The Allied victories in North Africa—not only Tunis, but El Alamein, and even earlier—might be classified primarily, as "petrol victories." Without an adequate and assured flow of petrol, no modern army can develop its offensive power, nor even maintain an effective defence —for this depends on the capacity to switch its reserves to threatened points.

The Navy and Air Force together succeeded in sinking the majority of the enemy's tankers in transit across the Mediterranean, and thus crippled his army, as well as restricting its size. The Air Force disrupted the local distribution of such petrol reserves as he had, and thus turned a cripple into a paralytic. The air force also disrupted his system of control, by shattering bombardment of his command and signal centres. But it was the navy, again, which blocked his line of retreat to the mainland, and was thus the primary means in producing the feeling of hopelessness that always tends to precipitate a collapse.

Loss of hope, rather than loss of life, is the factor that really decides wars, battles, and even the smallest combats. The all-time experience of warfare shows that when men reach the point where they see, or feel, that further effort and sacrifice can do no more than delay the end they commonly lose the will to spin it out, and bow to the inevitable. Exceptions to this rule are rare.

The victory in North Africa can best be epitomized by saying that the Army gained it, the Air Force cleared the way for it, and the Navy assured the possibility of it.

It is wise as well as just to recognize the essential part played by the Navy. Only by taking the full measure of it, can strategists build further plans on an equally sound basis. But it is also important to recognize that seapower has become as dependent as armies on airpower. What is the lesson? That the three spheres have become inextricably intertwined, and the three services inseparable. What is the natural deduction? That, being so bound together, they are bound to develop sooner or later from the stage of co-operation towards that of fusion. The main question is a time-question—whether it will be soon or later, and whether by hastening the natural process we could speed up progress towards security in the future.

Under pressure of war, and the war's earlier reverses in particular, many steps were taken towards increasingly close combination, both in the planning machinery and in the operational field. Significantly, the progress has been greater and quicker in the latter field than in the former. That is natural, if not logical—for direct contact with enemy forces brings a keener sense of realities, and is thus more effective in overcoming traditional, sentimental, or professional objections.

While direct experience, in contact with the enemy, has provided the strongest arguments for progress, the question remains whether we could not make more use of reason to hasten it. For war experience taught little beyond what was foreseeable by sheer logic before the war, and even yet we have advanced nowhere near as far as was suggested by logical thought years ago.

Within each of the separate services, *specialization* has increased under modern conditions, yet at the same time *integration* has become more marked in the field of operations. In the Army, for example, there has arisen not only a closer combination between the different arms but often an interchange of personnel that would never have been considered possible in the past, when the instruments of each arm were themselves less complex.

Why should this same dual tendency not apply, and be applied, between the three services? It has come to be recognized that the higher staffs must have a grasp of other spheres than that of their own service—the creation of the Imperial Defence College nearly a generation ago was an initial realization of that necessity. Lower down the scale, it has been recognized by the increasing attendance at courses, and attachments for duty, of officers from one service to another. But why do the services continue to move in slow time towards integration when the conditions of war urge a quicker pace?

Even now, although the inseparability of land and air components is manifest, and also that of sea and air components, the natural conclusion is hindered by extraneous factors and separatist feelings—diminishing but still powerful. Still less has the possibility of interchange between Navy and Army been appreciated. Yet there is, on balance, probably less difference of conditions between the action of tanks and warships than between that of tanks and infantry. A naval officer who was expert in handling a destroyer flotilla might well be more fitted to take command of an armoured division than an infantry officer who had spent thirty years in practising the 1914-1918 type of slow-action tactics. A soldier who was a master of mechanized mobility might make as good a naval commander as did several of Cromwell's generals, such as Blake and Monck.

It is true that there might have been dangers, as well

as advantages, if the movement towards integration of the services had been quicker. If the British Government had not been led, a generation ago, to convert the Royal Flying Corps into a separate service, the development of airpower might have been cramped as badly by conservative prejudices as the development of the Tank Corps in the Army—and as the air arm itself was retarded in France and the U.S.A. while it remained in a subordinate position. Even when given independence it suffered badly enough from the drawback of being the junior service. In any fusion, careful attention should be paid to the interests of minorities, especially when they are not an old-established element. It is also true, and should never be forgotten, that diversity is a source of vitality.

Nevertheless, the fact that the functional activities of the services are becoming so closely blended compels us to consider their organic blending. The separation of the Air Force from the Army, and from the Navy, is inherently unsound and logically absurd. Yet its division between them, as they have often desired, would be a step backward—and out of step with the trend of warfare. The obvious forward step, and the natural one, is the combination of the three Services in one. It would promise an increasing efficiency of operations in many ways. It would save a lot of the duplication, and triplication, of the "services" within the Services which too often entails a waste of man-power. Thus it would be a double step towards economy of force.

CHAPTER XIX

HAVE ARMOURED FORCES A FUTURE?

PACE WITH VARIABILITY IS THE SECRET OF MOBILITY

THE weight of the main types of tank in use has approximately trebled in the last ten years—as a result of continuous efforts to mount a bigger gun and thicker armour. At the same time the number of tanks in what is called "armoured divisions" has decreased. It is now a matter of common remark that the progressive effort to thicken armour has reached the limit of what is practicable and compatible with mobility. But the penetrative power of guns and projectiles has continued to grow. As a natural consequence there is a growing tendency among soldiers to argue that the penetrative power of the tank itself in operations has been curbed. It is even asserted that the tank has met its master in the anti-tank projectile, and that its military value is on the wane.

The argument would be more convincing if it had not been *so* often repeated, and *as* often refuted by experience. By tracing the sequence of "ups-and-downs"

213

through the past thirty years we can get a better light on the recurrent argument, and on the reasons why it has carried more weight than events have justified. That will also help to show how far we are from having reached the limit of what is operationally possible for armoured forces. Until we have tried to fulfil requirements which were apparent to clear-sighted thinkers thirty years ago it is foolish to conclude that the tank has "had its day."

I remember hearing such a conclusion expressed in November, 1919, by a distinguished soldier in a lecture on the "Possibilities of the Next War." His verdict seemed the more weighty because he had been concerned with the original production of the tank after the First World War had developed into a static war of trenches. Despite all the tank had contributed, and achieved, in breaking the deadlock in the last year of the war, he could see no further prospect for it. In his survey of future warfare he dismissed it in three sentences—"The tank proper was a freak. The circumstances which called it into existence were exceptional and are not likely to recur. If they do, they can be dealt with by other means."

His death sentence on the tank was applauded by most of the generals who were present. Only a small band of believers, mainly younger men, took a different view—and had a new vision of the potentialities of the tank.

Soon afterwards the first type of fast tank, capable of a speed of over 20 m.p.h., was successfully produced in England—carrying the practical promise of fulfilling the new vision. Yet, curiously, many soldiers who hoped to revive mobility and "open" warfare were antagonistic to the new means that might make such a revival possible.

That was particularly common among ardent cavalrymen, who still cherished the hope and faith that the reign of the horse would continue. Almost every time I met one of their ablest leaders, who then (in the mid-1920s) held the chief command in the British Army, he gleefully assured me that the tank was doomed because of impending improvements in anti-tank weapons. Such a view, and attitude, persisted in high quarters throughout the twenty years between the wars. Every demonstration of the potentialities of mobile armoured warfare was followed by a disparaging reaction.

The great pioneer, General Swinton, who in 1914 had seen the "armoured caterpillar" vehicle as a solution for the trench-deadlock, concluded his story of the much-resisted development of the tank in World War I by philosophically quoting the Persian proverb: "The dogs bark, but the caravan passes on." Once again he proved a true prophet.

For in spite of much doubt and obstruction, the tank and the conception of its use continued to progress in England during the years immediately following that war. That was due above all to Colonel Fuller, who had been chief staff officer of the wartime Tank Corps. He preached the idea of "sea warfare on land" conducted by completely mechanized forces—an idea which another member of its staff, Major Martel, had originally suggested as far back as November, 1916, in a paper entitled "A Tank Army"—and by his vivid presentation of the case brought it into the realm of practical discussion. Moreover, in his proposed "Plan 1919" and post-war writings, Fuller evolved the idea of a deep tactical penetration—driving right through to the enemy's divisional corps, and army headquarters, paralyzing the enemy's command system and spreading confusion in the immediate rear of his armies. Then, in considering the possibilities of tanks with much higher speed and longer radius than the 1918 type, I evolved the further idea that fast armoured forces could carry out a deep strategic penetration—an independent long-range drive to cut the enemy's communications far back, where his main arteries of supply could be severed. I illustrated it by a treatise on the lightning campaigns of Genghis Khan, drawing the conclusion that fully mechanized forces should be capable of a performance comparable to that of the all-mobile forces of the Mongols. This idea particularly appealed to Lindsay, who became Chief Instructor of the Central Schools on the formation of the Royal Tank Corps in 1923 as a permanent arm of the Army. The previous year, with the British armoured cars in Iraq, he had initiated the first trials of an embryo mechanized force.

In 1927 the British General Staff decided to create an Experimental Mechanized Force on Salisbury Plain for practical test of the new theories. It comprised one battalion of tanks, one battalion of armoured cars and "tankettes" (the forerunner of the light tank), one battalion of machine-gunners mounted in six-wheeled or half-track vehicles, a brigade (regiment) of tractor-drawn field artillery (with one self-propelled battery), and a motorized field company of engineers. Much of the value of the experiment was lost because of the cautious and cramped way in which the force was handled by the infantryman who was placed in charge of it. Nevertheless, the "fast group" under Pile (who became the C-in-C of Britain's A.A. Defence in the next war) provided a striking foretaste of what might be achieved by rapidity of movement and mind—above all in exploiting "unexpectedness." At the same time the Chief of the Imperial General Staff was persuaded to define a policy of training for the force—and future "armoured visions"—on modernized Mongol lines. Unfortunately, a prolonged reaction followed this spurt of progress. The force was disbanded in the autumn of 1928 after its second season of trials—partly as a way of getting rid of the slow-moving infantryman who had been appointed to command the force, and was cramping its potentialities. But the formation of a fresh force, a true armoured force, was deferred longer than had been hoped.

The British Mechanized Force of 1927 attracted the attention of the military world, and progressive soldiers in other countries were keen to try its possibilities. The next country to do so was America. Dwight Davis, the U.S. Secretary of War, attended one of the trials on a visit to England, and when he returned home gave instructions for the formation of a similar force in the United States Army. To soothe the fears of the older arms the announcement emphasized that the new type of force "would not displace" infantry or cavalry. The force itself had an even shorter life than its British forerunner —it was constituted in July, 1928, and disbanded in September. In the years that followed, the United States Army lagged behind the pace of developments in Europe —contrary to natural expectations. Colonel Chaffee, the leading spirit of the new school in America, had a heartbreaking struggle in his efforts to achieve an advance. General MacArthur was one of the few senior soldiers who had a vision of what mechanized mobility might achieve, but during his time as Chief of Staff he was hampered by opposition from static-minded contemporaries while handicapped by lack of financial resources. In Congress, Ross Collins was a lone voice crying in the wilderness when he constantly argued that mechanized forces would be decisive in a future war.

In America, armoured development was retarded because after World War I the heads of the Army, instead of maintaining a separate Tank Corps as the British did, had followed the example of the French Army in treating tanks as part of the infantry arm and keeping them subordinate. For France that proved a fatal policy. It can be traced to the complacency that was fostered by victory in 1918. The new school of thought gained some adherence in France, but for all their ardour they made little impression. They were borne down by the weight of superior authority, which rested on old doctrine. The heads of the French Army were supremely convinced that they knew more about war than any other army in the world and were apt to despise all others except the Germans as amateurs. Although not "too proud to fight" they were too proud to learn new ways of fighting.

The main current of mechanized development thus remained in Britain—so long as Germany was disarmed. It moved more slowly than ideas, but in 1931 a complete armoured formation, the 1st Tank Brigade, was at last formed for trial. One of the new school, Brigadier Broad, was this time put in charge of it. He worked out a force of battle drill training in tactics of indirect approach and variable aim. He also systematized the methods of control, laying a good foundation for a longer advance.

But another regrettable interval occurred before this first tank brigade was permanently constituted in 1934. Hobart, who was given command of it, not only developed the tactical methods and wireless control required for fast-moving operations, but set out to practise the method of deep strategic penetration—by an armoured force operating independently of the main Army.

These trials helped to confirm one's earlier theoretical exposition of its potentialities. But most of the senior generals were by no means convinced by the demonstration. They remained distrustful of the possibility of such long-range strokes, preferring to keep the armoured forces tied more closely to the main body of the Army, and to what they called "the main battle." As a result Hobart's opportunities to continue such practice of tank *strategy* were curtailed during the next two seasons' training.

The revolutionary possibilities of the new idea were more fully grasped in Germany—especially by Guderian, who was training the tank units which Hitler had just begun to build. For over ten years Guderian, as he has related, had been following British ideas with the keenest interest, and he now enthusiastically seized the chance to put them into practice himself. After the summer of 1935 had been devoted to practice in handling an experimental armoured division, three such divisions were formed in October that year. Each embodied four battalions of tanks and two mechanized "light infantry" battalions, together with artillery, engineers, a motorcyclist unit, and a reconnaissance unit. (By 1939 the number of armoured divisions had been doubled, and by 1940 increased to ten.)

More significantly still, Guderian directed and trained these new-style forces to carry out the idea of deep strategic penetration—operating independently and driving on far ahead of the main mass of the army. The older German generals were almost as horrified as the British generals had been at the unorthodoxy of the idea, as well as its hazards. They wanted to tie the armoured divisions down to the service of the infantry mass. But when war came, opportunity came—to cut loose from their cautious restraints. The campaign in Poland demonstrated the value of the new idea and diminished the Higher Command's tendency to impose checks upon it.

When the campaign in the West was launched, Guderian seized the bit in his teeth and bolted with the reins—his unchecked gallop from Sedan to the sea cut off the whole left wing of the opposing armies. The Belgians collapsed, the British barely escaped by sea, and a large part of the French Army was put in the bag. The armoured forces were then quickly switched south and east for a fresh stroke. After the new French front on the Aisne had been pierced, Guderian's sweep eastward to the Swiss frontier cut off the right wing of the French Army, and led to the fall of France. In each case the break-through itself only opened the way for a solution of the problem; the rapid and deep exploitation was the decisive part.

Guderian has epitomized the *blitzkrieg* method as "Mobility, Velocity, Indirect Approach." In a fuller definition of it—with which Guderian expressed emphatic agreement—I set it forth thus:

The secret lies partly in the tactical combination of tanks and aircraft, partly in the unexpectedness of the stroke in direction and time, but *above all* in the *follow-through*—the exploitation of a break-through (the tactical penetration of a front) into a *deep strategic penetration,* carried out by armoured forces racing on ahead of the main army, and operating *independently.*

The pace of such forces promises a decisively deep penetration *so long as* it can be kept up. It is kept up by a torrent-like process of advance, either swerving round resistance or piercing it at a weakened spot—in which case the tank-torrent contracts in pouring through a narrow breach, and then expands again to its original breadth.

It is the *persistent pace,* coupled with the *variability of* the thrust-point, that paralyzes the opponent. For at every stage, after the original break-through, the flexible drive of the armoured forces carries simultaneously several *alternative* threats, while the threat that actually develops into a thrust takes place too quickly for the enemy's reserves to reach the spot in time to stiffen the resistance there before it collapses. In effect, *both tactical and* strategical surprise are maintained from start to finish. It is a high-speed "indirect approach" to the enemy's rear areas—where his vital but vulnerable organs of control and supply are located.*

The points of this definition are worth keeping in mind when examining the course of operations throughout the war—those which brought quickly decisive results and those which did not.

These points, too, form a guide for the future—showing the conditions that will have to be fulfilled if armoured forces are to play a part in the future comparable to what they did in the immediate past. The improvement of counter-methods and counter-means are bound to make the conditions harder to fulfil, as they did in the last war after 1940, but this *blitzkrieg* method may again prove effective if the means for it are developed on the lines that reason long ago suggested. The armoured forces that triumphed in 1940 were of primitive composition— as Guderian himself and his fellow tankmen quite realized. They were limited by the means then available and their model was far short of the design that the original British exponents of armoured warfare had set forth in the 1920s. But it sufficed to dislocate the opposing armies because the heads of these armies had not really begun to understand the new method of warfare.

---

* Since Guderian described himself as my "disciple" in the field of tank warfare it may be of some historical interest to mention that the *concept* of this deep strategic penetration by armoured forces developed in my mind initially from study of the long-sustained drives carried out by Genghis Khan's all-mobile forces in the Mongol campaigns of the 13th century, while its application against modern mass armies dependent upon railways for supply was made clear in an analysis of Sherman's "marches" and Forrest's dislocating "raids" in the 1864-5 campaigns of the American Civil War. The conclusions were strengthened in a study of the effects that could have been produced by such forces in 1914 if they had then existed. As for the *method*, this was simply a strategic adaptation for armoured forces of the tactical "expanding torrent" attack which I had worked out earlier, at the end of the 1914-18 war.

The startling success of the German armoured forces in overrunning France aroused Britain's leaders to the practical value of the new theory that had been born there but neglected by them. Further armoured divisions were hurriedly formed to expand the small number then existing. A similar effect was produced in America. But in Germany, which had profited so much from the adoption of the theory, victory brought an increase of confidence rather than an urge to further development. Complacency has usually been an accompaniment of victory.

Before launching the invasion of Russia in 1941, Hitler wanted to double the number of his armoured divisions, for moral effect, but as the output of tanks was insufficient he chose the dangerous way of doing it by dilution—reducing the number of tanks in each division from a scale of 300 to 180. That reduction was contrary to the advice of the armoured warfare experts, some of whom considered that the pre-war establishment of 400 was the desirable figure—one company out of four in each tank battalion had been left behind on mobilization, to provide drafts. Moreover, no substantial improvement had been made in the mechanization of the other elements in the division. The ill-effect of those deficiencies was not very apparent in the opening phase of the campaign, since the Russian Command then was no better than the French in handling its own tanks or in applying suitable counter-measures. But as the Germans advanced deeper the inadequate mechanization of their so-called armoured divisions became an increasing handicap—Russia's poor roads proved a greater obstacle, especially in bad weather, than her tank forces. And as the German divisions shrank, through battle and mechanical casualties, the shrinkage became disproportionately crippling to their punch because their initial strength in tanks had been so limited. In the later stages of the campaign they often entered battle with less than a hundred tanks. It was hardly surprising that their attacks became decreasingly effective in results—even apart from the development of more efficient methods of anti-tank defence and the growth of Russia's armoured forces, equipped with new and better tanks.

It is also to be noted that, in the invasion of Russia, Hitler and the German military chiefs had agreed in putting a check on Guderian's desire to carry out the same kind of deep strategic thrust as he had done in France so decisively. He and the other "panzer-group" commanders were halted in their stride, when there was little to stop them. This top-level check was imposed on grounds of caution, coupled with an orthodox preference for completing the "classical" battle of encirclement. As so often in history, a predominant concern for security brought insecurity that might well have been avoided by audacity. In reflection, many of the more orthodox German generals came to recognize that the German Army had forfeited its best chance of decisive victory by the veto on Guderian's scheme of driving deep through to Moscow before the defence could rally.

Ironically, the British Army copied the errors of the German in the belief that it was applying the secrets of the latter's success. It would have done better to carry on the logical development of the organized British conception that the Germans had adopted.

At the outbreak of war, the British armoured division had comprised six tank units and one motorized infantry battalion—which was too small a foot-fighting element. By the autumn of 1940 this had been increased to three battalions, with six of tanks—a better proportion, though the value of the infantry element was diminished because it was mounted in unarmoured wheeled vehicles. But later the British Army swung too far the other way, under a mistaken imitative impulse. For in 1942, following the Germans' supposed lead, it changed to an organization for the armoured division similar to that which the Germans had adopted—to their cost—in 1941: reducing the tank units to three while increasing the infantry units to four. This served to ensure that the British armoured divisions would suffer a diminished effectiveness of punch similar to the Germans'. And as the infantry element was not mounted in tracked and armour-protected vehicles, capable of keeping up with the tanks on difficult ground and under fire, the power of the "follow-through" was also handicapped.

The faults of this composition were accentuated by faulty tactics and a mistaken aim, dictated by leaders who had grown up in the old style of warfare. The latter faults had already been manifested in the 1941 campaign in North Africa—then Britain's only field of military action. After the frustration there suffered, criticism concentrated on the deficiency of the British tanks in gunpower compared with the German. While the criticism was justified, it was too narrow. For it tended to ignore the way that the consequences of a deficiency in gunpower had been magnified by a tactical policy of directing the British tanks to seek out and destroy the enemy's tanks—rather than taking his unarmoured troops or exposed communications as their target. This tactical policy, on traditional lines, played into the hands of Rommel, who, using his 88 mm. guns in skilful combination with his tanks, laid traps for the attacking tanks on the lines I had advocated in pre-war years when urging the development of a new technique of defence. Rommel thereby cancelled out the numerical superiority of the British in tanks, and was able to deliver startling ripostes that turned their advances into retreats. (His repeated success with these defensive-offensive trapping tactics, even in the open desert, demonstrated how the Franco-British forces might have countered the German drive in 1940, and averted the disaster that overtook them.)

Even in 1941 the British had a superiority of force in North Africa sufficient to take the offensive with good prospects of success. But by concentrating primarily on the destruction of the enemy's tanks they not only made the worst of the main defect in their tanks but missed their offensive opportunity. The same mistake was repeated later. It was a legacy from old doctrine—a doctrine of "pitched battle" which hindered soldiers from realizing that the new mobility offered the means of fulfilling the true ideal of strategy: that of deciding the issue without a serious fight. The mistake was also a legacy from the habits of peacetime exercises wherein commanders of the old school had often begun by trying to cancel out one another's tanks so that they could proceed to conduct their battle on the lines with which they were familiar. Criticizing such a habit, one had pointed out long before the war that "to throw away such a potent piece as a tank force in fighting the enemy tank force is as foolish as for a chessplayer to begin by swopping queens."

When the policy was followed on the battlefields of North Africa in 1941 and 1942, the results shook the troops' confidence in their leaders and tactics—the phrase "doing a Rommel" became a common way among them of describing a good performance of any kind. The tactical faults magnified the technical disadvantages of British tank design. A change of policy came late in 1942,

when Montgomery took over command. As he wrote: "It
had been generally accepted that the plan in a modern
battle should aim first at destroying the enemy's armour
. . . I decided to reverse this concept and to destroy first
the unarmoured formations." This proved fruitful, but
its significance was partly obscured by the way that his
offensive at El Alamein was confined to frontal attack by
lack of an open flank.

Complaint of British tanks diminished with the advent
of new tanks in 1942, particularly the American-designed
"Sherman," but was followed in 1943 by renewed depre-
ciation of the tank arm and its place in warfare. This
trend of opinion had developed, curiously, after Montgomery's victory at El Alamein. The fact that the infantry
divisions were there employed to break into the enemy's
position, and open the way for the armoured divisions,
was seized on as a text to "boost" the infantry, and as a
pretext to disparage the tanks. The heavy losses which
the tanks suffered in slogging tactics following the frontal
penetration, and the subsequent failure of the armoured
divisions to cut off the remnants of Rommel's army, provided additional arguments for the disparagers of armoured mobility.

During the months that followed, many military voices
were again heard crying that the heyday of the tank was
past, and that it had declined from a primary to a secondary instrument of warfare. Few paused to consider
the question whether the armoured forces had been used
to the best advantage. Rommel's own diary comment on
his good luck in escaping is more to the point: "As always the British High Command showed its customary
caution and little forceful decision. For instance, they attacked again and again with separate bodies of tanks and
did not, as might be expected, throw into the battle the

900 tanks which they could, without risk to themselves, have employed in the northern part of the front, thereby using their vast superiority to gain a rapid decision with the minimum casualties."

The "anti-tank" chorus was momentarily silenced by the dramatic collapse of German-Italian resistance in Tunisia following the break-through of the 6th and 7th Armoured Divisions, and the decisive stroke of the former in cutting through the neck of the Cape Bon peninsula, thus cutting off the enemy's last bolt-hole. In that drive, riflemen were carried on the top of the tanks, so that they could come into action quickly in clearing obstacles. It was an improvisation that saved much time in bringing up lorried infantry, who would have had to dismount several miles back—but it was a reflection on the continued omission to provide armoured cross-country vehicles for the infantry element in an armoured division—a need one had urged for twenty years.

The slow, slogging advance through mountainous Sicily and the funnel-like length of Italy revived the chorus. Missed opportunities when the going was favourable forfeited repeated chances of quicker progress, but were not taken into account when the chance came to decry the future of armoured mobility. Moreover, too many believers in it lost faith by the time that the invasion of Normandy was launched. Churchill himself underwent one of his periodical reactions, and in February declared: "We have too much armour—tanks are finished." His doubts were deepened by his military advisers.

On a tour of the American forces in England early in 1944, one of the few ardent believers in armoured mobility I met was General Wood, commanding the 4th Armoured Division. But I found him very disturbed—

after a high-level conference which had been addressed
by Field-Marshal Sir Alan Brooke, Chief of the Imperial
General Staff. A keynote of it had been that warfare was
"back to 1918," and that lightning drives of the 1940 kind
were no longer possible. Wood felt that the American
High Command had been infected by this slow-motion
view. While pinning his hopes to Patton, who had just
arrived in England to take command of the U.S. Third
Army, Wood feared that even he might be led to swallow the majority conclusion.

At his urgent desire I went to see Patton. While the
latter's obvious dynamism was most refreshing, I was
rather disconcerted to find him saying that when the Allied armies invaded France they would not be able to
repeat armoured drives like that of 1940, but would have
"to go back to 1918 methods." While questioning this, I
felt it best to put the contrary arguments in the form of
an "indirect approach." He had told me that before the
war he had spent a long vacation studying Sherman's
campaigns on the ground in Georgia and the Carolinas,
with the aid of my book. So I talked of the possibilities
of applying "Sherman methods" in modern warfare—moving stripped of impedimenta to quicken the pace, cutting loose from communications if necessary, and swerving past opposition, instead of getting hung up in trying
to overcome it by direct attack. It seemed to me that by
the development and exploitation of such Sherman methods, on a greater scale, it would be possible to reach the
enemy's rear and unhinge his position—as the Germans
had already done in 1940.

This argument seemed to appeal to him—it fitted in
with his own mobile instincts better than did the arguments in higher quarters to which he had momentarily
acceded. At any rate, when I visited him again in June,

just before his army went over to Normandy, he no longer talked about 1918 methods, but on bolder lines. After the break-out from the bridgehead, his army drove from Normandy to the German frontier in super-Sherman style. Wood, with the 4th Armoured Division, was the spearhead of that drive; on reaching the Seine he wrote to tell me how successfully such methods had worked. But soon after that the momentum of the drive was checked— partly through excess of top-level planning and partly from deficiency of supply due to lack of preparation that was due, in turn, to lack of vision beforehand. Later, Wood wrote: "I feel that we could have done the job more quickly if our High Command had possessed an equal appreciation of the indirect approach." Referring to the Avranches break-through, he remarked: "There was no conception of far-reaching directions for armour in the minds of our people . . . nor of supplying such thrusts."

Here we may fittingly conclude the survey of the past that has been made to obtain a projection into the future. What it conveys is that armoured forces have not "had their day"—because, in the real sense, *they have not yet been tried.*

That may seem strange in view of the way that a handful of German panzer divisions overran Poland, France and much of Russia. But the German panzer divisions were not *armoured* forces. Nor were the so-called "armoured divisions" which the Allies used later in the war. The "armour" in an "armoured division" was a small pebble in a large sling. As the war went on the pebble became smaller, but not the sling. While the pebble comprised barely 200 tanks, the sling consisted of about 15,000 men and over 3,000 vehicles other than tanks. The tank regiments accounted for barely one sixth of the total manpower employed in the division. Since the war, the number of tank units has been increased from three to four, both in the British and in the United States Army, bringing the number of tanks up to 280 in the British armoured division and 300 in the American. That increase shows some recognition of a basic lesson of the war. But the sling remains as large as ever.

What is called the "armoured division" today may well be considered a much better striking weapon than the old-style infantry division—but it is not in any true sense of the word an *armoured* division. That name confuses the issue, and fosters a delusion. It would have been as reasonable, in the Middle Ages, to describe as an "armoured knight" one who had jumped out of bed in his nightshirt and merely pulled a gauntlet on his sword-hand.

The disadvantage is all the greater because the so-called "armoured division" has its legs shackled. Some nine-tenths of its vehicles still consist of wheeled transport, more or less road-bound. That has been a growing handicap as the scope of air attack increased, and likely to become worse. There has also been a multiplication of obstruction from the mining of roads. We have to reckon with the probability that any defence will be based on turning all the road-centres into formidable centres of resistance, so that any possibility of rapid and deep advance depends on our mobile forces being able to by-pass these "hedgehogs." If they have to pause while each of these obstacles is overcome in turn, they will hardly get anywhere before the enemy has assembled his reserves.

The small striking head of an armoured division can leave the road and dart round an obstacle, but the wheel-borne tail cannot. And what an immensely long tail it is!

If the division is confined to a single road this means that, at the customary spacing, it would stretch out some 200 miles. To put it more vividly, if the division was operating on the Continent, the tail would still be near Paris when the head was approaching Antwerp. Where an army is advancing, it is often impossible to allot more than one road to a division—especially in many parts of the Continent where roads are not numerous. Thus a division which is mainly wheel-borne finds its manœuvring power as restricted as that of a snake wriggling down a drainpipe.

Its present composition also has the effect of limiting the combined striking power of the army. All experience has shown—as theory pointed out long ago—that the best chance of delivering a decisive blow lies in the sudden concentration of a mass of tanks at a weak spot, so that the defence is assailed simultaneously by too many for his anti-tank guns to cope with. That is the method of the *Schwerpunkt,* which the German panzer divisions so effectively exploited in 1940. But they were lucky to find opponents who were very weak in anti-tank guns and had not grasped modern methods of defence.

Now, the problem is much harder—as later war-experience on all sides showed. The punch must be much heavier if it is to succeed. But with the so-called armoured divisions of the present type it is almost impossible for the concentration to be either massive enough or sudden enough. Each division forms such a bulky coil that even when it is coiled up close there is not room to concentrate many tank-fangs in one sector. Nor can they be concentrated quickly.

If we are to develop adequate striking power we must construct our "mechanical snake" on a clearly thought-out design—reducing the length of the tail and increasing the strength of the head. If we are to give it the power of penetrating deep we must so design it that the tail does not get stuck in a road rut.

Up to now the composition of an armoured division has been based on ideas that were more like a cookery recipe than a scientific design—"take a handful of tanks, mix with a pound of infantry, pour in a pint of artillery, and add a dash of armoured cars." We have even provided several different kinds of artillery unit—as if we were drawing up the menu at a luxury hotel—instead of trying to design one that would be adaptable to dealing with hostile infantry, tanks, or aircraft. We add something to protect an element that is only auxiliary, and are then led on to add something else to protect the protector—at each step multiplying transport, numbers, supply needs, and hence transport again.

Nearly thirty years ago I wrote a treatise on future mechanized warfare and the "Development of a New Model Army," which suggested how this might be achieved in two phases—the first "evolutionary," and the second "revolutionary." In the first phase, the new model divisions would be a blend of tanks with motorized infantry and artillery. In the second, the tank would swallow the older arms, and become the ground-partner of the aeroplane. The mobile divisions would become all-armoured, with the artillery on self-propelled armoured mountings and a smaller number of more skilled infantry carried as "tank-marines" in armoured vehicles. The treatise aroused much interest and discussion abroad, particularly in the German Army, which was then in the melting pot after defeat in World War I. Guderian and others have borne witness to its influence. But there is more significance in what was left undone than in what was done.

For it can be seen that even the Germans never went further than the first phase of that design. That sufficed for the defeat of France. It did not suffice for the defeat of Russia. And as the war went on, "armoured" forces of the existing type became increasingly checked by forces of similar mobility, while finding fewer opportunities of making rings round unprotected foot-marching forces which they could immobilize. That was natural and far less remarkable than the fact that the "evolutionary" phase of the new model had been sufficient to revolutionize warfare to the extent it did in the earlier period of the war. Yet the Anglo-American armies of the later period, when the tide turned, made no serious effort to develop a newer model—despite much superior industrial resources. They were content to batter their way to victory, by sheer weight, along the old-new lines.

There we remain. Armies and their armoured forces have got into the rut of a fresh orthodoxy. Except for improvements in detail, they are simply carrying on an operational convention that developed from a tentative and partial reorganization which, at the outset of World War II, happened to have a much more striking effect than could reasonably be expected. Armies must get out of this rut if they are to have any important influence in the future—otherwise they are likely to be both paralyzed and supplanted by airpower.

In order to give "armour" a fair chance we have to solve two problems—the break-through and the follow-through. The first is intrinsically the harder. The difficulties of the second are largely due to faulty organization under the influence of conventional thinking.

There are various possible ways still open to us for renewing the break-through power of tanks. Apart from new technical means of paralyzing anti-tank defence which it is undesirable to discuss publicly, we have by no means exhausted the tactical means. Since armoured forces were first introduced into war their more convinced exponents have always insisted that their value essentially depended on their being employed "in swarms —to swamp the defence." It is the principle of saturation —of confronting the defence with many more separate assailants than he can cope with. That principle was fulfilled in the German break-through at Sedan in 1940, where Guderian's corps of 900 tanks concentrated on a frontage of less than five miles in smashing through the successive French positions behind the Meuse. After a penetration of 15 miles in two days against considerable resistance, it was through into open country and the advance became a gallop. Similar saturation tactics were applied on the Aisne in the second break-through, where the follow-through produced the general collapse of the French armies. But the principle was rarely fulfilled in tank attacks later in the war—although its value was freshly attested in air attacks, beginning with the "thousand-bomber raids." The principle should be revived in designing future armoured forces if they are to have any chance of carrying out strokes of the Guderian type, either in the offensive or in the counter-offensive.

The possibility depends partly on the development of tank design and partly on the organizational design of armoured forces. It would be wise to recognize that the present trend of mechanical design towards bigger tanks, and thus fewer of them, is unfavourable to the fulfilment of the principle. We might gain much by a fresh effort to develop a lighter and cheaper type of tank, provided that the importance of obstacle-crossing capacity is kept in mind. That requires length of chassis, but not necessarily bulk or weight in proportion. Such tanks might mount rockets rather than a large-calibre gun—the Germans were going to concentrate on the production of rocket-tanks weighing under 20 tons if the war had continued.

Superior hitting power counts for much in the design of a tank, and even for self-protection is relatively of more value than thick armour; but the power of a body of tanks shrinks rapidly through casualties (battle or breakdown), and the smaller the number of tanks the more severe relatively the shrinkage becomes. Moreover, a superior gun can to a surprising extent be discounted by superior manœuvrability, especially in a fight between tank formations. A most striking example was the defeat of the Russian drive for the Ploesti oilfields in May, 1944, when the Stalin tanks made their first appearance in battle and gave the Germans an initial shock by opening fire at over 3,000 yards range with their 122 mm. guns. Yet, when this battle of Targul Frumos ended, Manteuffel's division of 160 tanks (of which only 40 were Tigers, with as much as an 88 mm. gun) had destroyed 350 of the attacker's tanks while losing only ten of its own. Even the small Panzer IVs managed to knock out a number of the opposing "Goliaths," by manœuvring swiftly under cover of ground to reach their rear, and closing the range—to 1,000 yards.

Although it was the German Army which took the lead in mounting powerful guns in tanks, its most experienced tank leaders emphasize, in the light of their war experience as a whole, that manœuvrability is even more important—for quickness in changing fire-positions and shortening the range, for more effective fire. Speed is an essential element in manœuvrability, but only one element. Cross-country mobility matters more than speed on the road; it might be defined as "loco-mobility," or agility. It depends not only on the performance of the tank itself, but on the tactical ground-sense of the crew and the wider tactical skill of tank unit commanders. When those who have tanks of superior speed and agility dwell on their inferiority in gunpower, the tendency recalls the proverb: "it is the poor workman who blames his tools." The complaint may be justified only where the weapon-inferiority is extreme or the terrain very unsuitable for manœuvre.

A superiority in gunpower, though desirable, can be purchased at too heavy a price where it results in a loss of manœuvrability *and* a reduced number of tanks. Both these handicaps are difficult to avoid with the growing size of tanks—which, in turn, is apt to be favoured by those who find it easier to follow a sedentary style of warfare. The very name of the post-war British "Centurion" tank is reminiscent of the pedestrian and over-laden Roman legionary rather than of the reborn Mongol cavalry idea that gave rise to the lightning style of operations ten years ago. It is time for a reversal of the elephantine trend in tank design, and a move towards the revival of tank-torrent tactics. The development of a new form of motive power for tanks, as well as a new and lighter form of hard-hitting weapon, would increase the prospects.

The tank of the future will have to be fitted with night-driving vision and probably with radar, as well as with wireless. It should be able to pass safely through a radio-active belt of country. If we try to combine all these requirements with a powerful weapon *and* provide over-all armoured protection of adequate thickness, the tank is bound to become an increasingly clumsy monster. The design must be simplified, to produce a mechanical David instead of a Goliath. That may be achieved by external mounting of the main armament—a rocket-launcher or recoilless type of gun—which should be sighted, fired and fed with ammunition mechanically. The armoured body could then be quite small—a cabin to house the directing apparatus with a crew of no more than three. A new kind of power unit would also help to diminish excessive bulk in the chassis.

Another possibility is the development of remote-control tanks for the spearhead. With crewless tanks there would be no spreading deterrent effect from heavy losses in swarm attacks. It would not matter that a high proportion were knocked out if an effective fraction penetrated the whole depth of the defence—then, the exploitation of the break-through could get going, and might better be carried out by manned tanks, for finer manœuvring, until another barrier-position was reached.

When such barriers are based on a river, mobile infantry are needed to achieve the crossing. But the scale of foot-fighters actually required is apt to be overestimated, and can often be reduced when and where skilful manœuvring creates a favourable opening. That was demonstrated in Guderian's forcing of the Meuse at Sedan, where two mobile infantry regiments sufficed to gain a crossing adequate for the passage of the whole panzer corps—although most of the higher commanders had argued that it would have to wait until the backing-up infantry divisions arrived. But the need could be further diminished by the development of new forms of tank-bridging and tank flotation. A vital difference could be made by the advent of a non-specialized amphibious tank, capable of swimming rivers without sacrifice of its general tactical value; and this problem calls for a fresh effort in research.

It can thus be seen that, in the sphere of tank design,

there are many possibilities still undeveloped by which the powers of a tank break-through may be renewed. Beyond these are the latest potentialities in the sphere of organization. As pointed out earlier, the chances of swamping opposition are much handicapped because the excessive size of present "armoured" divisions hampers a quick and ample convergence of real armoured striking power at the point of aim. It is difficult to concentrate the tank components of several such divisions on a narrow sector, and produce sufficient intensity of punch at short notice. To make it more possible, it is essential to cut down the other components in the division, thus raising the tank ratio.

As Manteuffel put it—in referring to Hitler's fatal decision on the further dilution of the German armoured division prior to the invasion of Russia—"The armoured division thus lost the impetus and penetrative force of its tank core, whereas everything should have been done to strengthen it. The pace of an armoured division's attack and much else depended now on the *infantry*—which was wrong. . . . An *armoured* division can only be strengthened by reinforcing the *tank core* . . . for it is that which invests it with the impetus necessary for attack." "On the basis of my long experience in practical service with troops in the war I fully agree with your opinion that the tank core *can never have too many tanks,* and that this is possible without rendering the 'tail' too heavy or unwieldy. I would warn everyone of the fatal disproportion between the number of vehicles in the combat echelons and the supply vehicles."

The "armoured division" has become more of a misnomer since the title was adopted in 1938 in place of "mobile division." Indeed, it is only a mobile division in the strategic sense, not in the tactical sense. The essential tactical idea of such a division is that of *fighting mounted* —to retain its impetus—as the cavalry did in the days when they played the decisive role on the battlefield. While the inclusion of men who can fight on foot is a tactical necessity—for dislodging enemy troops under cover behind obstacles, and for various defensive duties—it is a fundamental mistake of organization if the proportion of such "mounted infantry," dismounting to fight, exceeds or even equals the proportion that fights mounted, manning tanks and self-propelled guns (on tank chassis). "Armoured fighting men" should be preponderant in an "armoured division" if this is to justify its name and fulfil its proper purpose.

At the same time the foot-fighting element ought to be entirely carried in tracked vehicles, armour-protected, so that they have a cross-country mobility and manœuvrability equal to the armoured fighting units. That is essential in order that they can back up the tanks closely and come into action immediately they are required, to clear defended obstacles in the path of the tanks. Moreover, the quicker they can intervene, the fewer of them will be required—that is a matter of common experience in warfare. A company of such true "tank-marines" could often brush away opposition that a whole lorried battalion or more could not overcome an hour later, when the defending infantry have been reinforced by local reserves. The time-factor rules warfare.

A further reduction in the size of the foot-fighting element in the division might be obtained by the use of airborne troops, especially if the means of using these is improved and developed. In discussing the Ardennes offensive of December, 1944, Manteuffel emphatically agreed with what I had written at the time about the way that airborne troops could have been used to seize the awkward defiles in the Ardennes ahead of the tank advance. He considered that they might have made a decisive difference to the prospects of an early breakthrough, and "unlocked the door." In his reflections on the lessons of the war he has advocated that airborne troops should form part of all large armoured formations.

This brings us to the problem of the follow-through—which is, by comparison, simpler than the problem of the break-through. The basic conditions of a solution were epitomized in the definition of *blitzkrieg* set forth earlier in the chapter. *Pace with variability is the secret of mobility, and sustained momentum, in the follow-through.* But much depends on the development of technical means and the elimination of superfluities.

Armoured forces must move light, be able to operate self-contained, and develop more capacity to cut loose from communications—in the Sherman spirit—if they are to attain the degree of offensive mobility required for a decisive follow-through. The Germans went a good way towards this strategic ideal in 1940, but were greatly helped by the fact that the Allied armies were easily paralyzed as well as too rigidly rail-bound. It is no longer possible, for us at any rate, to count in future upon having opponents so susceptible to paralysis. And if we cannot cripple them in this way we shall run the risk of breaking our arms in striking—unless we can kick off our clogs and slip round their guard. Air transport offers one means towards greater freedom of movement and manœuvre. Cross-country transport offers another. The drastic reduction of impedimenta is a third. All these potentialities should be more fully explored and exploited.

The "armoured division" today is too much like an inverted turtle—with a small armour-clad head popping out of a huge soft-skinned body. This is so unwieldy and such an inviting target for air attack that its mobility is too easily turned into immobilized vulnerability. The un-armoured elements should be cut down to a minimum. So should the road vehicles. The maximum possible pro-portion of the infantry should be airborne. What is moved on the ground should be track-borne rather than wheel-borne. Supply *to* such mobile forces should be as far as possible by air transport rather than by land transport.

CHAPTER XX

HOW TO QUICKEN MANŒUVRE AND GAIN FLEXIBILITY

Every soldier knows that it is of vital importance to quicken the tempo of operations and the rapidity of manœuvre. That is the way to gain the advantage in modern battle, and to seize the chance of exploiting any advantage gained. The proverb that "opportunities are fleeting" has an intensified truth since armies have become mobile through motor-power.

Every soldier feels that there is something clogging the mechanism of manœuvre, even though he may be puzzled as to what it is. Missed opportunities remain very common, and operations often get stuck for some reason other than the enemy's opposition. If the operating speed is faster than formerly it has not quickened to anything like the extent represented by the difference between the old marching-pace and modern motor-pace.

Every soldier—except those directly affected—thinks that there are too many people on the staff, and not enough "on the job" with units. Headquarter staffs of all grades always have a tendency to grow in size as well as to multiply. And the shortage of efficient officers with troops is a source of constant complaint. Repeated efforts have been made to "comb out" the staffs, but their effect too often has merely been to upset the efficient working of these organs of control without adequate compensating gain.

Reflection on these different problems inspires the question whether there is not some common link between them. If so, in solving one we might go far towards solving all.

There are more ways to mobility than the use of motors. Mobility means, and needs, much more than mere movement along the road or over the ground. One way is by producing new weapons which ease your own path in face of opposition—by paralyzing the enemy's resisting power and mobility in counter-action. Another way is by developing new means of communication and transmission of orders. But all such technical developments entail a long period of research, experiment, and production. While pursuing research along these lines, we should not overlook the possibilities of a simpler and shorter way—by simplifying the system of control and, in particular, by shortening the chain of command.

Here reason and experience combine to show that each added link in the chain carries a quadrupled drawback. For it tends (a) *to cause loss of time* in (i) getting information back, and (ii) sending orders forward; (b) *to weaken the higher commander's power* by (i) making his impression of the situation more remote, and (ii) diminishing the force of his personal influence on the executives. The fewer the intermediate headquarters, the more dynamic the operations tend to become.

This problem is connected with another; that of improving the effective *power* of manœuvre by superior flexibility. A more flexible organization can achieve greater striking effect because it has more capacity for (a) adjustment to the varying circumstances; and (b) concentration at the decisive point.

It is easy to show this by comparison with the human hand. If a man had only two fingers and a thumb, he would find it much more awkward to get a properly adjusted grip on any object, or opponent, than he does with four fingers and a thumb. His hand would have less flexibility and less capacity for concentrated pressure than it actually possesses. If anyone doubts this, let them put on a fingerless leather mitten, and find how hampering it feels compared with an ordinary glove. That cramping condition has been reproduced in modern military organization. It has become the custom for units to be divided into only three manœuvrable parts, while the larger formations often consist of no more than two—if that. The modern structure of command tends to be more like a perpendicular line than a pyramid.

In the 1944-45 advance from Normandy to the Rhine, Montgomery's headquarters controlled only two armies, which in turn had only two and three corps respectively, and the corps operated only two to three divisions— sometimes, even, only one. The ratio of headquarters was no more economic in the American Army until a late stage. On top of both was Eisenhower's H.Q.—reputedly comprising some 30,000 officers and men. The abundance of headquarters was one reason why the "advance to victory" was so protracted, despite mobile instruments and exhausted opponents.

The command set-up in the Mediterranean had been even more overloaded. Thus for the invasion of Sicily there were three Corps H.Q. to handle a mere seven divisions, with two Army H.Q. on top of them, Alexander's H.Q. above these, and Eisenhower's H.Q. above that.

In Burma, at the start of the 1944 campaign, an even smaller force had two Corps H.Q., and above these successively an Army H.Q., a Land Forces H.Q., and a Supreme H.Q. (the highest but one of these H.Q. swelled to about 7,000 officers and men).

Nothing more cumbersome could be conceived than such absurdly long and narrow chains of command. They fettered mobility and flexibility at every turn.

The ill-effects might have been foreseen. They were pointed out more than a century ago by Clausewitz in his classic work "On War," where he remarked that: "there is nothing more unmanageable than an army divided into three parts except one that is divided into only two—in which case the chief command is almost neutralized." While emphasizing the difficulty of handling a force divided into too many parts, he reached the conclusion that eight to ten sub-divisions was the proper number for a higher commander to handle; and four to five, for a lower commander with a smaller staff.

Since Clausewitz's books are the "Holy Scriptures" of the military profession—though few of its members ever study them thoroughly—it is worth citing his argument on this score.

"Certainly, it seems that the supreme direction of an Army (and the direction of every whole) must be greatly facilitated if there are only three or four subordinates to command, but the Commander-in-Chief must pay dearly for this convenience in a twofold manner. In the first place, an order loses in rapidity, force, and exactness if the graduation ladder down which it has to descend is long, and this must be the case if there are Corps-Commanders between the Division Leaders and the Chief; secondly, the Chief loses generally in his own proper power and efficiency the wider the spheres of action of his immediate subordinates become. A General commanding 100,000 men in eight Divisions exercises a power which is greater in intensity than if the 100,000 men were divided into only three Corps. There are many reasons for this, but the most important is that each Commander looks upon himself as having a kind of proprietary right in his own Corps, and always opposes the withdrawal from him of any portion of it for a longer or shorter time. A little experience of War will make this evident to anyone."

The shrewdness of Clausewitz's argument is manifest, and since his time the facilities for extended control have been greatly improved by the development of new technical means of communication—especially radio. Yet in our time it has been a common practice to organize army corps consisting of no more than two divisions. This either means that the corps commander is almost neutralized, as Clausewitz said, or that he reduces the divisional commands to the function of "post-offices." Either he or they become superfluous and time-wasting. The outcome suggests a new proverb—"too many generals spoil the broth."

Moreover, since Clausewitz's time we have added two more links in the higher chain of command between the Commanders-in-Chief and the divisional commanders. Above the corps commanders we often insert army commanders, and above them army group commanders—all with large staffs. Each of these additional links carries an added risk of delay, misconception, and miscarriage of plans.

In finding our way back to a more rational organization we can "learn from history." Not until the generation before Clausewitz had soldiers discovered the far-reaching advantages of dividing an army into independently moving fractions. It is worth while to recall the story of that discovery and retrace the course of its development.

The Development of Flexibility by Fractionizing
(i.e. the Sub-division of a force)

A century and a half ago Bonaparte and other generals of the French Revolution achieved a military revolution. They overthrew the more highly organized professional armies of their opponents by an accelerated form of action. That achievement was the more remarkable because all armies then were limited to foot-marching pace, and so allowed small scope for the acceleration of actual movement. The greater factor in their success was due to exploiting the possibilities of the new divisional system. Earlier, armies had moved and fought as a whole—or at least a single body, with the cavalry wings hinged on to the infantry trunk. With its new organization in separate self-contained divisions, the army became a flexible grouping, much easier to manœuvre. This ease of manœuvre quickened its mobility both directly and indirectly. It could use more routes of movement, and could concentrate more quickly, while its concentration at any point could be stronger.

The lessons of that experience should be a guide in exploring the present problem. Motor-mobility has immensely increased the potential speed of manœuvre and rapidity of concentration. Yet it can be an impediment to both where it is misapplied, or the fundamental elements of the problem are misunderstood. Nothing is more self-obstructing than an accumulation of motor-transport that, through mistaken handling, develops into a congestion.

There is a further lesson to be found in earlier experience. Napoleon is often cited as the advocate of organization "in threes"—following an opinion he expressed when he became more partial to uniformity. It is significant, however, that in his earlier and most brilliant campaigns he usually operated with four to six divisions, of varying composition. By contrast, examination of his later campaigns, when his forces were organized in army corps—of two, three or four divisions—shows how much his effective control was impaired by the introduction of this intermediate link. And it suffered still worse when, as his forces grew, he inserted another link and tried to direct operations through army commanders.

The Past and Present Basis of Sub-Division

Before and in World War I some armies were organized on a basis of dividing formations and units into three parts, while others preferred four parts. In many cases the practice varied in different grades of unit within an army. On balance the Continental European armies tended to favour organization in "threes." But the British Army of 1914 was based on "fours" almost throughout— in a division there were three brigades (the equivalent of the regiment in other armies) but there were four battalions in a brigade, four companies in a battalion, four platoons in a company, four sections in a platoon. The American division of 1917 had four regiments, with three battalions in a regiment, and four companies in a battalion. But with the multiplication of new supporting weapons, the number of men and vehicles tended to make the formation too cumbrous—while at the same time modern conditions, and the need for mobility, clearly demanded a more handy rather than a less handy size.

A solution of the problem was sought by reducing the number of sub-units, and changing to the basis of organization in "threes"—as Continental armies had already done. It might have been better, instead, to reduce the number of intermediate links in the chain of command.

A tactical drawback of organization in fours was, in practice, that it encouraged the average commander to operate "two by two," spreading his effort evenly, instead of manœuvring to develop a concentration of force at a vulnerable spot. It fitted trench-warfare, simplifying the process of reliefs and "leapfrogging," but was less suited to open fighting. By contrast, organization in threes fosters the idea of manœuvre and concentration, compelling the commander to distribute his strength unevenly. That is its chief advantage. Nevertheless, four sub-units provides a skilled commander with more scope for effective concentration in attack and defence.

This is all the more important as warfare has become more mobile. But the need has not been met. On the contrary, the general reduction in the number of sub-divisions reduced the organic flexibility of units and formations, thus diminishing their *power* of manœuvre— i.e. the powerfulness of any concentration of strength at a particular point.

The Possibility of a New Basis

Weighing these factors, the question arises whether the reduction from "fours" to "threes" was not a retrograde step. It might have been better to go forward—to "fives." Operating with five sub-units would carry the same advantages as three in fostering the average commander's sense of manœuvre, but would multiply those advantages. It would also embody the advantages of the four-unit organization, while extending them—since a "five-finger exercise" has even more flexibility, and offers a greater range of combinations.

Indeed, in principle, the advantages would grow with every further increase in the number of sub-units—but for the limiting factor that the difficulty of control also increases. The problem is to determine the mean—for maximum operative efficiency. Organization in "sixes" has advantageous points both for tactical grouping and for administrative convenience, if it did not conduce to a "three and three" distribution. Organization in "sevens" might be the best of all for tactical flexibility, but stretches the power of control rather far—although the risk could be reduced by the use of a deputy commander. On balance, organization in "fives" probably comes nearest the mean of attaining increased flexibility without strain.

The idea that a commander cannot effectively control more than three or four sub-units has become a fetish. It is not difficult to find evidence from experience that such a limitation is unnecessarily narrow. In the 1918 "advance to victory" the British Commander-in-Chief, Haig, controlled five armies; while the Australian Corps under Monash, which played an outstanding role, handled five divisions throughout its advance, and at times as many as seven divisions. In the last war, the Russian "front commanders" frequently handled five or six armies, and their army commanders handled up to seven or eight divisions in some of their advances—without intermediary corps commanders.

It is not only in reduced speed and increased friction that we pay for additional links in the chain of command. The multiplication of headquarters swells the volume of the staff as a whole, draining the fighting units of far too many of their most capable personnel. The elimination of superfluous headquarters would go much further than mere combing towards a solution of this problem. It would release a large number of officers, and other ranks, for service with troops.

On all these grounds a shortening of the chain of command and a broadening of the commander's "hand" are desirable. In the light of experience the dual reform is clearly practicable. It offers the simplest and cheapest way of quickening the operative tempo and increasing operative efficiency.

But as it involves big changes—about which armies are always hesitant—it may be best to discuss its application on the successive levels, and to consider each of them separately. Even if a complete reorganization on the new basis were regarded as too far-reaching, much improvement on existing performance could be attained by carrying out one or more stages.

(1) *The Elimination or Enlargement of the Army Corps*

An army commander ought to be able to handle at least five divisions, and probably more, without having to deal with their commanders through an intermediate headquarters. The gain in time and personal touch would be very marked. (An army commander has, in reality, a less complicated problem than that of the commander of a division, which comprises many variegated elements besides its principal sub-units. And a corps commander has so few in comparison that he and his headquarters are the least necessary link in the chain.)

If the number of divisions in any army exceeds five or six, it would be simpler for the commander to control a "wing" through a deputy than to interpose several corps commanders. Only if the total exceeds ten, or perhaps eight, would the advantages of having corps commanders tend to outweigh the drawbacks.

This conclusion coincides with another which emerges from analysis of operations during the war—that two infantry divisions are the least number required to form an adequate pivot of manœuvre, and that three armoured divisions form the minimum necessary for a decisive manœuvre. A five-division corps of this composition, and with the infantry divisions motorized, would form a well-balanced instrument of great strategic and tactical power. (It is worth note that the German mechanized spearhead which pierced the French front at Sedan in 1940 was of exactly this composition.) But in any theatre where the forces were not large enough to form two or three corps of this kind, the balance of advantage would lie with the elimination of corps and, in their place, direct control of divisions by army headquarters.

This would mean (a) that corps would only need to be formed where armies were exceptionally large; (b) that in such a case the formation of corps would make it superfluous to form groups of armies, so dispensing with the need for army group headquarters. Thus in any case one link in the present chain would be eliminated.

Significantly, the Russians in the last war discarded the army corps except in the case of the armoured forces, and there they discarded the division—the armoured corps commanders handling brigades direct. Moreover, their armoured corps were considerably smaller than those of other nations, so that they gained in handiness as well as in the quicker control due to the elimination of a link. As they had a far smaller proportion of mechanized and signals equipment than Western forces, it would seem evident that the degree of mobility they nonetheless attained under such a handicap owed much to the way they had simplified and shortened their chain of command.

(2) *The Elimination of the Regiment and the Creation of a Handier Type of Division*

An obvious way of adapting the division to the "five-finger" basis is to reorganize it in two regiments of five battalions apiece—instead of three small regiments of three battalions apiece as at present.

On the other hand, such a change would improve the organic flexibility of a regiment at the expense of the division's. It would do nothing towards correcting the unwieldiness of the existing division, and diminishing the excessive number of vehicles that clog its mobility. It would not improve the internal mobility of the division —which can only be done by cutting out a link in the chain of communication and command.

Much greater benefits are offered by the more radical reorganization of the division—on a five-battalion basis. It would then be under the more immediate control of the divisional commander, without any interposing regiment headquarters. By eliminating these, the "overheads" would be greatly reduced—both in quantity and cost. Still greater would be the gain in quickening the speed of operations. Similar advantages might accrue if the field artillery of the division were reorganized in a single regiment of five batteries.

Such handy divisions would also be easier to move by road and sea. In holding a sector, while two of them would be roughly equivalent in scale to one of the existing type, their organization would make it possible for

them either to form a deeper defence or to cover a wider
frontage than is feasible at present. In mobile operations,
their compactness compared with the existing division
might be the means to achieve a greater advantage. For
most armies tend to operate in regimental groups (three
battalions with supporting weapons), so that on contact
one of these five-battalion divisions might promptly
achieve a decisive superiority sufficient to disrupt the
regimental group immediately opposed to it. By the
time the rest of the enemy division could intervene another of our compact divisions should also be able to
throw its weight in the scales, again tilting them in our
favour.

In man-strength, the new type division would approxi-
mate to the Revolutionary prototype of the late 18th century—which had a mobility and flexibility that the larger
division of more recent times has never attained. It
should be possible to revive those qualities within the
frame of modern conditions, if the design of the division
be properly thought out as a whole—a proviso that is
prompted by the results of an investigation which revealed that the early 20th century pattern had evolved
haphazardly, rather than logically, and that subsequent
attempts at modification had all been conditioned by this
legacy of custom.

It cannot be contended that the return to a smaller
pattern of division would be a leap in the dark, nor even
that a five-battalion basis is much too small for a divisional command. Before World War I, and during a
long period of it, the division in all armies comprised
twelve battalions, but in the later stages they were reorganized on a nine-battalion basis. When peace came,
the British Army—alone among the better European
armies—reinstated the former twelve-battalion pattern;

but shortly before World War II the General Staff was led to revive the less cumbersome nine-battalion pattern. At the same time, motor divisions were introduced, composed of only six infantry battalions. Moreover, in the later part of the war the German divisions were reduced to that same basic scale, of six infantry battalions—organized in either two or three brigades—in preference to reducing the number of divisions. While this reduction was initiated owing to heavy casualties, and the difficulty of maintaining man-power, many of the generals came to consider that the smaller divisions had a marked advantage in manœuvrability.

The difference between a total of six battalions and five is slight. On the other hand, a formation composed of two three-battalion regiments (or three two-battalion regiments) is organically less flexible than the earlier type of division, whereas one in which the divisional command directly controlled and manœuvred five battalions would be much more flexible than any of the types hitherto tried.

The proposed new basis is even simpler and more suitable in the case of the armoured division than in that of the infantry division. For the present armoured division falls into two distinct and heterogeneous parts: a regiment of tanks and a regiment of mechanized infantry (in wheeled or tracked vehicles). Thus from the divisional commander's point of view it amounts to organization in "twos"—in which case, as Clausewitz remarked, "the chief command is almost neutralized." The divisional commander has no real power of handling his armour in manœuvre unless he "sits on top" of the commander of the tank regiment and takes things out of the latter's hands—in which case the latter is "neutralized." The commander of the infantry regiment is also apt to be neutralized by the fact that his battalions are often used separately to support the tanks. It would be better if the tank units and the mechanized infantry units were organized in separate divisions of a handier pattern.

The habit of having a more or less equal proportion of tank and infantry units in the armoured division arose when the infantry were carried in unprotected wheeled vehicles as they could not follow the tanks closely, and were thus slow to come into action. The later that such supporting infantry arrive the more that are required. A much smaller proportion should suffice if this foot-fighting element of the armoured division is composed of "armoured infantry" mounted in armoured carriers that enable them to accompany the tanks and intervene quickly to help the tanks in overcoming defended obstacles.

Both in the British and in the American armoured division there are four tank units. One battalion of armoured infantry should be enough for immediate support in overcoming slight obstacles. That would make a five-unit division. When stronger support is needed it could be provided by calling up motorized infantry divisions of the handier type suggested.

A still better organization for the armoured division might be to have five tank units of battalion size, each with an armoured infantry unit of company size attached to it—though capable of being grouped.

Organization by "fives" could also be applied to the lower units with much advantage. In the armoured division it would not be possible on all levels without the formation becoming too big and radio control too complicated, but it could be applied on two of the three levels —the battalion and the company, or the company and the platoon. When I originally put forward, in 1942, the idea of organization by "fives" I found that a number of the ablest and most experienced commanders of armoured forces were strongly favourable to it, and seemed to see difficulty only in deciding which two of the three levels to choose. In the infantry division, "fives" could be made universal throughout if the number of men in the basic sub-unit—the American "squad," British "section," or French *"groupe de combat"*—were also reduced to five.

That should be practicable. A group of four or five men is sufficient to operate a light machine-gun—Lawrence in Palestine chose to operate with only two men for each. At the same time a group of that size is much less visible than a group of double the size—as in the present American squad or British section—and less vulnerable proportionately. Experience has often shown that the larger group may lose several men quickly, and then, when thus reduced in bulk, make a continued advance under fire with little or no further loss. Why expose superfluous men so that they become casualties early, and not available when needed? Several casualties within a group at an early stage are apt to diminish, disproportionately, its will to advance. There is less risk of this loss of morale if care is taken to avoid casualties that are caused by the excessive size of the target offered. Moreover the leader can keep a closer moral grip on the group, and carry it on more easily when it is small.

The novelty of the idea of organization by fives hindered its adoption when first proposed, in 1942. It has thus been the more significant to learn since the war that experience led one of the ablest General Staff officers in the German Army to put up a similar proposal, in 1944, shortly before the Allied landing in Normandy. The proposer was General Westphal—who was successively

Chief of Staff to Rommel in Africa, to Kesselring in Italy, and finally to Rundstedt in the West. In reflection on the lessons of the war he has come still more definitely to the conclusion that much would have been gained by adopting organization by fives. He points out that "the traditional organization in threes is much too uneconomical—as is shown by the excessive number of signal personnel required."

CHAPTER XXI

THE GROWING IMPORTANCE OF THE JUNIOR OFFICER

THE last chapter dealt with the problem of the chain of command, particularly with the higher links of the chain. This chapter is devoted to the lower links—and their essential place in the chain.

In wartime the newspapers tend to devote their attention to generals, admirals, and air chiefs—in so far as there is any to spare from the statesmen who temporarily meet the public's craving for a superman to whom they can trust their fate and future. It is time, however, that the influence of the junior officer received due recognition—not only because he makes the greater sacrifice, but because collectively he often carries more weight in the military balance. In examining the history of the First World War it can be seen in retrospect that the High Command counted for much less, except in the effect of their mistakes, than did the performance of the company officers. In the last war, where moves were more far-ranging and mobile, generalship recovered something of its old influence, yet the more recently developed

259

importance of the junior leadership in nowise declined as a result, and in some ways even increased.

It is of current value as well as of historical interest to trace how and why the role of the junior officer has grown with the changes in weapons and tactics.

Up to the middle of the 18th Century an army normally operated as a single compact body, so that only the army commanders had any scope for manœuvre, tactical or strategical. The subordinate commanders, higher and lower, could do little more than urge on their men, rally them when disordered, and show an example of resolution. Only in skirmishes between outlying detachments was there any opening for tactical skill.

Shortly before the French Revolution a wave of military reform was generated in France by Guibert and others. One result of it was that the army came to be reorganized in self-contained "divisions." When Napoleon exploited the value of this flexible distribution for his "*blitzkrieg*," a revolution in strategy and tactics was produced.

As these divisions were quartered and moved independently, and had wide intervals between them, their commanders gained the power of manœuvring. While operating on a common plan, directed by the army commander, they each had room for manœuvre, and could themselves be divided into parts, or limbs, that could tackle the opponent in front and flank simultaneously. As Napoleon's forces grew in size the divisions were formed into army corps, which operated in the same fluid way—flung out like a net and then drawn in swiftly round the flanks of an opposing force to catch it in a trap.

The infantry, however, continued to move and fight in close-knit formations, presenting a continuous front. Brigades operated normally as a solid body, and the smaller units were simply integrated fractions of it; the only exceptions occurred in outpost affairs, or when the opposing front became disordered. One corps of the army might grip the enemy in front while another struck him in flank, but for the infantry units in either corps their action was essentially direct and frontal, in attack and defence.

That limiting condition persisted for another century, down to the later stages of the 1914-18 war. It is true that "close-order" was eventually, and belatedly, superseded by "extended-order" as the range and effect of firearms grew. But this merely meant that the ranks opened out, to leave an interval of a few yards between each man and his neighbour, so as to diminish the appallingly vulnerable target that a closely packed body of men had offered when advancing. It did not mean that the infantry units were more manœuvrable.

Orthodox military doctrine still insisted that the power of the attack depended on its physical weight. It regarded distribution in depth, or successive lines of men, as merely a means of filling the bullet-torn gaps in the front line, and thickening this up prior to the frontal assault. The lines themselves were unarticulated, and too inflexible for manœuvre. The follies of the Crimea were repeated in the South African War, and again in the First World War. The middle years of that war saw worse tactical formations employed—and, naturally, much worse losses suffered—than those the British Army was driven to adopt by Boer marksmanship in the later stages of the South African War.

But the commonsense of the fighting soldier modified the dogmas laid down from above. When the unnatural mechanism of stiff-ranked lines broke down under sweeping machine-gun fire, the survivors instinctively formed themselves into little groups, and these often worked forward under some junior leader wherever they could find cover, and penetrated deep into the enemy's position, outflanking similarly improvised groups of the enemy.

In the last year of the war these infiltration tactics, born of close contact with front-line reality, came to be adopted and formulated as the basic method of all the armies engaged—and helped to inject some mobility into the deadlocked form of the struggle. Captain Laffargue of the French Army had been the first to set forth the new idea in writing, as early as 1915, and it was Captain Geyer of Ludendorff's staff who systematized it into the new tactical theory which the German Army applied in breaking through the British front in 1918. These pioneers were expressing and fulfilling the general trend of reflection among the alert-minded members of their generation who had learned from personal experience. It was the "Junior Officer," in the collective sense, who grasped the need for a change, and brought about its acceptance, in face of the reluctance of most of the seniors to consider anything radically different from the methods to which they were accustomed.

The development of fire-weapons enforced dispersion among the fighting troops. The confused conditions of the battlefield impelled men to break away from the regulation lines and work in natural groups, under a leader and together with comrades they knew. The combination of these factors produced the flexible chain of little groups, as a tactical formation, to supersede the continuous unarticulated line. The fact that there were, necessarily, intervals between them provided both the attacking and defending groups with opportunity for manœuvre, to outflank or enfilade opposing groups. As the supporting lines likewise became chains of groups, distributed in depth, these were able to help the forward groups by indirect manœuvring leverage on the points of resistance, instead of reinforcing the firing line direct where it was held up—which had too often meant merely piling up the human targets just where the enemy's fire was concentrated and the way was blocked. Now the reserves, in little groups or larger ones, could be diverted to follow in the wake of the more successful forward units, and then swing in from the flank against the enemy posts that checked the other forward units.

By thus exploiting small penetrations made by their leading sub-units, the platoon and company and battalion commanders in turn could fulfil the principle of surprise by striking from "an unexpected direction against an unguarded spot." They could take advantage of the "internal" flanks exposed by such progressively expanded penetrations. Thereby their segment of the battle was transformed from a mere straightforward push into a theatre of manœuvre, providing in miniature almost as much scope for tactical skill and tactical combination as generals, only, had possessed in the past.

All this gave the junior officer much more opportunity but also increased his responsibility, and raised the standard required of him. At the same time the demand on his mental powers was multiplied, and his problems complicated, by the variety of new weapons that were introduced. In 1914, the company commander had to think only in terms of the rifle, and even the battalion had merely the additional weapon-element of a couple of machine-guns, which were often treated as superfluous appendages. Before the end of the war, the infantry armament had been extended to embrace light machine-guns, mortars, hand-grenades, and rifle-grenades—both explosive and smoke-projecting.

The diversity of factors that had to be considered made the job of a junior officer inherently more complex than that of an infantry brigade commander,* who now had only three battalions to handle. Indeed, one of the best-known army commanders remarked to me some years later that he had come to the conclusion that, while the company and battalion commanders' jobs were about equally exacting, all the other and higher grades—that of brigade, division and corps commander—were simpler and easier until one reached the level of army commander, which he regarded as comparable in complexity to that of a battalion commander.

This does not imply that any competent company or battalion commander could equally well fill an army commander's place, and take the intermediate grades in his stride; for a somewhat different range of calculations and considerations arises with each enlargement of the scale of command, and some men are slow of adaptation while others are apt to be overwhelmed by the difference of scale. But it does suggest that a really good junior commander could ascend to the higher commands much more rapidly than is normally supposed, or allowed, if it were not for the artificial checks imposed by conventions that are based on professional interests, and the privileges claimed by age.

That conclusion is amply supported by the experience contained in military history. Examining the record of the outstanding commanders—the roll of those who are, significantly, termed "Great Captains"—we find that if we take the obvious "first fifteen" only four had served a

* This refers to the British Army—the equivalent in most other armies being the regimental commander.

lengthy apprenticeship in the lower ranks before they proved their powers in high command. Five were in their twenties, and six more in the thirties when they became famous. If we include a "second fifteen" of perhaps less familiar but equally strong candidates, we find that out of the whole thirty, only nine had such length of service as would now be required as a minimum.

Modern experience bears witness to the same effect, within the limits permitted by professional interests. Under the comparatively unexacting conditions of peacetime, an officer rarely attains command of a battalion until he is about forty years old, and is not considered fit to be a general until he is between fifty and sixty. But in World War I officers rose to command of battalions in their twenties, and to the command of divisions in their thirties. The only reason why the rise was not quicker still lay in the fact that it depended on vacancies caused by failure, not on the selection of those who were best fitted irrespective of seniority. In World War II the same mixed process operated, but rather more slowly, because casualties were fewer. Even so, several officers attained command of an army before they were fifty; others, command of an army corps when barely forty; and a few received command of a division when in their thirties. But such men might just as well have risen quicker and higher, if it had not been that promotion was still governed by the notion of "gradualness." (It is significant that in the Red Army, which underwent a much more severe eliminating test, a large proportion of the higher commanders were well under forty.)

It is to be noted, however, that the advancement of temporary soldiers was even more limited than in the previous war. This has a curious reflection, since the Services drew in the pick of the nation. It may be explained partly by the extra delay caused by the system of passing everyone through the ranks; partly by the feeling that a war is the professional soldier's time of opportunity; partly by the increased complexity of the technique that has to be mastered before a man can effectively exert his natural gifts of leadership—World War II saw the introduction of many fresh weapons and types of equipment, while operations became more mobile than in the first war.

A natural advantage which the regular soldier has over the temporary one is that he has become so habituated to military procedures that he can perform them instinctively, and thus is less affected by the "friction" of war, while being able to devote his thinking to the tactical problem of outwitting the enemy. It is a paradox of "total war" that the civilian entrant is expected to take over the most technical functions of soldiering—which fall to the junior officer—while he is unlikely ever to be considered for the higher posts—where more depends on wide knowledge, broad outlook and freshness of thought than on technical experience.

Long training tends to make a man more expert in execution, but such expertness is apt to be gained at the expense of fertility of ideas, originality, and elasticity. War is the realm of the unexpected; and adaptation to the unexpected comes more naturally to youth.

It should have been possible, after four years or so of war, to make better use of the nation-wide resources of mental power that were available. The potential value of doing so was shown in the previous war, where the Australian citizen-soldier, Sir John Monash, who had been little better than average up to brigade commander, became more and more outstanding the higher he rose. It is also significant how many of the leading generals in the last war originally came into the Army as temporary soldiers in the previous war.

It may help to open the way for a better and quicker utilization of talent in future if we come to realize more clearly the immense development that has taken place in the rôle of the junior officer, and the extent to which the gap between his functions and those of the higher commanders has been bridged by modern conditions. Such a realization may also help to increase his self-confidence and efficiency in leadership.

Since "close-order" has evolved into "dispersed-order," under pressure of fire-power and air-power, an army's success depends largely on the compound effect of many local collapses on the opposing side. Battle has become a serial process composed of momentary minor opportunities, and the exploitation of these naturally tends to turn even more on a general superiority in minor tactics among the junior leaders than on the major tactics of the generals—except on the highest levels, where strategy is called for, and where a bad strategical decision can undo a tactical advantage.

In other words, a battle has become a team-game on the largest scale, in which the junior leaders are players, not pawns. "Theirs not to reason why, Theirs but to do and die," is an out-of-date conception, and it is time that we gave full recognition to the implications of the change. The junior leaders have always borne the brunt of war, and do so still; but their intelligent initiative, and its cultivation, have now become vital factors in determining the issue.

CHAPTER XXII

THE "UNTIMELINESS" OF A CONSCRIPT
ARMY

Before the war Britain and the United
States were the only two powers which still relied on
long-service professional forces, raised by voluntary enlistment, to take the first shock of war. All others placed
their trust in compulsory service—and the mass citizen
army of large numbers, though short-service, which is the
natural product of the conscriptive system.

After the war the American and British Governments
decided to follow the example of other nations and adopt
the system of peacetime conscription. The former soon
suspended it, finding that it could raise by voluntary
enlistment forces much larger than before the war—and
as large as it can afford. The latter has continued conscription to help it in maintaining its forces on a similarly
enlarged peacetime scale—larger than it can really afford.

Britain's post-war change of policy has been welcomed
by her neighbours in Europe, who feel that it will increase her preparedness to help in the common defence.
The same idea was evidently uppermost in the mind of the

British Government and a majority of the public—60 per cent of which, according to a Gallup Poll, endorsed the decision.

"Better preparedness" has been the basic argument for conscription in every country. Is this idea true, or is it an illusion?

The first striking fact which bears on this question is that all the countries which collapsed under the shock of the German *blitzkrieg* in 1939, 1940, and 1941 relied on long-established conscript armies for their defence. The only one of Germany's original opponents which remained unconquered was the one that had rejected conscription until the eve of war, and relied mainly on voluntary forces during its supreme test.

Those who favour conscription will naturally reply that Britain also differed from most of the others in having a sea-ditch round her frontiers, and that she owed her survival to its protection. Is this an entirely convincing answer?

Norway had an even wider sea-ditch, but that did not save her. Moreover, while her army was small, the fraction of the British Army that was equipped and ready for action in the month or two following "Dunkirk" was also small. What deterred the vastly stronger German Army from invading Britain was the active opposition of the British Air Force and the latent threat of the British Navy.

This reflection leads to a further one. In numbers of men, the armies that faced Germany in the West were, on paper, as strong as her own. What paralyzed their resistance on the ground was the weakness of their armoured forces and of their air forces compared with hers. Britain's armoured force was also weak—hence her army was involved in the common disaster that overtook all the

Allied armies in the West. But her air force was relatively
strong compared with the others—hence it was able to
cover the withdrawal of her army, and then to deter the
Germans from trying to follow it across the Channel.

If Britain had earlier followed her neighbours' example
in adopting conscription, she might also have shared their
misplaced faith in numbers of men on the ground, and
devoted so much of her resources to building a mass
army as to leave her air force, if not her navy, as poorly
developed as theirs were. That is a sobering reflection.
The system of conscription has always tended to foster
quantity at the expense of quality.

After her defeat in 1918 Germany was forbidden to
continue conscription by the Versailles Treaty. For six
years she was consequently compelled to concentrate on
creating an élite professional force, the *Reichswehr*.
When Hitler revived conscription the German Army had
become so accustomed to think in terms of quality, and
had made such progress in developing specialist skill, that
the gradual infusion of a lot of conscripts did not completely alter the trend of its ideas and practice. It still retained the idea of having a core of élite formations within
the mass army, and did not sacrifice quality to equality in
the interests of uniformity—as is the usual military habit.
The newer arms, which required experts to handle them,
received priority. The results were registered in the victories of 1940, which were essentially a triumph of the
expert.

The *blitzkrieg* was carried out by relatively small spearheads—tanks and mechanized infantry, backed by dive-
bombers and in some cases by airborne troops. The world
has yet not clearly realized what a tiny fraction of the
whole they formed, and how little the bulk mattered. For

that reason, the composition of the thrusts deserves analysis—more fully than earlier in the book.

The decisive stroke in Holland was the disruption of the Dutch Army's rear, and the country's nerve system, on the opening day—May 10th, 1940. This was achieved by the use of 5 parachute battalions and a division of air-transported infantry, against the key cities of Rotterdam and The Hague, followed up by an armoured division which raced to their support through a gap that arose in the confused defence. These three striking elements numbered little more than 30,000 men. Their effect, in combination with the *Luftwaffe,* sufficed to produce the capitulation of Holland after five days, although the main Dutch defensive position remained intact.

If conscription were a good safeguard, the Dutch should certainly have been secure. For with its aid they had mobilized some 400,000 men—a total much larger than the German 18th Army which invaded Holland. They managed to withstand the mass of the invading forces, and could claim that their front was still unbroken at the end. But that did not prevent the issue being decided against them—by the menace in the rear.

The Belgians had a conscript army of 650,000 men mobilized since the autumn of 1939, and 900,000 in all were under arms in the final stage of mobilization. Their total was numerically much greater than the German 6th Army, which attacked the main gateway into Belgium. But it was of no avail. For the keys of the gate were captured by a tiny detachment of 500 parachutists, who descended out of the night sky and captured the bridges over the Albert Canal beyond Maastricht, as well as disabling the guns of Fort Eben Emael, which had been built to command the passage of that frontier water-barrier. This initial coup was exploited by a couple of armoured divisions which crossed the captured bridges next day and burst through the improvised line beyond, with the help of a cloud of dive-bombers. Once these thirty thousand mobile troops had poured through into the open plains of central Belgium, the whole frontier line had to be abandoned. From that point the retreat never ceased except for brief pauses.

The capitulation of the Belgian Army a fortnight later, however, was not the direct consequence of this thrust, but the indirect consequence of the way that the French front had in turn been ruptured on the Meuse, between Sedan and Namur, on May 13th.

On this sector three thrusts were delivered through the Ardennes by a total of seven armoured divisions. Their passage across the Meuse was covered by the same cloud of dive-bombers that had previously covered the Maastricht break-through. No airborne forces were employed by the Germans against the French front, as none were left available.

After the break-through from the Ardennes, these armoured divisions swept on westward, 160 miles in a week, to the Channel coast. By reaching the sea so quickly they cut off the whole of the Allied forces in Belgium—comprising the best third of the French Army and almost all the British Army, as well as the Belgian Army. The barricade across the Allies' rear was soon cemented by a few motorized divisions followed by a number of marching divisions which arrived before the Allied forces had recovered from the shock of being severed from their bases. After this disaster the remainder of the French Army proved incapable of checking the invaders when they turned southward in the next, and final stage of their offensive.

The fate of France was virtually decided by the opening stroke and its follow-through. The decisive breach, at Sedan, was made by nine hundred tanks, covered by a thousand aircraft. The mass of the German Army only played a "walking on" part in the principal act, and merely came on the scene to confirm the issue.

The mass of the French Army was no more effective in preventing the disastrous issue. Conscription had provided France with trained reserves amounting to some five million men, a far larger total than Germany's. A greater proportion of the French had undergone military training than in any other European nation, and for a longer period. All this counted for little in face of the shock of a comparative handful of more up-to-date forces.

In the light of the experience of World War II it is hard to see justification for the hoary notion that conscription spells security. Rather does it appear to foster a false sense of security, and impede preparedness to meet new forms of danger. The countries which placed less trust in the system were quicker to adapt themselves to the real needs. The countries that were so quickly overrun in 1939, 1940, and 1941 might have fared much better—and could have fared no worse—if they had relied instead on smaller professional forces of higher quality, training and equipment.

When we turn from the past to the future, the value of conscript armies looks even more dubious. They are no answer to the menace of attack by atomic bombs and long-range rockets. Indeed, they are more of a menace to the defence, by cluttering up the strategic points and communications with a useless mass of unspecialized manpower that places excessive burdens on the system of transport and supply.

The idea that such so-called "trained" reserves will be valuable in making a counter-offensive against the enemy's atomic and rocket bases is the craziest of illusions. Months, if not years, would elapse before they would be ready to undertake such offensive action.

The conscript armies that were overrun in 1940 had enjoyed nine months after mobilization before they were called on to tackle the simpler task of defensive action, and even then were under-trained. It is unlikely that those who may have to meet aggression in the future will be allowed nine months' grace before the attack starts.

Beyond all these drawbacks is the more fatal one that any such counter-offensive by an army launched months after atomic warfare had begun could not redeem the devastation already suffered. Belated intervention of this kind could save little or nothing of the wreckage, which would probably have gone so far that any such military effort would be stillborn.

If the warring nations refrain from employing atomic weapons, for fear of common destruction, that natural limitation would not revive the value of conscript armies. For the alternative form of aggression to be feared in that case lies in the sudden penetration of a borderland by mobile mechanized forces, or the infiltration of disguised forces to support a disaffected section of the people in the land concerned.

Neither of these threats can be met except by a professional force that is standing by ready to intervene like a fire brigade. A conscript army, besides being slow to mobilize, can be mobilized only when the emergency has arisen—and that is too late. Moreover, it is itself more liable than a professional army to contain disaffected elements within its own body. This is more certainly an era of ideological warfare than of atomic warfare. A crafty aggressor will organize his sympathizers among the men conscripted into the opposing army, and use this infiltration to paralyze its action when he starts his more open moves. A professional army is "purer."

In sum, the more deeply the system of conscription is studied in the light of modern conditions, the more out of date it appears. In the military field, it is the equivalent of the prehistoric mammoth. The European nations would show more sense in changing to a professional system than Britain has shown in becoming the last convert to an antiquated idea.

PART FIVE

TIMELESS

Some Basic Problems of Yesterday and Tomorrow

CHAPTER XXIII

CONSCRIPTION—THE BASIC QUESTIONS

Various aspects of the conscript system as now working have been discussed in earlier chapters, but it is important to examine the more fundamental factors. The following summary of the "pros" and "cons" represents conclusions reached in long study of the question—conclusions which, on the balance, altered my own initial tendency to favour the system.

The system of conscription has a number of marked advantages. It is the most *systematic* method of raising armies, and the easiest to organize. It is thus a boon to planners. They can make their calculations with precision, and can count on filling their columns without any headaches. No imaginative effort is required in recruiting, or in improving Service conditions. The men must come when called, whether they like it or not.

It is the *cheapest* system—in proportion to numbers enlisted. Men of good quality and technical ability may be obtained without regard to rates of pay. That is im-

possible with a professional army recruited on a voluntary basis.

It appears the most *democratic* system, since it demands an equal extent of service from all. But its fair-
ness may be found dubious on deeper analysis of the
social and psychological factors, after taking account of
mental and temperamental diversity, as well as of the
practical workings of the system. There can be no true
equality in uniform treatment of those who are naturally
suited to military service and those who are not—and it
is a most obvious truth of human experience that the
more that men increase in civilized value, the more they
are inclined to lose the pugnacity that is desirable for
fighting. Nevertheless, the appearance of equality has an
obvious appeal in a political system that is aiming at
equalitarianism.

Conscription seems more democratic, also, in that the
power residing in skill at arms is distributed among the
citizens of a country, instead of being confined to a section. It thus carries the promise of checking an abuse of
such power by a professional caste whose interests may
run counter to those of the community as a whole. Here
again, the experience of history suggests that this assumption is an illusion. But such appearances tend to be
comforting.

Another argument for conscription is that it gives the
youth of a nation a necessary discipline and spirit of service to the community. Although it has too often been a
favourite argument of war-minded leaders abroad, and
is therefore suspect, it should not be lightly discounted
on that score. A sense of discipline is needed, in one way
or another, for good citizenship. The lack of it has become marked since the breakdown of parental authority,
and the ill-effects are rampant. Military service often

brings an improvement. But the use of such a substitute is a confession of educational failure, in the home and in the school. It would better be remedied by concentrating on the problem early instead of leaving it until late and hoping it may come as a secondary product of training for war. The very fact that leading soldiers have tended to advocate conscription for its value as social discipline raises a doubt about the ulterior motive and whether the system is really essential on pure military grounds.

Conscription is the only system that can produce a very large army. This is its principal justification, and is important so long as the chief assurance of a nation's security in peace and victory in war rests in the *number of men* under arms. From a military point of view, largeness has other advantages of which any government's military advisers are conscious, though they would hesitate to use them as arguments. The larger the army, the larger the number of high-grade appointments, and thus the better the prospects of promotion—which is the very natural explanation why those professional soldiers who are most scornful of "civilians" welcome their conscription into the army, even though it means a weakening of the soldierly spirit. It would be unreasonable to blame them for promoting their interests—for that is normal human nature—but we should understand, and take account of, the subconscious motive.

Even from a military point of view, however, the conscription system carries a number of *serious disadvantages* that have to be weighed against these apparent advantages.

In the first place, we have to consider its underlying effect on efficiency. The longest possible period of conscript service in peacetime is not long enough to develop the standard of skill attainable with long-service volunteers, and the time required increases with the technical complexity of weapons. But beyond the time factor lies a psychological factor. Enthusiasm is the mainspring of efficiency, and is inherently incompatible with compulsion.

This, of course, does not imply that a compulsorily enlisted man cannot develop enthusiasm for his job, or that an army on a voluntary basis carries on without compulsion. Moreover, a fair degree of efficiency can be attained without men being very keen on their job. But the higher degrees of efficiency arise from a dynamic impulse that is essentially spontaneous, and this in turn depends on the least possible sense of compulsion. A modern army cannot afford to aim at less than the higher degrees of efficiency, and therefore of enthusiasm.

Conscription also tends to weaken the reliability of an army, especially under stress and strain. An unwilling soldier is a germ-carrier of demoralization, likely to spread infection out of all proportion to his enforced contribution. With growing experience of modern war, the fighting services have learnt that it is wiser to discard men whose morale is dubious—whether from temperament or prolonged nerve-strain—rather than force them to go into action, as was the former habit. Nothing is so infectious as panic. In the increasingly individualistic conditions of modern warfare, any weak element becomes more dangerous. The system of compulsory service naturally multiplies the chances of such weakness.

Conscription runs counter to the *qualitative* trend of modern warfare. It fosters the fetish of numbers, at a time when real superiority of force is coming to depend more and more on specialized skill and individual initiative. In this connection it is significant that the German leaders were led, by experience, to give increasing emphasis to the use of *special storm troops* for all important tasks. The Nazi movement itself was essentially a voluntary movement, exclusive rather than comprehensive, while the most vital sections of the German forces—the air, tank, parachute, and S.S. units—were recruited on a semi-voluntary basis. There is little evidence to suggest that the ordinary "mass" of the German Army had anything like the same enthusiasm, and considerable evidence to suggest that it contributed a basic weakness in Germany's apparent strength.

A conscript army also has the drawback of being slow to mobilize, and in a democratic country there is a natural inclination to delay its mobilization. It can never have the same readiness for action as a professional army. It is thus far less fitted to meet the danger of a modern *blitzkrieg* type of invasion—and still less suited to meet the dangers of atomic attack. At the same time it tends to preserve the old view, now an illusion, that the strength of a country lies in its weight of armed numbers, and thus fosters a false sense of security.

Beyond these general disadvantages, a military system based on conscription is particularly unsuited to countries, such as Britain and the United States, whose military problems lie mainly overseas. The former has always had to maintain a large part of her forces overseas. In contrast to Continental States, the primary task of Britain's land forces is the defence of territories abroad, not of her home frontiers. That need can only be met by a voluntary, professional army, as all the advocates of compulsory service are compelled to admit. At most, conscription is only a supplement, not the main solution of the problem.

But in advocating that supplementary purpose, they overlook the drawbacks of mixing compulsory service

with voluntary recruitment. Experience provides reason
to fear that the effect tends to reproduce, in the military
sphere, the adage that "bad coinage drives out good."
Between the First and Second World Wars, military
opinion in France came to see the importance of creating a professional mechanized striking force in addition
to the conscript army. But efforts to recruit an adequate
professional element had disappointing results—in a country that was habituated to the idea of short-term compulsory service. The lack of such a force, instantly ready,
was a decisive factor in preventing the French from
checking Hitler's reoccupation of the Rhineland in 1936.

It can thus be seen that the military advantages of the
system are accompanied by a still greater number of
disadvantages which are qualitatively more serious. But
beyond this reckoning, due account must be taken of the
disadvantages in a wider sphere.

In the first place, conscription causes a larger subtrac-
tion than a long-service professional force from the man-
power available for industry. The British are now beginning to feel, acutely, the economic draught of the military drafts. There is no country whose economic system
is less suited than Britain's to bear the extra strain of
military conscription.

A second fundamental drawback of conscription is that
it gives the military hierarchy greater influence, and creates a bigger vested interest in warlike activities. In a
country such as Britain and the United States, and other
democracies, the danger of it fostering aggressive tendencies may be discounted, but even in a peaceful country that increased influence may promote greater military
demands than the national economy can safely bear.

A more subtle danger of conscription is that it weakens
patriotism. That is natural, for compulsion atrophies the

sense of personal responsibility, and fosters the spirit of evasion. The countries that have long been habituated to the compulsory system have shown a high percentage of deserters and "fifth columnists," together with a marked disposition to sudden collapse.

This reflection leads us to the most fundamental conclusion of all. Conscription immensely increases the power of the State over the individual. It has been of great service to dictators as a means of enslaving the people to their own purposes. Liberty-loving peoples are foolish if they help to preserve such a system as a natural and proper custom. For conscription has been the cancer of civilization.

CHAPTER XXIV

THE PROBLEM OF AN INTERNATIONAL FORCE

THE idea of creating an International Force as the "arm" of the League of Nations was much canvassed during the decade that followed World War I. It remained a subject of constant discussion until the breakdown of the League—following Japan's unchecked aggression in Manchuria, Hitler's rise to power in Germany, and Mussolini's still more open defiance of the League over Abyssinia. However, a second world war brought a revival of the idea, and its adoption in principle by the "United Nations."

At the San Francisco Conference, the victors jointly agreed that the United Nations Organization should be provided with its own armed forces—to "put teeth" into its Charter. Early in 1946 the Military Staff Committee of UNO, sitting in New York, started to consider the problem. It comprised official representatives of the so-called "Big Five"—Americans, Russians, British, French and Chinese. After a year's deliberation they produced a report laying down the principles on which this world force should be organized.

286

The report comprised 41 articles, and the members of the Military Staff Committee succeeded in agreeing on a large proportion. While they differed on a number of important points, they were unanimous in recommending that "Unoforce" should be composed of separate national contingents, instead of being an integrated force directly enlisted for the service of UNO.

Since then the increasingly manifest rivalry between the victors has made the "United Nations" a synonym for dangerous disunity, and as a natural consequence has paralyzed the continuation of plans to create a "Unoforce." In these circumstances study of the problem appears an academic exercise unrelated to current affairs. Nevertheless it is conceivable that, sooner or later, there may be a change of political conditions that will give fresh relevance to the problem. So it is worth while to collate what has been learned in exploring the problem. Moreover, the conclusions have a bearing on the problem —which is not so remote—of organizing an "international force" that is not a completely representative "world force" as visualized by the hopeful sponsors of UNO.

The problem of an international force is a subject to which, with the aid of a Leverhulme Fellowship, I once devoted a lengthy period of research. A prime conclusion reached was that while the "national contingent" basis seemed to be the simplest, and had more hope of gaining political acceptance, it was the most difficult in a technical and practical sense. Its path would be strewn with fissures and overhung by potential avalanches. It was the problem of past allied forces *multiplied*.

There are many cases in history of different national contingents operating together. Their effectiveness has

tended to vary with the number concerned. Forces of two
nations have frequently combined with success.

The partnership between English and Prussians in the
final campaign against Napoleon worked well during the
crisis of 1815, thanks to good co-operation between Wellington and Blücher, though it degenerated as soon as
victory was assured. Still more notable was the degree of
co-operation between the British and American forces in
World War II, thanks to tact on both sides and the way
their association was crowned by a supreme commander
of Eisenhower's supremely tactful personality. Even so,
there was a good deal more disagreement than appeared
on the surface.

With the inclusion of more national contingents, the
difficulty has always grown. A glaring example was the
friction in the Macedonian campaign of 1915-18, when
six national contingents combined—French, British, Italian, Serbs, Russians and Greeks. No quite comparable
situation arose in World War II. For while the number
of national contingents participating in some of the later
campaigns—especially in Italy—was almost equal to that
in Macedonia, they were all small compared with the
British and American, and were dependent on supplies
from the two bigger allies. Nevertheless, there were times
when their contribution was outweighed by their complications.

Closeness of contact is apt to accentuate divergences.
That is another lesson of experience between allies—
similarly to what so often happens when grown-up members of a family live together under the same roof. A
famous example was in the alliance against Louis XIV's
bid to dominate Europe. The English and Austrians co-
operated smoothly for a long spell, thanks to the way
Marlborough and Eugene blended, but for much of the

time it was a long-range co-operation. On the other hand there was a frequent clash of purposes and wills between the English and Dutch, who fought alongside one another. British histories paint a picture of a clear-sighted and angelic-tempered Marlborough being repeatedly frustrated by the exasperatingly cautious and short-sighted Dutch. But when one comes to see the Dutch point of view better, one can appreciate that they had cause for concern over Marlborough's inclination to gamble audaciously on the issues where they had much at stake and he had little. A slip would expose their country to invasion, whereas England was safely out of reach.

Friction was frequent in the coalitions against Napoleon. That is one reason why the uncommon degree of co-operation between Blücher and Wellington in the brief Waterloo campaign has caused that interlude to be so greatly applauded. Disagreement was also a normal accompaniment of most of the battles of World War I that were conducted on a joint basis.

Cross purposes and mutual criticism have been prevalent whenever forces of different nations have fought alongside one another. They tend to blame their allies for any reverse suffered and to claim for themselves most of the credit for any success gained.

Differences can be diminished—up to a point—by the creation of a single commander. Such an appointment has worked best when one of the nations has been unmistakably the senior partner. Between more or less equal partners, a unified command has been more difficult. In World War I it was not established until the fourth year, when the crisis of March, 1918, led to Foch's appointment to that position. Yet the supreme command remained only a name, as Foch himself remarked. His power was in reality limited to co-ordination and conciliation. He could only coax his team, not drive it. If Eisenhower's appointment in World War II became more effective, that owed much to the fact that he had only to deal with two major national armies, instead of three like Foch—while both spoke a similar language.

The "agreed" recommendations of the Military Staff Committee of UNO did not appear to take account of these lessons of experience. The kind of international force they proposed would have comprised a larger number of national contingents, on an equal basis, than in any of these cases of inter-allied operations. The nearest parallel to it in history was provided by the international army that was formed to advance on Peking to deal with the common threat to European interests arising out of the Boxer Rebellion of 1900 in China. For it, eight nations furnished contingents. The course of events suggested that this temporary international force was fortunate in not meeting more serious armed resistance in executing its tasks. Moreover, joint action here generated an ill feeling between the associates that had wider reactions. The common purpose was soon forgotten, and each nation had the impulse to use its contingent to gain an advantage for its own interests in the subsequent settlement of that sphere.

The scheme visualized by the Military Staff Committee of UNO repeated these faults of the past with some fresh ones added. The military experts of all the powers represented on it agreed, in their report, that the various national contingents should retain their "national character," including their distinctive system of control and discipline. Each was to provide its own reinforcements, supplies, and transport.

At first thought, such recommendations may seem a wise precaution. But when these principles are translated into practical terms, the creaking of the machinery can be heard in advance—the competition and controversy over the respective use of ports, railways, and roads between so many equal partners, especially in any region where such facilities were scanty. The administrative area is the weakest spot of any force. That weakness would be multiplied where the numerous component parts were intent to maintain their "national character" —each requiring different rations to feed its men; different calibres of ammunition to feed its weapons; different spare parts and tools; and each functioning on a different staff system. They would be talking different languages both metaphorically and literally. The sum of all these differences would make the tower of Babel sound like a symphony.

The points of difference in the report of the Military Staff Committee were also significant. While a majority of the representatives recommended that each member should make "comparable initial overall contributions," others interpreted this broad formula to mean that each contingent should be equal in size and composition. But this would imply that if one member had a very small tank force, the proportion of tanks in the whole force would be low; and that, as some of the members had no aircraft carriers, there would be none in the force. An international fleet that was limited to the scale of what the Chinese Navy could have contibuted would not have been very impressive!

A more practical arrangement, in any scheme, would be one that allowed the members to make their contribution in different ways. Some are better suited to furnish land forces; others, sea forces; others, air forces. It would simplify the problems of operation if not more than two or three national contingents were represented in each

sphere—land, sea, or air. The smaller nations might contribute to the cost or the facilities rather than to the actual forces. This way of sharing in the maintenance of
international justice by proxy may not appear to fulfil
the principles of equity and equality, but it would diminish complexity.

As might have been expected, the most awkward disagreement in the Military Staff Committee's report
turned on the problem of bases. The French representatives urged the need of arranging for a network of bases
that could be handed over immediately to Unoforce
when an emergency arises. The Americans, British and
Chinese endorsed the principle that bases should be
available everywhere, but made reservations about putting the principle into practice. The Russians contended
that the bases of any national contingent should be confined to its own national territory or waters, except for
ex-enemy territories—a limitation that would obviously
cramp essential flexibility in the strategic use of an international force. This reflected the underlying realities of
the situation—the mutual suspicions that were rampant
in the "United Nations" from the outset.

If the project of an international force should be revived in more favourable circumstances, or on a less complete basis, it would be advisable to discuss a different
plan. A realization of the many difficulties that hedge
round a national-international force lead us to consider
the other form of such a force—composed of men directly
enlisted for the permanent service of the international
body. They would be men of all nationalities, though the
proportion of each would presumably be governed by a
quota.

Politically, the creation of such a truly international

force is the more difficult of acceptance, but it would be superior in several respects to the other from a practical point of view. It could be organized and trained homogeneously. Its system of command, of communications and of supply would be uniform, together with its equipment and armament.

It would, preferably, have to adopt a single language for its usage. Even if two were insisted on, to meet political considerations, the difficulty would be no greater than in many imperial armies, past and present. Indeed, it would be less, for the personnel would be of higher intelligence than the natives who are enlisted in most colonial forces.

As regards the provision of arms and equipment, to draw the supply mainly from one or two nations in the interests of uniformity would give these nations a manufacturing advantage that would also be a potential military advantage. That would be unfortunate if a split threatened to develop. The drawback might be met by arranging to draw particular articles from particular nations—tanks from one, artillery from another, fighters from another, bombers from another, anti-aircraft guns from another, and so on. Such a system might in any case be necessary for initial supply. Later, the international force might have its own design department, the designs being executed, on a quota, by different nations. This would pave the way for the international authority itself to take over the manufacture of the major weapons —which would be the safest system.

An objection commonly raised against the idea of an international force of this kind is that of morale. It is argued that it would lack the will to conquer which inspires a national army, and thus be at a disadvantage against troops of an aggressive nation who were conscious

of fighting for their country's cause. The objection is exaggerated, I think—both morally and technically. In most
professional armies, national spirit has been a factor secondary to the soldierly spirit. It grows out of training,
discipline, and comradeship, flowering into a sense of be-
longing to a mystical cult of a martial kind. Isolation
from ordinary national life tends to strengthen it. If we
look back in history we can see its strength. In the
Roman Legions, from the time of Marius on, patriotism
counted for little. Their triumphs were produced by
training and soldierly spirit. Cæsar had only to address
his men as *quirites*, civilians, to quell a mutiny. The same
elements were predominant in the Swiss, Scottish and
Irish soldiers of fortune who long formed the *corps d'élite*
of many of the European armies.

Composite nationality has made little difference. The
French Foreign Legion has achieved great feats of
bravery and endurance despite it. Composite nationality
should all the less affect an international force, because
its members would not be fighting under the flag of one
foreign nation. If called on for action, against a member-
state, the section that belonged to the offending nationality would, naturally, not be employed.

We need not have much fear of the morale of a true
international force. *Esprit de corps* would soon grow. If
any doubt remains, it should be dispelled by reflection on
the way that the importance of pugnacity is decreasing
in the more modern types of force, and replaced by the
dispassionate determination that accompanies pride of
craftsmanship. Pugnacity matters less in a tankman than
in an infantryman. It is not required in the artilleryman.
It may help the airman when he is under fire, but except
when fighting another aircraft it has no place in his action. Both the gun-crew and the bomber-crew despatch

their missiles in an essentially impersonal spirit. Patriotic ardour will hardly improve their aim.

The more mechanical that weapons become, the less will the absence of a national spirit be felt. This leads on to a further deduction—that if an international force mainly employs long-range weapons it will avoid many difficulties that now loom large.

The world would be safer for all peoples if the more powerful offensive weapons, especially the longer range ones, were entrusted solely to an international force. Such a force would in any case need to possess a pre-dominance in them if it were to have any chance of en-forcing the decisions of the international authority. But if the various national forces also retain these weapons that would entail the international force being propor-tionately larger—and the larger it has to be, the more difficult its creation would be.

A similar problem is involved in any scheme of organ-izing an international army on the same comprehensive lines as the national armies. If it includes a mass of in-fantry it is bound to be of such bulk as to increase, im-mensely, the difficulties both of creating and operating it.

A possible solution of both problems might be found by making the international force of a more specialized nature. Thus, apart from the air and naval components, it might comprise only the more powerful types of land force—armoured and airborne divisions, long-range ar-tillery and rocket units—with the minimum of infantry required for their immediate protection. The main body of the infantry required to follow up and occupy the troublesome area might be provided by contingents from the various national armies.

Whatever the composition of the force the question of adequate and suitable bases will remain the basic problem. The possessive disposition that expresses itself in vehement insistence on the rights of national sovereignty is a primary obstacle. But the concession of bases on national territory would not really suffice. They would be too exposed to interference. For security, a base needs a covering zone that cannot be easily dominated or penetrated. That need calls for the creation of international territories in different parts of the world—a chain of larger "Tangiers."

It might be met to some extent by the internationalization of portions of ex-enemy territory and mandated territory. But to make it adequate the members would also have to hand over pieces of their own territory in various quarters. The political objections are obvious. But the conclusion has to be faced that there can be no security for any nation without a partial surrender of national rights to a higher authority in which each shares.

CHAPTER XXV

DISARMAMENT WITHOUT DEFENCELESSNESS

D ISARMAMENT" was a late starter in the race, at snail's pace, for international security following the First World War. After protracted preliminary discussions the World Disarmament Conference finally assembled at Geneva in 1932. A few months before it opened, Japan had tentatively started on its long course of aggression in the Far East. At the outset of 1933 Hitler vaulted into the saddle of Germany, and the hopes of a general disarmament agreement faded away—along with the Conference itself.

In the second year after the end of the Second World War, there was a revival of the project. Disarmament suddenly came to the fore in the proceedings of the United Nations although there had been no mention of it in the agenda when the General Assembly met in New York in the autumn of 1946.

The revival came in an indirect way, arising out of a Soviet proposal for a census of the troops which each nation was maintaining abroad. This led at first merely to a series of wrangles. But it led on to an unexpected res-

297

olution for a general reduction of armaments, and then, surprisingly, to acceptance of international inspection in principle—which had previously been opposed as an infringement of national sovereignty. At the same time the existing proposal to abolish the atom bomb was widened to embrace any other weapons of "mass destruction."

It was, and is, easy to be cynical about such far-reaching proposals. The temptation, and the incentive to obstruction, was all the stronger because the process of settling the "peace" by the victorious nations had already begun to look like the marshalling of forces for battle. Cynicism and political manœuvring combined with mutual distrust to nullify the prospect of agreement on any such comprehensive scheme of all-round disarmament.

But time brings changes, and some day the opportunity as well as the idea may be revived—in a more favourable atmosphere and better conditions. So it may be of value in the interval to carry out an objective examination of the problem of disarmament, and to collate the lessons of experience that have a bearing on the subject.

The idea of a universal scaling down of armaments has the most obvious appeal, but numerical scales form the most difficult way of tackling the problem. When numbers come into calculation it is very hard to reach a general agreement as to the scale that the different countries require for their security. Each country is naturally inclined to exaggerate its own special circumstances and overestimate its own minimum needs, while failing to see the justification for what others claim.

Discussion of the relative *size* of national forces commonly leads to interminable wrangling, and to no definite conclusion. The idea of fixing relative scales of military *expenditures* is quite as difficult to carry out, while it is by no means a satisfactory method of disarmament. For it does not touch the core of the problem—that of curbing the possibility of successful aggression.

To concentrate on dealing with *weapons* is a more promising line of approach. If particular types of armament could be universally abolished by mutual consent, and adequate checks on their manufacture created by a universally accepted system of international inspection, that would be a real measure of *disarmament*.

A further safeguard would be the creation of a collective organization, like the proposed International Atomic Authority, which could continue research and experimental development with the types of weapons that the individual states had agreed to discard. If a directly recruited International Force were created, on the lines discussed in the previous chapter, it could be used to carry out the necessary practical tests.

If the International Inspectorate should ever have reason to suspect that any individual state was secretly developing the banned weapons, the others would naturally be released from their obligations in this respect. Although the evader might gain a start, there is always a time-lag before any fresh development is ready for use. Moreover, it would not be easy for him to catch up the experimental lead enjoyed by the International Authority—with its wider facilities for research, wider access to raw materials, and control of all existing plants.

It would probably be wiser to abandon the idea of "sanctions"—the polite name for punishment—which figured so largely in the programme of the League of Nations, and proved so difficult to apply. Attempts at punishment where a great country is concerned are more likely to precipitate war than to prevent it—and such a

cure can be more fatal than any failure to prevent evasion
of the rules. What is really more important is early notice
of any evasion. This should be assured by an adequate
system of inspection—acceptance of which would be a
pre-requisite of any disarmament agreement between
nations.

The best check on any reintroduction of prohibited
weapons lies, not in sanctions, but in the likelihood that
it may turn into a boomerang. Sanctions did not check
Italy's invasion of Abyssinia, nor her use of poison gas
to help her to victory. Yet during the six years of the Second World War no one ventured to employ gas—because
all knew that the others could retort in kind, and feared
the mutual consequences of competitive gas attacks.

In bomber strength, one side enjoyed a clear superiority at the outset of the war, and the other side later, so
there was no inherent check. A similar one-sided advantage attached to the V-weapons in 1944 and the atom
bomb in 1945. But with gas there was always a state of
balance—based on the certainty that either side had
stocks of gas, and reinforced by mutual uncertainty as
to how effective these were. So the mutual restraint was
never broken.

It was a significant lesson, from a fresh angle, in the
restraining value of a "balance of power." That principle
of policy has been unjustly criticized in recent times. Because it was upheld by statesmen in the 19th century,
and because the First World War broke out nevertheless
in 1914, most people jumped to the conclusion that it was
a fallacy. But deeper examination corrects such hasty assumptions. It was not the principle that proved faulty,
but the balance itself—which became so uneven as to en-
courage German hopes of a quick victory. Even so, the
outcome showed that such hopes were mistaken. The

same *disequilibrium* occurred in 1939—with similar results.

These successive experiences suggest that we ought to give more attention, rather than less, to the practical problem of maintaining a balance of power. It becomes more and more foolish to count on ultimate victory. We should concentrate on the problem of nullifying any prospect of a quick victory. No one will venture to strike if there is clearly no chance of that.

For that reason, disarmament should not stop short at the abolition of atomic bombs and other weapons of mass destruction. If they were ruled out, massacre would be reduced and war would be less likely to destroy civilization, but war would not be ruled out. Armies would still be able to invade the territory of other nations, and might even be more likely to make aggression pay. So a Disarmament Plan should cover the weapons on which a land offensive depends for its chances of initial success. To check the power of the offensive is to put a real check on aggression—and thus on war.

The root of the problem is to make armies offensively impotent—incapable of achieving a successful penetration of other countries. If we can do that, armies would become, in fact as well as in name, a means of defence, and no more.

A solution of the problem is much simpler than it sounds. To realize that we need only look back at the 1932 Disarmament Conference, and its upshot.

There had been prolonged debate about different methods of *quantitative* disarmament—limiting the number of troops, the number of arms, the size of military budgets. Then the Conference came round to the idea of *qualitative* disarmament—the principle of restricting particular weapons. To anyone who had pondered the ex-

perience of the First World War, it was not difficult to
pick out the weapons that were most dangerous to the
security of nations.

In 1914 the Germans had only been able to penetrate
their neighbours' frontiers by bringing specially heavy
guns into the field to crack the fortresses that barred the
main avenues of invasion. Then, from 1915 onward, a
state of deadlock was produced by a new *small* weapon,
the machine-gun, which could sweep any path of attack
with such a stream of bullets that offensives withered
away.

Defence was definitely on top. Ordinary field-guns had
little effect on entrenched machine-guns. It was only by
bringing masses of heavy guns into the field, to smash the
trenches flat, that attacks made headway at all. Even
then, the process was so cumbrous that by the time
the original defences were penetrated, fresh lines were
dug in rear. An acceleration came later in the war with
the invention of the tank. After the war the improvement
of this new-born arm continued, and a new theory of armoured warfare was conceived—first, in England. This
promised to produce, in the future, the rapid break-
through that had never been completely attained
throughout the First World War.

It thus seemed clear that to curb the development of
these particular weapons would be the best way to make
a success of disarmament. That would also be the
simplest way. It would cut out the mathematical tangle,
and wrangle, into which the quantitative method—of fixing numerical ratios for each country—was bound to drag
any conference.

To propose the abolition of all guns and tanks would
have been too much for the nations to swallow, and it
was not necessary from a practical point of view. The

lighter types of armoured track vehicle might be easily improvised from commercial motor parts, so that it was unwise to include them in the ban, but neither they nor ordinary field artillery were capable of cracking modern defences. On balance, they tended to help defence more than attack.

All that really mattered was to stop the production of heavy tanks and heavy guns. Even if the manufacture of such bulky machines could be concealed, they would have to come into the open for testing, for the training of their crews, and for practicing their effective use in tactical exercises. That multiple and prolonged process would be almost impossible to conceal. It thus provided its own inherent check on secret evasion. Such evasion would be far more difficult than with quantitative forms of disarmament—budgetary expenditure can be camouflaged, and the number of troops discreetly increased.

For an early exponent of mechanized warfare it was not pleasant to advocate a ban that was bound to frustrate the fulfilment of the ideas one had been preaching so long. As a military theorist, one had seen in armoured mobility the solution of the military problem of reviving the power of the offensive. But when one came to look at the problem from the wider point of view—of peaceful nations wishing to check aggression—the sensible solution was to nullify such a rebirth by abolishing the means of it.

That solution, however, was bound to have an adverse effect on many professional interests, while the very idea of eliminating weapons that favoured the offensive was naturally repugnant to most military minds. These were quick to react. With numerous quibbles they strove to sap the basic agreement that the Governments had reached on the principle of qualitative disarmament.

Concentrating on the literal sense, instead of on the practical sense, of the term "offensive weapons," they argued that a distinction could not be drawn between offensive and defensive weapons. That argument missed the essential point. Obviously, all weapons are offensive in that they inflict damage; and all can be useful to the defenders as well as to the attackers. This fact was so obvious that the amount of breath spent in discussing it was palpably intended to create a verbal smokescreen round the real issue—that *the* offensive depended for success on certain weapons above all, and would be impotent without them.

It was also argued that a country defending itself against aggression would need these weapons in order to eject the invader—forgetting that, if they were abolished, there could be no invasion in the first place, and hence no need of these means for a counter-offensive.

Threatened with the disappearance of the heavier type of tanks, the General Staffs of Europe momentarily showed an appreciation of its value that was in remarkable contrast to their attitude before, and after. The British War Office had recently built a mere half-dozen medium tanks, weighing 16 tons. It was so anxious to preserve this handful that its military representatives at the Disarmament Conference were instructed to argue that only tanks of more than 20 tons should be classed as "offensive." Thereupon the French, who had a few experimental monsters of 70 tons, proposed that the limit should be set above this figure! It reduced to a farce the principle of debarring anything larger than commercial vehicles—i.e. a maximum of 6 to 8 tons.

The worst of such technical quibbles was that they delayed the progress of the Conference just at a time when the political situation in Europe made it urgent to

hasten the conclusion of a definite arrangement. Before
the matter was settled the Nazi regime came into power,
the Conference broke down, and the new rulers of Germany were allowed to re-equip themselves with weapons
such as the other Powers retained.

It is not fair, however, to blame the soldiers entirely for
the delay. Their objections were supported by many
shortsighted, though often well-meaning, politicians.
Even Mr. Churchill attacked the qualitative principle of
disarmament "as a silly expedient," asserting that it was
not practicable to attempt a definition of "offensive
weapons."

Hitler provided the clearest answer to that view, as we
know now, by ordering that the German rearmament
programme should *"concentrate on offensive weapons,
principally heavy artillery and heavy tanks."*

An ironical sequel to the breakdown of the Disarmament Conference was that, although all nations remained
free to build tanks, it was only the Germans who took
full advantage of the opportunity. When 1939 arrived,
the British authorities had not yet produced any further
medium tanks beyond the handful they had imperilled so
much to preserve seven years earlier! The French had
more, but were burdened with a larger quantity of obsolete types which gave them a false impression of their
real strength compared with the more mobile Germans.
They would have lost nothing, and might have gained
much, if there had been a general scrapping of tanks by
agreement in 1932. It would then have been more difficult for Germany to go ahead in this respect, and even if
she had, the French would have had a better chance of
keeping pace if they had likewise started from scratch,
unhandicapped by old ideas and old machines.

Looking back on the events of 1939-41, it can be seen

that all the main successes that the aggressor achieved were due to the very weapons that were to have been abolished under the 1932 scheme. Without these "tin-openers" it is clear that the offensive—and thus aggression—would have had no chance of succeeding. Poland, Holland, Belgium, France, the Balkans, and Russia were penetrated in turn by these means, and only the last escaped decisive defeat.

The significance of the primary offensive weapons is engraved in the experience of two World Wars. In the light of this experience, coupled with a scientific forecast of new trends, it should be possible to devise a new and comprehensive plan of qualitative disarmament that would deprive armed aggression of any prospect of success—while nations would keep the security conferred by the more truly defensive kinds of armament. The hindrance to it is political rather than technical.

It was through the improvement of fortifications that aggression was strategically cramped in the 18th century. It was thanks to the improvement of small arms that tactical defence began to gain the upper hand in the 19th century, and still more in the early 20th century. Just as there is no menace in developing fortifications, so there is none in multiplying the lighter automatic weapons. The more numerous they are the more the prospects of the attack are reduced—and so the stronger becomes the deterrent to a would-be aggressor.

The idealist may lament the existence of armies, and the expenditure on them, but the practical man must realize how much they are influenced by the instinct of self-preservation. The statesman must reckon with human nature as it is; only exalted spirits can rise above the craving for material security. But, accepting this instinct as inevitable, the security could be made non-aggressive by an agreement to scrap those weapons on which offensive prospects principally depend, and a scheme of supervision to see that they do not reappear.

If these conditions were universally accepted, the problem of limiting the scale of troops, reserves, and expenditure would become as immaterial as it is insoluble—although once a feeling of security grew it is probable that the nations would start on their own to reduce their forces, in order to reduce taxes.

The core of the whole disarmament problem lies in convincing the aggressive that victory is unattainable from the start. The most effective means is to annul the chances of successful attack. To sterilize offensive potency is to sterilize war itself.

CHAPTER XXVI

THE LIMITATION OF WAR

CAN war be limited? *Logic* says—
"*No*. War is the sphere of violence, and it would be il-
logical to hesitate in using any extreme of violence that
can help you to win the war."

History replies—"Such logic makes nonsense. You go
to war to win the peace, not just for the sake of fighting.
Extremes of violence may frustrate your purpose, so that
victory becomes a boomerang. Moreover, it is a matter of
historical fact that war has been limited in many ways."

Even if there has been a bad relapse in our time, it has
not been as bad as the normal practice of war in earlier
ages that we regard as highly civilized. Shocking as has
been the Germans' treatment of conquered people, they
have not massacred the population of captured cities as
the Greeks and Romans often did. Their deportation of
civilians for forced labour was not so barbarous as what
the Greeks and Romans considered a merciful alternative
to the rule of "death to the conquered"—that of selling
men, women, and children wholesale as slaves. Still less

have the Germans slaughtered the conquered armies, as was a common practice in Greek and Roman warfare.

Read Julius Cæsar's own account of his campaigns in Gaul, and you may realize that Hitler was quite a gentleman compared with that much praised missionary of Roman civilization—who is revered by so many students of the classics.

But the Romans at their worst were mild compared with the ancestors of all the Western European nations during the Dark Ages that followed the collapse of the Roman Empire—and the *Pax Romana*. It was the habit of the Saxons and the Franks to slay everyone in their path—men, women, and children—and to indulge in the most reckless destruction of towns and crops.

It is important to understand how the "total warfare" of those times came to be modified, and gradually humanized. It is a story of "ups and downs"—but far more *up* than down.

The first influence in the rescue of humanity was the Christian Church. Even before it converted the pagan conquerors of the West, it often succeeded in restraining their savagery by exploiting their superstitions. People who took refuge in its sanctuaries were often spared from the general massacre. After the conversion of the barbarians the Church was able to exert an increasing restraint—by slow degrees. One of its most notable efforts was the two-branched "truce of God." The *Pax Dei* introduced in the 10th Century sought to insure immunity for non-combatants and their property. It was followed by the *Treuga Dei*, which sought to limit the number of days on which fighting could take place, by establishing periods of truce.

These efforts of the Church were reinforced by the

growth of the power of kings, over the feudal lords. This reduced the quantity of wars.

A wider reinforcement came from the Code of Chivalry. This seems to have been of Arabic origin. Here, it has to be admitted that the followers of Mahomet were much quicker than the followers of Christ, in the West, to develop humane habits—although Mahomet himself had shown much more of the Old Testament spirit revealed in Moses. In the Crusades, the Muslims behaved like gentlemen compared with the Christians. The difference may have been due to the fact that they had their roots deeper in civilization than the recently converted pagans of the West.

Contact with the East, however, helped to foster the growth of chivalry in the West. That code, for all its faults, helped to humanize warfare—by *formalizing* it. Economic factors also helped. The custom of releasing prisoners in exchange for ransom may have depended more on a profit-motive than on a sense of chivalrous behaviour, but was essentially *good* sense—it worked for good. At first, it applied only to those who could afford to pay a ransom. But the habit grew, as habits do, and gave rise to a general custom of sparing the lives of the defeated. That was an immense step forward.

This progress in civilized behaviour reached its peak in 15th Century Italy. As Machiavelli tells us—"The lives of the defeated are nearly always spared. They do not remain prisoners for long, and their release is very easily obtained. A town may rebel a score of times; it is never destroyed. The inhabitants retain the whole of their property; all they have to fear is that they will be made to pay a levy."

This increasing habit of limitation was aided by the spread of mercenary soldiers—that is, professional soldiers. First, these came to realize the mutual benefit of restraint in dealing with one another. Then, their employers came to realize the mutual benefit of curbing their tendency to plunder the civilian population on either side. By contrast, it had been noted that, even in the supposedly ideal democracies of Greece, citizen soldiers tended to be much more passionate, and hence more ruthless.

In the late Middle Ages, the growing tendency to limit the degree of violence, for mutual convenience, had a profound psychological effect. Passions were not cured, but they were kept more under control. Wars did not disappear, but their damage was diminished. *Good* sense came increasingly to prevail.

Unhappily, a severe setback came from the Wars of Religion, which arose from the Reformation. Religious fervour incited barbarous behaviour. The split in the Church broke up its moral authority, while turning it from a restraining influence into an impelling agent. It heated the fires of hatred and inflamed the passions of war.

The climax of this period was the Thirty Years' War, when more than half the population of the German states perished directly or indirectly from the war. That terrible period had a lasting effect on the development of German civilization—some historians have reckoned that it was put back two centuries. Yet the savagery of such warfare was not so great as it had been in the Dark Ages.

Moreover, this excess of violence produced a widespread revulsion—which, in turn, led to a great advance, greater than ever before.

Reason stepped in where religion had failed. It showed men that the impulse to violence, if carried to extremes, simply led to mutual destruction. It showed them the dangers of having too strong a conviction of their own rightness. To proceed to extremes in war might be *logical,* but it was not *reasonable.*

Another important influence was the growth of more formal and courteous manners in social life. This code of manners spread into the field of international relations.

These two factors, reason and manners, saved civilization, when it was near the verge of collapse. Men came to feel that behaviour mattered more than belief, and customs more than creeds, in making earthly life tolerable and human relations workable.

There was an increasing limitation of violence in warfare—by mutual consent—in the last part of the 17th Century, and still more in the 18th Century. The remarkable change that took place is to be seen in the general reaction towards one of the rare exceptions to the new and humane rule—for when Marlborough burnt the villages and crops of Bavaria in 1704, as a means of forcing its king to make peace, even England's allies protested against the brutality of such a method.

The improvement made during the 18th Century in the customs of war, and in reducing its evils, forms one of the great achievements of civilization. It opened up a prospect that the progressive limitation of war, by formalization, might lead to its elimination.

The improvement was helped by the fact that there was no radical change in the means of warfare during this period. For experience suggests that an increase of savagery in warfare is apt to follow new developments—technical or political—which unsettle the existing order.

The bad effect of a big political change was shown at the end of the 18th century, when the code of limitations on violence in war was broken down by the French Revolution. The new Republic, finding itself surrounded by hostile neighbours, went to war partly in self-defence, and partly as a missionary for the spread of "liberty." But this soon developed into a war of ever-expanding aggression—for the subjection of all nations to French imperialism.

The new conscription of citizens as soldiers multiplied the passion and the violence—as it had done in ancient Greece. Although a tendency to give "no quarter" was short-lived, the maltreatment of non-combatants and the habit of plunder were revived. Dangerous breaches were made in the embankments that had been built in the 18th Century for the protection of civilization against the flooding passions of war.

But the wars of the French Revolution never, at their worst, became so terrible as the Religious Wars of the 17th Century. And the restoration of civilization was helped by the wise moderation of the peace terms imposed on France after the fall of Napoleon—thanks largely to England's influence, as represented by Wellington and Castlereagh. The best testimony to it was that half a century passed before there was another serious war in Europe.

The 19th Century saw, on the whole, a continuance of the trend towards humane limitations in warfare. This was registered in the Geneva conventions of 1864 and 1906, which dealt mainly with the protection of the wounded, and the Hague conventions of 1899 and 1907, which covered a wider field.

But this humane progress was endangered by three factors. One was the survival of conscription. While the French were glad to be released from it, one of the victorious nations chose to preserve it. That was Prussia. In liberating herself from Napoleon she thereby made herself the slave of war.

Another factor was the growth of a new theory of war which embodied all the most dangerous features of Revolutionary and Napoleonic practice. That theory was also evolved in Prussia—by Clausewitz. Pursuing logic to the extreme, he argued that moderation had no place in war —"War is an act of violence pursued to the utmost." As his thinking proceeded he came to realize the fallacy of such logic. Unfortunately, he died before he could revise his writings—and his disciples remembered only his extreme starting point. When they conquered Austria in 1866 and France in 1870 all the world became convinced that Clausewitz's original theory was correct—although both those wars had been marked by moderation both in the waging of the campaign and the making of peace. But the results of quick conquest intoxicated the next generation.

Another dangerous factor now developed—the terrific scientific development in the weapons of war. By becoming far more destructive, they were less controllable. Moreover, the advent of submarines and aircraft did not fit the limiting rules of war that had been evolved, and thus tended to break down these limitations.

Under the combined influence of these factors the 1914-18 war started in a bad way—and went from bad to worse. Excess of logic led Germany's leaders to the conclusion that ruthlessness was the best policy. Their opponents responded in kind. The new development of propaganda made the most of every brutal tendency, and hid every surviving example of humane restraint. The war itself was pursued to the bitter end under the influence of Clausewitz's misinterpreted theory of the "absolute" aim.

The ill effects of the war were deepened by the nature of the peace settlement—so different from the wise moderation shown in the treatment of France after the defeat of Napoleon. Any people whose spirit was not permanently broken would have striven to evade such crippling and humiliating terms. Those who imposed them showed no understanding of history, or of human nature. The silliest feature of all was the way that the new Republican government in Germany was compelled to be the agent of accepting and fulfilling them. That helped to ensure its downfall, and the rise of Hitler.

The prospects were made worse by the state of exhaustion and chaos to which Europe was reduced by the time the peace was made, and by the general degeneration of standards produced by the years of unlimited violence. The soil of Europe had been all too well fertilized to bear a crop of revolutions that would ripen into tyrannies.

The Second World War

The nature of these revolutions, as in the case of the French Revolution, ran counter to the former customs of civilized behaviour. Coupled with the trend of weapon development, it tended to make war more *total* in every sense.

The first effect was seen before the war began in the more complete organization of the people for the service of the state. The second effect was seen in the more drastic, and often atrocious, treatment of conquered populations during the war.

It is important to realize that it was simply the external application of a mode of ideas and manner of behaviour that had already arisen from the internal revolution. War conditions merely produced, and were bound to produce, the intensification of its evil characteristics that Europe has suffered in these recent years. But it was a civil development, carried out by organizations of a "political police" type. It should be distinguished from military developments. If it is to be checked, it must be tackled in the political field.

On the military side, in contrast, the level of behaviour was better in a number of respects than in the First World War. Even at its worst, it never fell back to the pre-18th Century level. The armies in general continued to observe many of the rules contained in the established code of war. Indeed, military atrocities seem to have been fewer than in the First World War. That is a significant feature —and a hopeful one for the future. It might be turned to good account.

Unfortunately, such a gain for civilization was offset by the development of new weapons for which no clear limitations had been thought out—and no code of rules established in time. As a result the immense growth of air power led to a sweeping disregard for humane limitations on its action, in carrying out bombardment from the air. This produced an extent of devastation, and in many areas a degradation of living conditions, worse than anything seen since the Thirty Years' War. Indeed, in the destruction of cities, the record of this war exceeds anything since the campaigns of Genghis Khan and Tamerlane.

Yet this appalling development, of unlimited warfare, cannot be traced to the same source as that which produced the enslavement of nations in the service of war and the brutal treatment of conquered peoples. The main part of the devastation from the air was produced, not by the original aggressors, but by the opponents of aggression—when they began to gain the upper hand. That is an uncomfortable fact which we must honestly face.

But the reflection at least offers a better hope for the future, if we do face the facts.

The bombing policy which the Allies pursued was the product of a theory which arose after 1918, when Britain gave the world a lead in creating an Air Force separate from the older fighting services. Instead of being limited to narrowly military objectives, it was argued that the Air Force should be used independently, to strike at the sources of an enemy's war effort. That was a logical extension of Britain's old tradition of naval warfare, in which the fleet had been used as a means of economic pressure, and had often carried out devastating raids on the enemy's coast towns. Significantly, the British Manual on the rules of warfare rejected the general Continental view that bombardment should be limited to military objectives. It maintained that "destruction of public and private buildings by bombardment" was a justifiable means to impress upon the civil authorities "the advisability of surrender."

The only other Manual which claimed a similar freedom from limitations was the American. When the American Air Force reinforced the British, in 1942, it was thus the more certain that bombing would be carried to the utmost pitch of devastation.

Originally, Air Chiefs had suggested that industrial objectives might be destroyed by precision-bombing, without damage to the ordinary civil population. But any attempt at humane limitation on these lines was naturally subject to a wide margin of error, thus provoking reprisals, and was likely to be abandoned as the war mood became more bitter.

German air theory took a different course. That was not due to humanitarianism, but to a different line of military reasoning. Although some of the Luftwaffe chiefs

favoured the British air theory, the General Staff was the
predominant influence in Germany. They held that the
bombing force should be used mainly to aid the army in
its battles, rather than independently against the interior
and industry of the opposing country. Their view prevailed, even with Hitler.

The trend of German ideas was seen in Hitler's proposal of 1935, repeated in 1936, for a universal agreement
that bombing should be confined to the fighting zone. He
suggested that this should be reckoned as covering a
depth of 100 kilometres beyond the front line.

When we examine the German air operations in the
early stage of the war, it has to be recognized that their
practice kept close to this proposal, as well as to their
theory. The bombing of Warsaw and Rotterdam horrified the world, but it did not take place until the German
troops were fighting their way into these cities. It thus
conformed to the 1935 definition, as well as to the old
rules of siege bombardment. Yet in 1940 the Germans had
such a vastly superior Air Force that they could have used
it as they chose.

The first clear departure from this rule was in the
bombing of London. That followed upon six successive
attacks on Berlin by the R.A.F. They were thus, in fact,
justified in claiming that their action was a reprisal. Moreover, they took the initiative a few weeks later in propos-
ing a mutual agreement to restrict such city bombing—
although they still had the immense advantage in bombing strength. This shows, not that they were humane,
but that they had a long-term realism. Having studied
war more closely than we had, they could see the ultimate
drawbacks—even to the victor—of destroying cities and
industry.

Their attitude then accorded with other evidence from

history—that a calculating aggressive power is more apt to see the wisdom of limiting destruction than the nations which have to meet aggression. It recalls the proverb that "A burglar doesn't commit murder unless cornered." He wants to get his gains intact, and with the least risk to himself. That calculating tendency might be turned to good account by the opponents of aggression—if they kept a cool head. It is worth remembering when we are trying to devise methods of limiting the destructiveness of war.

By contrast, it has to be admitted that cool-headed and far-sighted measures to meet aggression are exceptionally difficult under a democratic government. Democracy is a system that puts a brake on preparation for war—defensive as well as aggressive—but it does not conduce to the limitation of warfare, or the prospects of a good peace. As the history of ancient Greece showed, no political system becomes more easily out of control when passions are aroused. This defect has been multiplied in modern democracies, since their vaster size produces a larger volume of emotional pressure. Too often it overwhelms reason, and drives the leaders to extremes—in order to keep their lead. That has been seen in the waging of both the First and Second World Wars, and in the making of peace after the wars.

In 1940 these emotional "gases" propelled the British Government into trying, with an inferior bomber force, the so-called "master-plan" of bombing Germany's industrial centres—which was like throwing pebbles against an enemy who could throw boulders in return. It merely tended to precipitate the "blitz" on Britain's own cities, with disproportionate damage to herself. Such an unequal competition in devastation could have spelt nothing better than slow suicide for Britain, if she had not been saved by Hitler's decision to invade Russia, instead of concentrating his resources on building a bombing force sufficient to finish off Britain.

The same kind of pressure then led to the abandonment of precision-bombing for area-bombing—an unlimited attack on non-combatants that revived the horrors of ancient times. In the end, it culminated in the use of the atom bomb against Hiroshima and Nagasaki. Even Genghis Khan and Tamerlane could never have imagined that so many could be killed so quickly by so few.

It was ironical that nations who had entered the war to preserve civilization should have come to practise the most uncivilizing means of war that the world had known since those Mongol exponents of wholesale massacre.

Atomic Weapons and the Future

Now that atomic energy has been unleashed in warfare, the outlook for the world appears dark. To many, it seems hopeless. Many of the scientists confirm this pessimistic view by telling us that there is no defence against it.

Even if they prove wrong, it is difficult to see how any antidote could be brought into operation before hostilities have begun. That is a handicap on the defence. An attack by atomic bombs might come without any declaration of war, or indication of war—delivered by civil aircraft, by rockets, or other agents. It may thus seem that the rest of the lives of all people now living will be spent under the chilly shadow of "atomization" without warning.

Yet, if we look closer, we may see possible breaks in the cloud.

"Total warfare," such as we have known it hitherto, is

not compatible with the atomic age. Total warfare implies that the aim, the effort and the degree of violence are unlimited. Victory is pursued without regard to the consequences. In the chaotic aftermath of the Second World War, we are coming to realize how the lack of limitations in waging the war has made nonsense of the victory. An unlimited war waged with atomic power would make worse than nonsense—it would be mutually suicidal.

That realization should be a curb on the reckless use of such weapons which is generally assumed. Once both sides possess such a devastating weapon there may be more rather than less hesitation to unloose it—as happened with poison gas in the recent war. An aggressor might hesitate to use it, because of a doubt whether it could be counted upon to ensure immediate victory. Aggressors tend to be more calculating than their victims. Although a number of cities might be quickly demolished, their fate would not necessarily spell a nation's surrender. Some nations are less dependent on their cities than others. All should have learned a lot about dispersing and "earthing" their vital resources in such ways as to maintain the power of resistance. On the other hand, the other side might equally hesitate to start atomic warfare if the aggressor refrained. They would suffer too much themselves before they could turn the balance.

The limitless destructiveness of the weapon forms its own practical limitation. Its use cannot be adjusted to circumstances like that of a body of troops. For that reason troops are a more effective lever in a frontier argument. With the atomic bomb, it is a case of all-out destruction or nothing.

Many popular assumptions may be nullified in the atomic age. For the moment, the atomic bomb seems to have increased the power of the Great Powers. But once atomic energy can be more easily released, Small Powers may gain an equality with Great Powers that they have never yet known. Given the use of atomic weapons, a Small Power with a low density of population might have an advantage over a Great Power that was highly industrialized and densely populated. Brazil might defy the U.S.A.; Norway might defy the U.S.S.R. The atomic age may even see, as a result, a "democracy of nations" established by this levelling process.

It is at least clear that such devastating weapons as the atomic bomb have more limitations than have yet been realized. That may eventually help to improve the chances of securing their formal restraint, by general agreement, under a scheme of international supervision.

Conclusions

Experience should have taught us the mistake of concentrating exclusively on the perfectionist policy of preventing war. We have tended to neglect the practical necessity, if that policy fails, of limiting war—so that it does not destroy the prospects of subsequent peace. It is the peaceful nations, above all, who need to learn that moderation in war is the best guarantee of subsequent peace. For they are more inclined to carry matters to an extreme than any calculating aggressor who thinks of gain.

The most favoured idea for the prevention of war has been the creation of a World Federation. It has become painfully clear, however, that the theory has small chance of being put into practice—though there may be more prospect of a Federation of the West. The defects of the United Nations Organization are only too apparent. As so often before in history, a rivalry between victorious allies developed as soon as the counterpoise was removed —by the overthrow of Germany.

Is there any way of diminishing the dangers of that rivalry within the so-called United Nations? The dangers are dangers of war, and particularly of one or other side gaining an early advantage. Peace rests on preserving equilibrium—physical as well as mental.

The maintenance of an effective balance of power has been discussed at length earlier in this book. Also, the importance of maintaining balance of mind—a need which is less often recognized in democracies. In the previous chapter, we have examined one possible aid to equilibrium—a comprehensive scheme of qualitative disarmament coupled with an adequate system of technical supervision. The real question is not as to its practicability, but as to the possibility of its acceptance by the present Greater Powers.

Failing that, the best chance may lie in trying to revive a code of limiting rules for warfare—based on a realistic view that wars are likely to occur again, and that the limitation of their destructiveness is to everybody's interest.

The more that warfare is "formalized" the less damaging it proves. Past efforts in this direction have had more success than is commonly appreciated. Even in the bitter struggle which has engulfed the world in the present decade, the battling armies to a large extent observed rules which developed in the period of limitation, rules which would have seemed incredible to the men who fought in earlier "total wars"—for example, the rule of taking prisoners instead of massacring all the defeated army.

The value of rules was aptly summed up in Montesquieu's *Esprit des Lois*, where he remarks that, just as many wise things are conducted in a very foolish manner, so some foolish things have been conducted in a very wise manner. The point of his remark can be all the better appreciated by comparing 18th Century war with 20th Century war.

At present it is difficult to see any check upon the destructiveness of warfare—if war breaks out between nations that have different systems of government, different ideals, and the power to convert the resources of science into instruments of destruction. Through present-day eyes, it seems vainly optimistic to hope that any civilized limitations can be revived. Yet a view of history provides ground for hope. Sanity was recovered, and civilization restored, after that prolonged orgy of violence in the 17th Century known as the "Thirty Years' War." Salvation came simply through a revival of reason and manners. So it is not impossible that a similar reaction may follow the "Thirty Years' War" of the 20th Century.

INDEX